IMPROVING ONLINE PUBLIC ACCESS CATALOGS

Martha M. Yee
and
Sara Shatford Layne

AMERICAN LIBRARY ASSOCIATION
Chicago and London
1998

While extensive effort has gone into ensuring the reliability of information appearing in this book, the publisher makes no warranty, express or implied, on the accuracy or reliability of the information, and does not assume and hereby disclaims any liability to any person for any loss or damage caused by errors or omissions in this publication.

Cover by Tessing Design

Composition in Goudy on Xyvision by the dotted i

Printed on 50-pound White Offset, a pH-neutral stock, and bound in 10-point coated cover stock by Victor Graphics

The paper used in this publication meets the minimum requirements of American National Standard for Information Sciences—Permanence of Paper for Printed Library Materials, ANSI Z39.48-1992. ∞

Library of Congress Cataloging-in-Publication Data

Yee, Martha M.
    Improving online public access catalogs / by Martha M. Yee and Sara Shatford Layne.
        p.   cm.
    Includes index.
    ISBN 0-8389-0730-X (alk. paper)
    1. Online catalogs—United States.   I. Layne, Sara Shatford.   II. Title.
    Z699.35.C39Y44   1998
    025.3′132—dc21   98-6217

Printed in the United States of America.

02 01 00 99 98   5 4 3 2 1

To Betty

Contents

Figures

Preface

We have long regarded existing online public access catalogs (OPACs) with frustration, seeing in them an unrealized potential for using the riches of existing catalog records to provide the catalog user with new and wonderful ways of navigating the bibliographic universe. We are therefore pleased to have the opportunity this book provides to talk to librarians and system designers about our ideas for improving OPACs.

In 1996 we published an article, "Online Public Access Catalogs," in volume 58, supplement 21, of the *Encyclopedia of Library and Information Science*. Encouraged by colleagues and by Marlene Chamberlain at ALA Editions, and with the permission of the publishers of the encyclopedia, we decided to use that article as the basis for a separate publication, this book, that would be useful to anyone involved in the design of OPACs.

In order to write this book, and the article that preceded it, we collected and examined as much of the significant research as we could identify concerning catalog use. In addition, we both have extensive experience as catalogers of a variety of materials, as well as some experience in the public service side of libraries, and considerable experience in searching different OPACs. We have used the research of others, in combination with ideas that we have developed during years of conversations with each other and with any colleagues willing to listen, to produce the recommendations contained in this book. We have illustrated many of the recommendations with examples of bibliographic and authority records. Although these records were current at the time the manuscript was submitted to the publisher (April 1997) it should be noted that records are revised over time, and we make no claim for the continuing currency of these records.

We would like to acknowledge here the contributions of some of those colleagues who have listened to us, and who have given us valuable advice regarding this book. In alphabetical order, we wish to acknowledge Allyson Carlyle for reading and commenting on the book when it was still an article; Jo Crawford for informed ideas about systems; Stephen Davison for his programming expertise; Crystal Graham for her careful reading of the published article and for her serials perspective; Thomas Mann for his encouragement and for his reference perspective; and Joan Mitchell and Terry Ryan for comments and encouragement. We would also like to acknowledge the support of our families, especially Wei, Charles, Mao, and Xiaomei, and assure them that we will now be able to spend more time at home.

Objectives, Interfaces, and Building Blocks

Our primary goal in writing this work was to improve the design of online public access catalogs (OPACs). We cite considerable user research that indicates that users are having a hard time using current systems, which are paradoxically both overly complex and not complex enough. One user, Nicholson Baker, was so desperate he went to the lengths of writing a long article in the *New Yorker* in part about the problems he was having using OPACs.[1] This book contains many suggestions for making OPACs appear to be simple to use while in fact carrying out effectively the inherently complex operation of searching and displaying bibliographic records.

OPACs are currently very complex in the array of commands they make available to users. They provide commands for searching particular ways in particular indexes, for combining searches, for limiting searches, and for displaying records. Before the OPAC came along, users did not have to learn any commands at all. All they had to do was walk up to a drawerful of cards and begin to shuffle through them. Some user research indicates that many of our users balk at learning more than a few basic commands.[2] In his intensive study of actual searches done on the MELVYL® system[3] (the large online union catalog containing the holdings of the University of California), Michael Berger found that the real problem was not that users did not find anything, but rather that they conducted suboptimal searches; in other words, they found a few things, but not everything or even the best things they were looking for.[4]

Catalog use research reveals that users rely heavily on defaults.[5] One of our goals in this book is to recommend the best possible default search for each of the three types of entities commonly sought by users in library catalogs: authors, works, and subjects. Our recommendations are based on a close and careful study of all of the available research on problems users are having with OPACs. While as expert OPAC users we certainly make extensive use of all of the powerful and complex searching capabilities OPACs offer that were unavailable to us in the days of book and card catalogs, we also recognize that it took us a long time to learn to use these powerful and complex searching capabilities. We also recognize that much of our power derives from our intimate knowledge of the records we are searching and that it is unreasonable to expect library users, who are busy with other vocations, and who have no idea what they will find when they begin to search, to be able to be equally successful. Instead, we use our expertise to recommend to users, by means of the default searches, the best way to begin each of the three main types of searches: author, work, and subject.

We also recognize, however, that no one search will ever be ideal for every particular information need. After recommending a few simple default searches, we recommend a number of backup strategies to suggest to the user for whom the default search is not working.

1

The design of online public access catalogs is more and more moving out of the hands of system designers and programmers and into the hands of librarians, who are given the responsibility for configuring their systems for use in their particular libraries. Librarians now often have a great deal of power and flexibility in deciding which fields to index in a given index, and what fields to display in various types of display. This book intends to address the issues that will arise in either the design process conducted by system designers and programmers in the creation of an overall OPAC system or the design process conducted by librarians who have purchased such a system and need to determine its local configuration. Our intent is to indicate some of the pros and cons of making particular decisions, in order to aid in effective decision making for system design of online public access catalogs.

Another goal of this book is to record what is known about user problems with existing systems, in order to point the way to future improvement. There are problems inherent in the design of any effective catalog. Many of these have not yet been completely solved in the design of online public access catalogs. In this book, we explore these problems and suggest potential solutions. Not all suggestions made will be currently implementable, but perhaps they will be in the future if enough people ask for them. The book briefly considers the history and development of online public access catalogs, but the focus will be on design.

This book focuses on the public access component of online catalogs, and as such it does not deal directly with integrated systems that also provide for functions such as circulation, acquisition, and serials check-in. However, to the degree that users of the system are allowed to see these other aspects of the system, the same design principles should be applied. The more seamlessly these other aspects are incorporated into the online public access catalog function, the easier they will be for users to comprehend and use. For example, a single display of serial holdings that also contains item-level information (e.g., which volumes are checked out or have been declared missing), acquisition information (e.g., which volumes have been claimed), and bindery information (e.g., which volumes have been sent to the bindery) could be very helpful to users trying to find journal articles; even better would be a command that would allow the user looking at a particular serial record to specify the volume sought and immediately be given circulation information about that volume, even if it is associated with a different but related record because of a serial title change.

This book does not deal with the inclusion in the OPAC of pathways to abstracting and indexing databases, community information systems, or the wealth of other types of information available over the Internet. Also not included are the various means currently available or being developed for delivering the full text of materials identified through searching the abstracting and indexing databases. There are many unsolved intellectual problems with providing users with pathways to other databases and information, stemming from the variety of design decisions made in those different systems, such as the use of different controlled vocabularies, or of no controlled vocabularies at all, or quite different indexing and display decisions. The World Wide Web is the most current attempt to deal with these problems. Perhaps the ultimate solution is to try to standardize bibliographic practice over all these systems or to develop highly sophisticated mapping programs that could automatically translate queries from one system to another.

This book attempts specifically to address the system design improvements that could aid users with the problems they are having with OPACs. We have not attempted to discuss the many ways in which changes in cataloging practice (i.e., record design, if you will) could also aid users with problems they are having with OPACs. The latter topic could take another book. However, some of the improvements in record design that might be worth investigating in the future include (1) devising a way to create a unique entry for each particular work; (2) devising a way to provide access to name authority records by characteristics of persons or bodies, allowing users to search the authority file for Afro-American filmmakers or museums in Chicago, for example, and then to retrieve bibliographic records attached to authority records for people and corporate bodies of interest; (3) cleaning up our subject access systems so as to make a clear distinction between topical subject access and form/genre access, but ensuring that a user who searches on a form/genre term is shown both works about that form/genre and exemplars of it; (4) improving Library of Congress Subject Headings (LCSH), making the headings more consistent, with a cleaner syndetic structure, with fewer topical subjects buried in subdivisions, and with more current terminology; and (5) with the emerging recognition of the importance of visual materials, devising a better and more consistent way to distinguish between depictions of a person, place, etc. and discursive works about that person, place, etc.

This book is primarily organized around the two main types of searching that users do in OPACs: (1) searching for particular authors and for their works; and (2) searching for works on a particular subject. Design for each of these two main types of searching is broken down into three categories: (1) file and index structure; (2) indexing; and (3) display.

The first category, *file and index structure*, deals with the partitioning of the database into pieces, such as the bibliographic file and the authority file or the name/title index and the subject index. In this category we are most concerned with partitioning that affects searching. We are less concerned with partitioning that is invisible to the user. An example of partitioning that *can* have an effect on searching might be a system that creates a title index and a name index and then requires a user looking for a particular work to do either a title search or a name search, thereby forbidding a search using both author and title. Another example might be a system that requires a name used as a subject (e.g., Beethoven's name attached to a book about him) to be either in the subject file or in the name file but not both, so that a user who looks in the wrong file or index will fail to find works about Beethoven.

The second category, *indexing*, deals with the actual indexing algorithms used to match a user's search to the data contained in various kinds of records in the OPAC. Two of the major types of indexing algorithm are keyword indexing and phrase indexing, both of which will be defined further and explained in chapter 3. The predominance of one of these types of indexing over the other in any particular system can have a profound effect on the types of problems users will have with that system, as well as on the types of information needs that can be easily met using that system.

The third category, *display*, is one that is often neglected in the discussion of OPAC design. There still seem to be many system designers who build systems under the assumption that every user is looking for one particular item represented by one particular record in the database and is capable of pulling up that one particular record on the first search. If that were the case, display design would indeed be a rather trivial part of the design of any given system. On the contrary, however, we cite research that shows that users frequently pull up large numbers of records, and we demonstrate logically that any entity sought by a user (an author, a work, or a subject) is *always* represented by multiple records in any OPAC. In systems that have inadequate displays for summarizing large numbers of records, users can be at a loss as to how to proceed to narrow their searches to the most useful materials retrieved. Effective displays of large numbers of records can be an immense help with this problem.

Both of the authors are catalogers intimately familiar with cataloging practices. Because of that background, we are painfully aware of information riches locked away in our records and not yet extricated by catalog systems to benefit the users they were intended to benefit. We make many recommendations for how OPACs could do a better job of passing on to the users the benefits of the expensive intellectual effort that goes into creating catalog records.

There are currently two schools of thought in the area of information organization. One looks at the expense of cataloging (i.e., of human beings looking at an item, describing it, determining its author(s) and title, and assigning subject headings and classification numbers to it) and the delays in the provision of timely information due to the time it takes to catalog it and concludes that the work of cataloging ought to be assigned to computers, using artificial intelligence algorithms.

The other school of thought, aware of the complexity of the recognition and matching tasks involved in cataloging, is pessimistic about the possibility of computer programs ever being able to function effectively as the sole organizers of information for access, although they can be extremely helpful as assistants to the human organizers.

The authors fall into the latter school of thought. We wish it were not so expensive to organize the cultural record to enable future generations to gain access to it, but it is. As a society, we have already invested billions of dollars in creating US-MARC (USMARC format for bibliographic data) records to describe the priceless and irreplaceable cultural heritage housed in the nation's libraries. Let's devote ourselves to designing more effective catalogs to enable our users to mine this treasure.

Notes

1. Nicholson Baker, "Discards," *New Yorker,* April 14, 1994, p. 64–86.

2. "Although there are a multitude of MELVYL indexes, statistics indicate that users generally use only a small number." Michael George Berger and Mary Jean Moore, "The User Meets the MELVYL System," *DLA Bulletin* 16, no. 1 (fall 1996): 14; "Users rarely appear to realize that they could combine author and subject/title searches, or that they could start with a broad search and refine it in subsequent iterations with the AND command. Most searchers continue to use the same search code from search to search. Reformulation of a search is generally done by changing the key words used, not by trying different search codes." Thomas H. Martin, John C. Wyman, and Kumud Madhok, *Feedback and Exploratory Mechanisms for Assisting Library Staff Improve On-line Catalog Searching* (Washington, D.C.: Council on Library Resources, 1983), p. 3; "Most users stick to a few basic commands." Dorothy McPherson, "How the MELVYL Catalog Is Used," *DLA Bulletin* 5, no. 2 (Aug. 1985): 17; see John E. Tolle, *Current Utilization of Online Catalogs: Transaction Log Analysis* (Dublin, Ohio: OCLC, 1983), p. 108. Tolle found that in each of the catalogs studied there were search features that were used infrequently.

3. MELVYL is a registered trademark of the Regents of the University of California.

4. Michael George Berger, "Information-Seeking in the Online Bibliographic System: An Exploratory Study" (Ph.D. diss., UC Berkeley, 1994), p. 155; "252 searches in the random sample achieved zero results; of these, 87 were modified by users and redone with success; 53 truly had zero results (i.e., search variations still retrieved zero results), and 102 could have been redone with success had the user continued with additional searches." Berger and Moore, "The User Meets," p. 16.

5. Michael Berger, *The User Meets the MELVYL System: An Analysis of User Transactions*, Technical Report no. 7 (Oakland, Calif.: Division of Library Automation, University of California, 1996), p. 48.

Objectives of the Catalog;
History of OPACs;
Research in Catalog Use

Objectives of the Catalog

The *ALA Glossary of Library and Information Science* defines *online public access catalog* as follows:

> A computer-based and supported library catalog (bibliographic database) designed to be accessed via terminals so that library users may directly and effectively search for and retrieve bibliographic records without the assistance of a human intermediary such as a specially trained member of the library staff.[1]

Note that this definition does not exclude CD-ROM (compact disc read-only memory) catalogs, even though, technically, they are not *online* in the sense that updating of the catalog is instantaneous. Because most of the problems of catalog design for user access are the same between truly online catalogs and CD-ROM catalogs, however, it is wise to consider them together.

An online public access catalog is a catalog and as such should try to meet certain objectives in order to serve its users. Since these objectives were first formulated, the technology to achieve these objectives has changed several times, from book catalog, to card catalog, to online catalog. While the means to achieve the objectives have changed, the objectives themselves have not.[2] Charles Ammi Cutter first stated the objectives of the catalog, or objects, as he called them, as follows:

OBJECTS
1. To enable a person to find a book of which either
   (A) the author
   (B) the title   } is known.
   (C) the subject
2. To show what the library has
   (D) by a given author
   (E) on a given subject
   (F) in a given kind of literature.
3. To assist in the choice of a book

(G) as to its edition (bibliographically)

(H) as to its character (literary or topical).[3]

The objectives of the catalog were adopted as an international standard by the International Conference on Cataloguing Principles in Paris in 1961 in the following form:

> 2. Functions of the catalogue
>
> The catalogue should be an efficient instrument for ascertaining
>
> > 2.1 whether the library contains a particular book specified by
> > > (a) its author and title, *or*
> > >
> > > (b) if the author is not named in the book, its title alone, *or*
> > >
> > > (c) if the author and title are inappropriate or insufficient for identification, a suitable substitute for the title; and
> >
> > 2.2 (a) which works by a particular author and
> > > (b) which editions of a particular work are in the library.[4]

The objectives adopted in Paris were limited to those served by descriptive cataloging and did not include those served by subject cataloging and classification, which Cutter's original objectives did include. The Paris Principles, which include the objectives, continue to be an international standard for descriptive cataloging.

There is some research to support the continuing value of the first part of the second objective, 2.2 (a), which calls for displaying all of the works of an author. Peter Mann summarizes research that shows that public library fiction readers will look for works under a particular author of interest and select any work they haven't read.[5] Not much research has been done on this question in other types of libraries, however.

Some have questioned the value of part of the second objective, 2.2 (b), wondering how often users wish to see all the editions of a work. These doubters have failed to realize that the second objective was designed to serve the following users: the user who can use any available edition of the work; the user who doesn't know ahead of time that there is more than one edition of the sought work and might find another preferable to the one in her or his citation, such as the latest edition of a scientific text or a particularly reliable text of a work of belles lettres; the user who has an inaccurate citation for a particular edition sought; or any user who enjoys and profits from the operation of serendipity in the catalog. Research might well reveal that most users would fall into one or more of the above categories. We do know that in one study, when users of both card and computer catalogs were asked to define a successful search in their own words, 13 percent of the computer catalog users and 19 percent of the card catalog users stated that finding something more than they were looking for was a criterion of success.[6] Disturbingly, another study reports user concern over a loss of serendipity in the switch from card catalogs to online catalogs.[7] As Thomas Mann, who works as a reference librarian at the Library of Congress, puts it, "While it is true that users do not want to *end* their research with 'everything' in the library, it remains true that they do wish to *start* with the best possible retrieval pool, from which they then make their selection."[8]

It is important for all catalog designers to realize that users often cannot specify in advance the terms that will be used in the catalog to describe the author, work, or subject they seek. One job of the catalog is to facilitate *recognition* on the part of the user, rather than to demand exact *specification*.

It is also important for all catalog designers to realize that what users are looking for, no matter what type of search they are doing, may often be represented by multiple records. An author is represented by at least one authority record (and often several),[9] as well as by all of the bibliographic records for that author's works. A work is represented by all the bibliographic records for editions of that work, as well as by records for works containing it, related to it, or about it. A subject is represented by an authority record for a subject heading, authority records for any subdivisions[10] that are attached to that heading, by a point or points in the classification with every classification number under it in the hierarchy, as well as by all bibliographic records with the relevant subject heading(s) or classification number(s). The ideal catalog ensures that all the records representing the author, work, or subject sought by the user are linked together and available for display to the user at every point that an individual record is displayed to the user. A catalog should never display a single record, even one that matches a user's search exactly, without indicating in some way the existence of related records and, if possible, the nature of those relationships. The keys to these relationships are the headings for authors, works, and subjects assigned by catalogers. Heading displays have the effect of demonstrating relationships to the user. OPACs that offer only bibliographic record displays, or that emphasize bibliographic record displays rather than heading displays, mask these relationships from users. Movement within a card catalog was essentially movement in and around a fixed, single, linear arrangement of records or references to records. Because of the way each bibliographic record contains several headings, the online catalog can be more like a kaleidoscope, which can be changed from one pattern or arrangement to another within seconds.

Some existing systems make it as easy as possible for users to explore the catalog by means of author, work, or subject relationships by allowing a user to select an entry on a retrieved record to obtain further retrievals.[11] For example, the user could choose to see other works by the same author, or the user could identify a useful subject heading attached to a record retrieved on a title search and ask to see other works to which that subject heading has been attached. This function is sometimes called *navigation*. Walt Crawford also refers to this type of search as "related-record searching," "jump" searching, and "bridge" searching.[12] The Music Library Association guidelines,[13] and Leslie Troutman,[14] suggest that we ought to be able to link editions of a work through their common uniform titles; this would work particularly well for music materials, which so frequently have authority controlled uniform titles. It ought to work fairly well for classic works of prolific authors, but less well for the rest, because of the lack of control exerted over titles in standard cataloging practice. If we could devise means to link together all editions of works, whether alphabetically (using uniform titles) or by other means (e.g., mechanical links), we could carry out the second cataloging objective of always showing the user all the editions of a sought work better than we have ever been able to do before using previous catalog technologies. The user who reaches a particular edition by means of a search that did not retrieve all editions of the work could still be assured of being led to, or at least informed of, all editions of the work.

A catalog should always assume that its fundamental goal is to put the user into place in a complex web of relationships and then to set the user free to explore that web.[15] The danger to be averted, as Thomas Mann eloquently puts it, is that "readers who retrieve 'something' very often miss most of what is actually available without realizing they've missed anything at all." Michael Berger has done a catalog use study that reveals the frequency with which users do suboptimal searches, in which they retrieve some materials but not the best materials for their information need.[16] As Mann goes on to point out, a good catalog ensures "predictability, serendipity, and depth of access."[17]

In addition to carrying out the objectives described above, which are required of it as a catalog, an online public access catalog also should follow the principles of good software and system design in order to be as easy to use as possible as well as to be as powerful as possible. An OPAC should always let the user be in charge; at any given step in the searching process, the user should be in complete control and able to determine what is done next. Systems should avoid the rigidity of algorithms that guess at the user's needs based on sketchy information; it is unlikely that algorithms will ever be developed that can figure out what a user wants—the searching process is just too complex. Instead, the user should always have at his or her fingertips a LOOK HARDER command or button that can be invoked at the user's discretion and suggest more complex types of searches and displays when the default searches and displays seem inadequate to the user. The user should be free to back out of these more complex approaches at any time.

There are a variety of online catalog systems with an array of options currently available for purchase "off-the-shelf"; many of these are "configurable," or "customizable." That is, the library that purchases the system is given a great deal of decision-making power about the system design of the catalog. For example, the library may be able to determine which fields will be indexed in which indexes, what searches will be available and what they will be called, how multiple retrieved records will be arranged, which fields will display in individual record displays, as well as the wording of *HELP* screens and terminology of field labels. Choosing among systems or among options within a system gives the individual library a great deal of power to ensure the design of an effective catalog that meets the needs of its own particular users; with power, as usual, comes responsibility. The ways in which the catalog should serve the library user should be kept firmly in mind in making decisions about systems or options within a system.

In discussing decisions to be made about the online public access catalog, the following assumptions are made: (1) users know very little about the database: what is in it, what vocabulary is used to index it, or how it is organized; and (2) users are the only ones competent to judge which items in the database are truly useful to them, that is, *pertinent* to their particular information need. The goal of effective online public access catalog design is a database that reveals its organization to the user as it is being searched, not by forcing the user to make many choices before arrival at her or his goal, but by informing the user at all times of all the available pathways from that point. The catalog should also provide the user with as many records as possible that may be relevant to his or her query but then allow the user to indicate which are truly relevant and to make all subsequent pertinence decisions.[18]

In making decisions about system design, we should try to build in devices to guide the user to all possible relevant records, but not to those that are clearly irrelevant, as well as devices to give the user the power, and enough information, to decide whether to exclude records in the doubtful cases. While we should build in as much power as possible to allow sophisticated users to narrow, expand, and combine searches at will, it is very important to provide a few simple and powerful defaults at every level of searching and displaying records so that the novice searcher has the best chance possible of doing an effective search without any training. There is evidence that most searchers use only a few commands, regardless of how many are provided.[19]

Another design principle is that the system itself should be as *unobtrusive* and *invisible* as possible. No command, even one that makes no sense to the computer, should cause the system to crash, come to a halt, or hang up. When a command makes no sense, the computer should give the user a clear but tactful message to that effect and suggest the commands that would make sense at that point. To the degree that it is possible, all commands should be available and work the same way at any point in a search. The computer should recognize many forms of the same command.[20]

One caveat: Whether you design your own system or purchase a configurable system, document all decisions carefully and make them readily available to sophisticated users by means of *HELP* screens. It is rare to find a system that provides its users with information such as which USMARC fields were indexed for which files or indexes or whether keyword matches are performed within a single field or within the whole record. This kind of information can be very helpful to the sophisticated user who wants to design the best possible search. It can also be helpful for staff training. Documentation can also be crucial for debugging the system. For all these reasons, be sure to document all decisions carefully.

History of OPACs

Many OPACs started out as circulation systems or local processing systems, with the public access interface added later. It wasn't until the 1980s that systems began to be designed specifically as OPACs.[21] The word *OPAC* was apparently coined in 1981.[22]

Perhaps the first automation project in a library occurred before World War II, when Ralph Parker of the University of Missouri Library began using IBM punched cards for circulation. However, it wasn't until the 1960s that automation projects began to occur frequently. In the late 1950s and early 1960s, the first computer-output microfiche catalogs began to appear. In 1963, the Yale University Medical Library began printing catalog cards from machine-readable data on punched cards. In the same year, the University of Toronto began a project to computerize production of book catalogs. The first computerized cataloging system may have been the one created at McDonnell Douglas in 1961. Throughout the 1960s and the 1970s, locally developed, noncommercial library automation projects established through college and university funding and federal matching funds proliferated; pioneers in these types of projects were Stanford University, University of Chicago, and Massachusetts Institute of Technology. These systems tended to be designed to support processing rather than public access: in 1966, Illinois State Library in Springfield introduced a circulation system; in the late 1960s, Oregon State University at Corvallis introduced an acquisitions system; the University of Chicago Library Data Management System was mainly an acquisitions system but used USMARC format records; and in the early 1970s the University of California at Los Angeles Biomedical Library introduced the precursor of ORION (UCLA Libraries online information system) in the form of a serials check-in system.

In 1967, OCLC launched its online system, which some would describe as the first successful, widely accepted library automation project. The next year, 1968, the Library of Congress published the USMARC format, which, for the first time, provided a standard structure for machine-readable cataloging data, so that data could be moved from system to system without record conversion.[23] Between 1969 and

1972, BALLOTS (Bibliographic Automation of Large Library Operations using a Time-sharing System) was founded, the precursor of RLIN (Research Libraries Information Network) and one of the first automation projects to make use of advanced retrieval software.

In the 1970s, a radical change in mass-market computer technology occurred, making possible faster systems with increased storage at a lower price; by the early 1970s, minicomputers were commercially viable. This made it possible for companies to sell off-the-shelf, or "turnkey," automation to libraries. In the early 1970s, CLSI (Computer Library Services International, Ltd.) introduced the first turnkey library system, designed initially only for circulation; its first installation was at the Cleveland Public Library in 1972.

It was only in the early 1980s that systems began to be designed specifically for public access; early examples were MSUS/PALS (Minnesota State University System) and the MELVYL system. Libraries began to build integrated systems and make multi-institutional arrangements. In 1980, CLSI installed the first OPAC offered by a commercial supplier, the public access catalog or PAC at the Evanston Public Library in Illinois. It was a module of a circulation system and did not use full USMARC records.

By the late 1970s, the first microcomputer systems began to appear; the Apple Computer Company was begun in 1975, the IBM PC was introduced in 1981, and the Apple Macintosh was introduced in 1984.[24] The microcomputer offers smaller libraries the power to program their own software to tailor their catalogs to meet the needs of their users. It also offers flexibility to larger libraries by permitting multiple interfaces to the same catalog.

Although the OPAC has its roots in nearly forty years of library automation history, its public access aspect is a relatively recent phenomenon; that no one has yet attempted a history of OPACs is evidence of their relative newness. It is not surprising that we have not yet managed to solve the problem of how to make such powerful and complex systems easy to use.

Research in Catalog Use

Research in catalog use is very difficult to carry out for a number of reasons. Among them are the following:

1. users do not have a vocabulary to use to discuss the bibliographic universe or the problems they are having dealing with it;
2. users are often unaware of the problems they are having so are unable to report them;
3. searching is a very complex process, and much of the recall and recognition work being done by the searching user is silent and unarticulated;
4. searching is an iterative process, in which trial and failure are followed by further trial; it can be hard to define the beginning and ending of the searching process;
5. searching involves a negotiation between the user and the system, during which the user learns about how the system works and applies this knowledge in further searching; the user's behavior is constantly being influenced by the system itself, making it difficult to evaluate the system by studying the user's behavior; and

6. there are a multitude of factors that affect the success of a given search, including, but not limited to

   (a) system design factors, such as the type of index chosen by the user, the type of indexing available, the file design of the system, the types of commands necessary for searching and displaying records, and the displays available;

   (b) the size and nature of the collection being searched;

   (c) the user's world knowledge and powers of observation; and

   (d) cataloging practices that affect record design.

This makes it very difficult to isolate one factor and study it in such a way that the results are not being influenced by all of the other factors affecting success.

In this book, we cite extensively from the research in catalog use that has been done so far. A list of all of the user studies consulted can be found in appendix A. It should be noted, however, that the research done so far just scratches the surface of the complexity of the searching process described above. It tends to focus on the types of things that a machine can identify. For example, the most common type of research studies searches that result in no hits, with the assumption that all no-hit searches are failed searches. However, there are many cases in which a no-hit search is a successful search, e.g., when the collection does not hold a work on the topic sought, when no one has written a work on the topic sought, when the work sought is not in the collection, etc. There are other cases when the no-hit search is the only possible response, e.g., when the user has typed in a hopelessly misspelled word or an egregious typo. It's unlikely that any algorithm can ever be developed to recognize all the possible misspellings and typos that users can come up with. Meanwhile, this type of research ignores what Berger calls suboptimal searching, in which the user does retrieve some material but not the best material available.[25]

It may be that we will never be able to design research methodologies sophisticated enough to penetrate the complex cognitive processes going on in the course of a user's search of an OPAC. For that reason, it would be wise to devise other ways to learn how to improve OPAC design. Professional librarians who are knowledgeable about both OPACs (records and systems) and the types of problems users are having with them are a largely untapped resource in this regard. Design processes that involve extensive testing using real users with real information needs have not been widely tried so far, to our knowledge, but could hold great potential. Use of concrete examples of citations and the records they need to match, such as those examples we cite frequently in this book, could also be used to test OPAC performance.

Notes

1. *The ALA Glossary of Library and Information Science* (Chicago: American Library Association, 1983).

2. Martha M. Yee, "What Is a Work? Part 1, The User and the Objects of the Catalog," *Cataloging & Classification Quarterly* 19, no. 1 (1994): 9–28.

3. Charles Ammi Cutter, "Rules for a Printed Dictionary Catalogue," in *Public Libraries in the United States of America, Part II* (Washington, D.C.: Govt. Print. Off., 1876), p. 10.

4. International Conference on Cataloguing Principles (1961: Paris), *Statement of Principles*, annotated ed. with commentary and examples by Eva Verona (London: IFLA Committee on Cataloguing, 1971), p. xiii.

5. Peter H. Mann, "A Browser's Catalogue," *New Library World* 83 (Oct. 1982): 143–145.

6. N. C. Kranich, C. M. Spellman, D. Hecht, et al., "Evaluating the Online Catalog from a Public Services Perspective: A Case Study at the New York

University Libraries," in *The Impact of Online Catalogs*, ed. J. R. Matthews (New York: Neal-Schuman, 1986), p. 109, 127; N. C. Kranich, *A Study of an Online Catalog from a Public Services Perspective* (Washington, D.C.: Office of Management Studies, Association of Research Libraries, 1984), p. 18.

7. C. Walton, S. Williamson, and H. D. White, "Resistance to Online Catalogs: A Comparative Study at Bryn Mawr and Swarthmore Colleges," *Library Resources & Technical Services* 30 (Oct./Dec. 1986): 392.

8. Thomas Mann, letter to Martha M. Yee, August 5, 1994.

9. For example, authority records for the author's various pseudonyms and authority records for the author heading with various subject subdivisions.

10. *Subdivisions* are subsequent pieces of a subject heading that are added to the main heading. The following is an LCSH heading:

CHINA—HISTORY—OPIUM WAR OF 1840–1842.

The main heading is *China*. *History* is a topical subdivision. *Opium War of 1840–1842* is a chronological subdivision.

11. Among these are:

1. BLIS (Biblio-Techniques Library and Information System, WLN), described in Curtis W. Stucki, "BLIS: Biblio-Techniques Library and Information System," *Library Hi-Tech* 11 (1985): 73–84.

2. CARL (Colorado Alliance of Research Libraries) ("Express Search"), described in Walt Crawford, *The Online Catalog Book: Essays and Examples* (Boston: G. K. Hall, 1992), p. 165.

3. Dynix ("Related Works Menu"), described in Crawford, *Online*, p. 240.

4. ILLINET online music subsystem ("K" command keeps the headings on a particular record; "F" and no. of line redoes the search), described in Leslie Troutman, "The Online Public Access Catalog and Music Materials: Issues for System and Interface Design," *Advances in Online Public Access Catalogs* 1 (1992): 25–29.

5. Marquis ("Related Works"), described in Crawford, *Online*, p. 375.

6. NLS (Network Library System) at the University of Wisconsin-Madison, described in Donna Senzig, *Network Library System Public Access Catalog* (Madison, Wisc.: University of Wisconsin-Madison Board of Regents, 1985); *NLS User's Guide*, preliminary edition (Madison, Wisc.: University of Wisconsin-Madison Libraries, 1985).

7. TINman, described in Helen L. Henderson, "TINman: Information Made Easy," in *Online Public Access to Library Files: Proceedings of a Conference Held at the University of Bath, 3–5 Sept. 1984*, ed. Janet Kinsella (Oxford, Eng.: Elsevier International Bulletins, 1985), p. 183–185; Kathleen T. Bivins Noerr and Peter L. Noerr, "A Microcomputer System for Online Catalogues," in *Future of Online Catalogues*, ed. A. H. Helala and J. W. Weiss (Essen, Germany: Gesamthochschulbibliothek, 1986), p. 360–392; Peter L. Noerr and Kathleen T. Bivins Noerr, "Browse and Navigate: An Advance in Database Access Methods," *Information Processing and Management* 21 (1985): 205–213.

12. Crawford, *Online*, p. 17.

13. Lenore Coral, Ivy Anderson, Keiko Cho, et al., "Automation Requirements for Music Information," *MLA Notes* 43 (Sept. 1986): 14–18. (A report of the Subcommittee on Music Automation of the Music Library Association.)

14. Leslie Troutman, "The Online Public Access Catalog and Music Materials: Issues for System and Interface Design," *Advances in Online Public Access Catalogs* 1 (1992): 17.

15. For a related discussion on the importance of giving users access to the *catalog*, not simply to individual *records*, see Sara Shatford Layne, "Integration and the Objectives of the Catalog," in *The Conceptual Foundations of Descriptive Cataloging*, ed. Elaine Svenonius (San Diego, Calif.: Academic Press, 1989), p. 189.

16. Michael George Berger, "Information-Seeking in the Online Bibliographic System: An Exploratory Study" (Ph.D. diss., UC Berkeley, 1994).

17. Thomas Mann, letter to Martha M. Yee, August 5, 1994.

18. *Relevant* is used here to describe documents that are about the subject, are by the author, or represent the work that is sought by the user. Relevance is an important concept in online systems, because it is easy for keyword searching to retrieve documents that match the input keywords but are not actually what the user was looking for. *Pertinence* is

a further refinement of this concept to take into account the fact that a user may have other reasons for rejecting retrieved documents, even when they are relevant; for example, the user may have already read a particular retrieved document. It should be fairly obvious from this example that only the user can judge pertinence, although a good system can retrieve documents likely to be relevant; because of the existence of synonyms, homonyms, and homographs, it may be necessary for the system to refer some relevance decisions back to the user. The distinction between relevance and pertinence was originally made by Kemp and Foskett: D. A. Kemp, "Relevance, Pertinence, and Information System Development," *Information Storage and Retrieval* 10 (1974): 37–47; D. J. Foskett, "A Note on the Concept of Relevance," *Information Storage and Retrieval* 8 (1972): 77–78. It was further discussed by Lancaster: F. Wilfred Lancaster, "Pertinence and Relevance," in his *Information Retrieval Systems: Characteristics, Testing and Evaluation*, 2nd ed. (New York: Wiley, 1979).

19. Berger, "Information-Seeking"; Michael George Berger and Mary Jean Moore, "The User Meets the MELVYL System," *DLA Bulletin* 16, no. 1 (fall 1996): 13–21; Michael K. Buckland, Mark H. Butler, Barbara A. Norgard, et al., "OASIS: A Front-End for Prototyping Catalog Enhancements," *Library Hi-Tech* 10, no. 4 (1992): 9. See also the following for a lengthy bibliography of research on the principle of least effort: Thomas Mann, *Library Research Models: A Guide to Classification, Cataloging and Computers* (New York: Oxford University Press, 1993), p. 91–101, 221–242. Johnson and Connaway found that one of the criticisms of the NLS system the users they interviewed had was, "I hate the many different ways there are to search for an author." Debra Wilcox Johnson and Lynn Silipigni Connaway,

"Use of Online Catalogs: A Report of Results of Focus Group Interviews," typescript (Feb. 1992): 11.

20. This was a specific request of users interviewed by Johnson and Connaway, "Use of Online Catalogs," p. 12, 28.

21. Historical information was taken from the following works: James Barrentine and Trudy Kontoff, "Library Automation Software," *Library Technology Reports* 26 (July/Aug. 1990): 475–483; Audrey N. Grosch, "Hardware for Library Automation," *Library Technology Reports* 26 (July/Aug. 1990): 463–474; Ernest A. Muro, "The Library Automation Marketplace," *Library Technology Reports* 26 (July/Aug. 1990): 455–462; Richard W. Newman, "Four North American Bibliographic Networks," *Library Technology Reports* 26 (July/Aug. 1990): 485–495; Dennis Reynolds, *Library Automation: Issues and Applications* (New York: Bowker, 1985), p. 13–16, 72–102; William Saffady, *Introduction to Automation for Librarians*, 3rd ed. (Chicago: American Library Association, 1994), p. 219–220.

22. Charles Hildreth, e-mail communication to Open Library and Information Science Education Forum, March 9, 1994.

23. *USMARC Format for Bibliographic Data, Including Guidelines for Content Designation*, 1994 ed. Prepared by Network Development and MARC Standards Office (Washington, D.C.: Cataloging Distribution Service, Library of Congress, 1994).

24. Michael J. Miller, "Looking Back: Introduction of the PC," *PC Magazine* 16, no. 6 (March 25, 1997): 108–136.

25. Berger, "Information-Seeking"; Berger, *The User Meets*; and Berger and Moore, "The User Meets."

2

Interfaces

Interfaces are changing rapidly, and this book may become quickly outdated on the topic of interfaces because of this rapid change. What is driving the change is the rapid change in the microcomputer market. Libraries are just the tail on that dog, and that is as it should be, to some extent. Libraries must follow the culture, not vice versa. We must use the language of our users rather than imposing our own fabricated terms on them. Similarly, we should try to use the computer interfaces with which our users are most familiar. There is just one qualification to this principle, however: we must ensure that the interfaces we use do not prevent users from finding the authors, works, and subjects they seek by imposing unreasonable restraints on the OPAC design process.

Command-Based, Menu-Based, and Form Fill-In Interfaces

Walt Crawford provides an extensive discussion of the pros and cons of command-based systems versus menu-based systems.[1] Menu-based systems and their variants, touch-screen systems, as well as graphical user interfaces and hypertext systems with point-and-click functions provide novice users with more guidance, and require less typing on the user's part, but can be slow and inflexible.[2] The inflexibility is inherent in these systems, as there are a limited number of choices you can fit on any screen; whichever choices you decide to offer first may not be good fits for the user's actual information needs; if you add many subsequent layers, the user can get lost in a maze of hierarchies. Because there are potentially an infinite number of questions a user could ask a catalog, menu-based systems can be frustrating to use.

Command-based systems usually provide the knowledgeable user with speed, power, and flexibility, but they take some time to learn. Prompted-entry (fill-in-the-blanks) interfaces, like menu-based systems, can be slow and inflexible but have the advantage of allowing the user to be quite precise about the nature of search terms being input, without having to learn complex labels for these terms.

One way that most current online catalogs are harder to use than the old card catalogs is that in most the user must often choose among different types of searches (e.g., keyword or exact search) and different indexes (e.g., subject or author) without really understanding what the differences are among them.[3] Form fill-in systems can make a system easier to use.[4] For example, the user who is looking for a particular work and has a citation that includes the names of two authors and a title should be able to tell the computer to look for a first author, a second author, and a title; a well-designed prompted-entry system could collect this data properly without the user having to know the system very well, although it would require the user to have accurately identified the categories of information in her or his citation, which is not always a simple matter.

If the searching software knows precisely what kind of data is being searched, the terms can be searched in a more sophisticated manner; for example, author surnames can be searched only in surname subfields in all bibliographic and authority fields known to contain author names, and author forenames can be severely truncated, so as to retrieve forms of name that have forename initials. Rebecca Denning and Philip Smith describe a system (ELSA, Electronic Library Search Assistant) that shows the user lists of authorized headings in a window next to a form fill-in window, prompting the user to choose authorized forms for each box filled in on the form.[5] Of course, command searching should always be available for the more sophisticated users who are willing to learn more about the system, in order to have increased speed. Figure 2.1 contains some examples of form fill-in screens that designers might find thought-provoking, if not yet ideal.

Menu-based or prompted-entry systems could be better designed to offer searches that correspond more closely to what most users are looking for. The objectives of the catalog and user studies coincide in stating that the three most common searches done by users are (1) a search for a particular work; (2) a search for the works of a particular author; and (3) a search for works on a particular subject.[6] Not one of the systems described in Crawford's *Online Catalog Book* offers the user the option of a search for a particular work; the choice most often is *either* author *or* title, although a few do offer an author-title combined search, often only in command mode, which means it is only available to the sophisticated user.[7]

Frequently, several different cryptically named searches are offered for author and subject, without any explanation or suggestions about which might be preferable as a first search. For example, one system offers a "Subject" search and a "Subject Keyword" search. Another offers a choice among "Author," "Title," "Subject," and "Key Word." By all means, systems should offer every possible degree of flexibility and power to knowledgeable users, including a number of different author, title, and subject searches. However, it would be helpful to the novice user if the best first search was made readily available; for example, the opening menu (which could be overridden by the sophisticated user who prefers to use commands) could list the three main types of searches—a search for a particular work, a search for a particular author, and a search for a particular subject. In a form fill-in system, such as the one shown in figure 2.1, if the user chose one type of search, the appropriate form fill-in screen could be brought up.

Client-Server Interfaces

Crawford's chapter entitled "Distributed Power" is a good introduction to the concept of the client-server model and to the ANSI/NISO Z39.50 standard, Information Retrieval Service Definition and Protocol Specifications for Library Applications. The

The following examples of form fill-ins are offered just to help the reader visualize better how this might work. No examples in this book are meant to be prescriptive.

Initial Menu Screen

Please Choose One Type of Search
   1. A particular work (or title)
   2. A particular author, artist, actor, musician, etc.
   3. A particular company, association, institution, or conference
   4. Works on a particular subject or in a particular form or genre
   5. Other

Form Fill-In Screen for User Seeking a Particular Work

Please fill in anything you know about the work; feel free to leave lines blank when you have no information or doubtful information.

Author 1: Last name: _____

            First name: _____

Author 2: Last name: _____

            First name: _____

Title: _____

Please indicate preference: ____ Find all of the words above*

                            ____ Find at least one of the words above

                            ____ Find all of the words above exactly in the order they
                                 were typed in

                            ____ Find the first word or two of the above exactly in
                                 the order they were typed in

                          *Default search

Subject of work: _____

Conference: _____

Company, association, or institution connected with the work:

_____

Form Fill-In Screen for User Seeking a Particular Author

Last name: _____   First name: _____

Form Fill-In Screen for User Seeking a Particular Corporate Body

Company, association, or institution connected with the work:

_____

Conference: _____

Figure 2.1   Examples of form fill-ins

Form Fill-In Screen for User Seeking Works on a Particular Subject

If the subject you are interested in has several different aspects or covers several different concepts, please put each aspect or concept on a separate line below:

Term or phrase 1: _____

Term or phrase 2: _____

Term or phrase 3: _____

Please indicate preference: ____ Find all of the words above*
____ Find at least one of the words above
____ Find all of the words above exactly in the order they were typed in
____ Find the first word or two of the above exactly in the order they were typed in
*Default search

Form Fill-In Screen for User Who Chooses Other

Please type in any words or names you would like to have searched:

_____

_____

Please indicate preference: ____ Find all of the words above*
____ Find at least one of the words above
____ Find all of the words above exactly in the order they were typed in
____ Find the first word or two of the above exactly in the order they were typed in
*Default search

Note: This "other" search might be useful for a user whose citation is so garbled that he or she is not sure whether a particular word is from a title, a conference name, or a series (or even a subject heading). There should always be some type of search available for users who don't know what types of words are in a citation.

client-server model allows different interfaces to be overlayed on existing systems, either to allow users to design, or at least choose, their own interfaces or, as in the case of Z39.50, to standardize the user's interface to many different systems.[8] For example, if the system knows a user is a science student, it could ask her if she would prefer a default sort order that puts the most current publications first, and then remember that for every search session. If this is done, however, it should always be easy for the user to change the default for a particular search, for a particular session, or permanently. Such customized systems could also offer users a kind of Selective Dissemination of Information, or SDI, service in which a particular search strategy could be run against new acquisitions each month, with results automatically reported to the user. If users are allowed to design their own desktops and toolbars, and name the buttons on their toolbars, the client-server model could be said to come close to allowing users to design at least parts of their own user interface.

It should be noted that the client-server interface generally depends on the client being a fairly powerful computer in its own right, and one that is networked to the server. One danger of client-server interfaces can occur when the client is not sufficiently powerful to sort and display large numbers of records. In the mainframe world familiar to many large research libraries, time-sharing allowed any user theoretically to tap the immense power of the entire mainframe for a fraction of a second; this allowed users to retrieve and sort tens of thousands of records. Even though servers can appear to approach the power of older mainframes, this is somewhat deceptive, as the power from a server comes from adding up the power of all of the various modules that comprise it, and the entire power is never available to one particular user. Thus, client-server systems need to be carefully engineered so as to be able to handle long searches and large retrievals that require complex displays.

The client-server approach is currently under attack in the world at large. The current buzzword is "thin-client computing," meaning less powerful clients. As one writer puts it, "Large businesses are looking for a way back to the mainframe model, because the networked PC is simply too expensive and too much of a hassle. . . . Maintenance and upgrade costs have turned out to be budget-busters."[9] If the library world eventually follows the corporate world, as it has in the past, this may mean the eventual end of the client-server interface.

Separating the interface from the database, as is done in the client-server model, is not as easy as some would like to think, as the design of the database profoundly affects the nature of the interface, and to consider them separately is highly artificial.[10] A Library and Information Technology Association (LITA) program on implementing Z39.50 included many reports of problems due to differences in underlying indexing and display software, including differences in valid commands from one system to another, differences in the rules for entering data in valid commands from one system to another, and displays that did not include the fields that led to the record being retrieved.[11] Gary Klein warns that designing interfaces that use Z39.50 is going to be made even more complicated by the fact that different sites using the same configurable software have made many different configuration decisions.[12] Also, as Denise Troll points out, maintaining a number of different interfaces means more programming, more hardware and software testing, and more management and makes the system designer's job considerably more complex, especially when changes in the system are required.[13] There are costs associated with the development, maintenance, and distribution involved, and libraries rarely have a lot to spend. Finally, the maintenance of many different interfaces makes difficulties for reference librarians and systems staff who must aid the public with problem solving at remote sites on interfaces the library staff may never have seen.

However, these efforts to allow a user to have the same interface on any system he or she may choose to search reveals a longing for greater simplicity and standardization of interfaces for the user, which is probably a healthy impetus. The current complexity is staggering. It is hard for even a trained librarian to learn to search so many different systems.

Graphical User Interfaces

A graphical user interface (GUI) is defined as "a combination of windows with pull-down menus, icons (pictures to represent things or ideas), and a pointing device, such as a mouse or trackball, to manipulate information."[14] We have dealt with the point-

and-click and pull-down-menu aspects of GUIs above in the section on menu-based interfaces. However, we have not yet dealt with the graphical aspect, that is, the use of pictures to represent things or ideas. The bibliographic universe is not an inherently visual one; what image would represent the concept of *imprint* to most of the population of library users, for example? Thus, it is difficult to devise graphical images that communicate the complexities of the search process adequately. However, there is an effort at the international level (at the International Federation of Library Associations and Institutions, or IFLA) to establish a standard set of icons for use in bibliographic information systems.[15] If this effort were to succeed to the extent that the standard icons became familiar to library users all over the world, these visual images might have the potential to facilitate communication across language barriers.

Web Interfaces

Much energy is being devoted these days to the design of Web interfaces. Because of the rapid expansion of the World Wide Web, most users can now be assumed to have some type of Web browsing software already on their computers (e.g., Netscape or Microsoft Internet Explorer); in essence, this standard and widely used Web browsing software becomes the client to which the library's Web catalog "serves" up Web pages. This has the advantage of freeing the library from having to develop, maintain, and distribute a proprietary piece of software that users will need to be guided through a search of the catalog and to display records from it. The library can say to a user, if you have Netscape or Internet Explorer on your computer, you can search our catalog. Also, the library can design one user interface for all clients and avoid some of the problems that arise with Z39.50 applications, in which users may have many different interfaces. Web access allows access to much more than just text, including, for example, digitized maps, images, and sound that can be linked to catalog records that describe them.

However, there are some disadvantages as well. The Web interface must be designed using Hypertext Markup Language (HTML), and in the current state of this evolving standard, this requirement can impose significant constraints on the design process.[16] Right now, the fundamental model on the Web is the hypertext link, which assumes that you will choose one link at a time. This model does not accommodate the pattern in many catalogs that allows users to choose more than one entity at a time or in which one-to-many links can be made. Another potential problem is due to the "stateless nature of the Web."

> A web server responds to page requests either by returning an HTML page or by triggering an external application via a server API. [Application Programming Interface] Once the page is delivered or the application executes, the transaction is complete and the connection closes. The server makes no provision for storing vital information about the application and the user within the application. This approach is fine for delivering hypertext documents, but creates huge headaches for anyone trying to design a tight multipage database application.[17]

Ray Larson et al. remark, for example, that "because HTTP is a stateless protocol, with each query/response pair considered a complete transaction, the ability to do relevance feedback is very limited in the current WWW implementation."[18] This does not sound like a good model for a system that needs to support complex and iterative searching of library catalogs. Already ways to register users at a Web site using IP (Internet Protocol) addresses are being developed, so that their previous searching actions can be remembered over time, but lots of development will be necessary before the Web environment can be made truly hospitable to catalog applications. Use of a Web interface also means that all users of the system must have powerful enough computers to run Web browsing software. Users who have older computers and older modems may find the slowness of the Web frustrating. The Web is also suffering telecommunications growing pains at the moment that make its use frustrating for all users.

Notes

1. Walt Crawford, *The Online Catalog Book: Essays and Examples* (Boston: G. K. Hall, 1992), p. 9–11.

2. Christine L. Borgman, Sandra G. Hirsh, Virginia A. Walter, et al., "Children's Searching Behavior on Browsing and Keyword Online Catalogs: The Science Library Project," *Journal of the American Society for Information Science* 46 (1995): 663–684.

3. Nicholson Baker, "Discards," *New Yorker,* April 4, 1994, p. 81.

4. Systems with form fill-in: LaserGuide (Charles Hildreth, *Intelligent Interfaces and Retrieval Methods* [Washington, D.C.: Cataloging Distribution Service, 1989], p. 62–63); TECHLIB Plus (Hildreth, in Crawford, *Online*, p. 459); TINlib (Hildreth, *Intelligent*, p. 24).

5. Rebecca Denning and Philip J. Smith, "Interface Design Concepts in the Development of ELSA, an Intelligent Electronic Library Search Assistant," *Information Technology and Libraries* 13 (June 1994): 133–147.

6. An example of a work is Shakespeare's *Hamlet.* A work can exist in many editions and, therefore, be represented by many records in the catalog. When a user has a citation to just an author and a title, the citation is to a particular work. When the citation gives a publisher, a date, an edition statement, etc., it is a citation to a particular edition of a particular work. For further discussion of this rather complex area of cataloging theory, see Martha M. Yee, "What Is a Work? Part 1, The User and the Objects of the Catalog," *Cataloging & Classification Quarterly* 19, no. 1 (1994): 9–28; Martha M. Yee, "What Is a Work? Part 2, The Anglo-American Cataloging Codes," *Cataloging & Classification Quarterly* 19, no. 2 (1994): 5–22; Martha M. Yee, "What Is a Work? Part 3, The Anglo-American Cataloging Codes," *Cataloging & Classification Quarterly* 20, no. 1 (1995): 25–46; Martha M. Yee, "What Is a Work? Part 4, Cataloging Theorists and a Definition," *Cataloging & Classification Quarterly* 20, no. 2 (1995): 3–24.

7. Systems that allow combined author and title searches: CL-CAT ("Author and title"; Crawford, *Online*, p. 183); DOBIS ("combined Boolean" must be chosen; then fill-in screen provided; Crawford, *Online*, p. 221); IO+ ("Author-title"; Crawford, *Online*, p. 312); Josiah ("start AUTHOR/TITLE search"; Crawford, *Online*, p. 326); MARCIVE ("combined search"; Crawford, *Online*, p. 357); MELVYL (FPA AND FTI); Okapi '84 offered two choices to users: "Specific books" and "Books about something" (Stephen Walker, "The Okapi Online Catalogue Research Projects," in *The Online Catalogue: Developments and Directions*, ed. Charles Hildreth [London: Library Association, 1989], p. 85); ORION (FNT); TECHLIBplus (form fill-in; Crawford, *Online*, p. 459); Unicorn ("author with title"; Crawford, *Online*, p. 484); USCInfo ("Author/Title"; Crawford, *Online*, p. 497).

8. Crawford, *Online*, p. 89–94. Also see the following: Library of Congress Z39.50 Web page: http://lcweb.loc.gov/z3950/agency/; David S. Linthicum, "Client/Server Unraveled," *PC Magazine*, March 26, 1996, NE1–25; William E. Moen, *A Guide to the ANSI/NISO Z39.50 Protocol: Information Retrieval in the Information Infrastructure* (Bethesda, Md.: NISO Press, 1996); Karen G. Schneider, "Z39.50: Beyond Your Wildest Dreams," *American Libraries* (June/July 1996): 86.

9. John C. Dvorak, "The Decline of Desktop Computing," *PC Magazine*, Jan. 21, 1997, p. 87.

10. Martha M. Yee, "System Design and Cataloging Meet the User: User Interfaces to Online Public Access Catalogs," *Journal of the American Society for Information Science* 42 (March 1991): 78–80.

11. Donna L. Hirst, "Z39.50 Implementation and Impact," *LITA Newsletter* 15, no. 4 (fall 1994): 13–15.

12. Gary M. Klein, "A Bibliometric Analysis of Processing Options Chosen by Libraries to Execute Keyword Searches in Online Public Access Catalogs: Is There a Standard Default Keyword Operator?", typescript.

13. Denise A. Troll, "The Mercury Project: Meeting the Expectations of Electronic Library Patrons," *Advances in Online Public Access Catalogs* 1 (1992): 114–135.

14. Richard P. Hulser, "Overview of Graphical User Interfaces," *Advances in Online Public Access Catalogs* 1 (1992): 1–8.

15. The Web site for this project is located at http://lorne.stir.ac.uk/iconstd/

16. A critical examination of bibliographic displays in Web-to-catalog interfaces in academic libraries has been carried out at the University of Toronto School of Information Studies, and they have noted "inherent limitations imposed by HTML." See their Web site at http://www.fis.utoronto.ca/research/displays/

17. "Web Database Tools," *PC Magazine*, Sept. 10, 1996, p. 206–207.

18. Ray R. Larson, Jerome McDonough, Paul O'Leary, et al., "Cheshire II: Designing a Next-Generation Online Catalog," *Journal of the American Society for Information Science* 47 (July 1996): 564.

3

The Building Blocks: The Structure of Bibliographic and Authority Records

In this chapter we examine the basic building blocks for an online public access catalog that uses USMARC records. The basic building blocks are the USMARC bibliographic record and the USMARC authority record. Also available are US-MARC holdings and community information records, but these are much less widely used, and to a great extent their use has not yet stabilized, so we will not cover them here. We also describe the basic types of indexing algorithms that are available to system designers, so that we can refer to them later in describing solutions to various design problems.

Introduction to the USMARC Bibliographic Record

See figure 3.1 for a portion of a USMARC bibliographic record. Let us begin with some definitions. Each three-numeral number is a *tag* that begins a separate *field*. All the fields put together make up a *record* that describes a book by Hunter S. Thompson. The tags indicate what type of data is contained in the field that follows. For example, in the record in figure 3.1, the tags are defined as shown in figure 3.2. Each field is made up of *subfields*, which are identified by a *delimiter* and a *subfield code*. For example, the 260 (or imprint) field in the record in figure 3.1 contains the subfields shown in figure 3.3.

There are a number of different ways to analyze the types of data that can be found in a USMARC bibliographic record. First, the data can be analyzed into the following three different categories: transcribed data, normalized data, and composed data. *Transcribed data* are copied by the cataloger from the item being cataloged. For example, the 245 field in the record in figure 3.1 contains the title, subtitle, and statement of responsibility as they appear on the title page of the book itself. In the record in figure 3.1, the following fields are transcribed: 245, 250, 260.

Normalized data are manipulated by the cataloger in order to provide consistency in the indexing of the catalog. For example, one form of name is chosen for each author, with *see* or *search under* references from other forms of name that may appear on other title pages. Thus, the normalized data are *not* transcribed. The fields containing normalized data are sometimes called *heading fields*. Each heading field can be extracted from the bibliographic record and placed in an index to the bibliographic records. For example, the subject heading fields in the record in figure 3.1 could be extracted and placed in a subject index. In the record in figure 3.1, the following fields are heading fields: 100, 600, 650. *Controlled vocabulary* is another term that is used for *normalized data* when it concerns the subject matter of the item cataloged.

The sharp-witted reader may have noticed by now that the 245 field is somewhat anomalous in this analysis. It is a transcribed field, but it is also used as a heading field in most OPACs; in this instance, we make one field do double duty, performing both as transcribed information and as a heading. Of course, if a particular work needs to be represented in the catalog under a different title than the title that appears on the item, a normalized title can be inserted between the author and the title on the

100	10	≠a Thompson, Hunter S.
245	10	≠a Fear and loathing in Las Vegas : ≠b a savage journey to the heart of the American dream / ≠c by Hunter S. Thompson ; illustrated by Ralph Steadman.
250	__	≠a 1st Vintage Books ed.
260	__	≠a New York : ≠b Vintage Books, ≠c 1989, c1971.
300	__	≠a 204 p. : ≠b ill. ; ≠c 21 cm.
600	10	≠a Thompson, Hunter S.
650	_0	≠a Journalists ≠z United States ≠x Biography.

Figure 3.1   A portion of a USMARC bibliographic record

100	Main entry—personal name
245	Title statement
250	Edition statement
260	Publication, distribution, etc. (Imprint)
300	Physical description
600	Subject added entry—personal name
650	Subject added entry—topical term

Figure 3.2   Definition of tags shown in figure 3.1

≠a	Place of publication, distribution, etc.
≠b	Name of publisher, distributor, etc.
≠c	Date of publication, distribution, etc.

≠ is a delimiter. a, b, and c are subfield codes.

Figure 3.3   Subfields in the 260 field in figure 3.1

record; such a normalized title is known as a *uniform title*. The even more sharp-witted reader may have begun to notice that, while each author and each subject is represented by a single heading field in the bibliographic record, each work (or at least each work that has an author) is actually represented by a combination of two fields, the author main entry and the title field.

These two observations about the way data are stored in the USMARC record—the fact that the title field does double duty, functioning as both a transcribed field and a heading, and the fact that a work is often represented by a combination of two fields, not just one—will have a bearing on our future discussions of the difficulty of providing users with access to particular works in the OPAC.

It might also be useful to mention here the problem that arises when a topical subject sought by a user is found in more than one subject heading, rather than in a single heading field. This will be discussed more thoroughly in later chapters, but the record in our example (figure 3.1) illustrates the problem. If a user was looking for a biography of Hunter S. Thompson, and used both his name and the term BIOGRAPHY in the search, the search would fail unless it searched both subject heading fields simultaneously.

The third type of data, *composed fields*, is created by the cataloger, rather than copied from the item being cataloged, but they are not normalized fields. The only composed field in the record in figure 3.1 is the 300 physical description field. Most note fields are also composed by catalogers, including summaries describing the subject matter of a work.

Some have looked at the fact that a USMARC record may contain the same data in more than one form, e.g., transcribed and normalized or composed and normalized, and have criticized the USMARC format for encouraging redundant storage of data.[1] These critics have failed to realize the value to some users of the catalog of knowing exactly what appeared on the item cataloged, even if that form is not used to index the name, subject, or work sought.

Another way to analyze the data in the USMARC format is to approach it from the point of view of information about the topical subject content of the work being cataloged, i.e., what the work is about. From this point of view, the data can be divided into *free text data* and normalized data. The free text data consist of transcribed and composed fields that contain words that can help the user deduce what the work is *about*; free text data are contained in fields such as the title or a summary note composed by the cataloger. However, because this information has not been normalized, the user searching directly and exclusively on this data would be left to her or his own devices to think of all synonyms and variant spellings for the concept or concepts sought, as well as broader or narrower topics that might be of use. Because of the existence of homonyms, words that are not controlled can pull up undesired material; for example, an engineer who searches using the word POWER may pull up political science materials. Also, the user would be likely to miss works that had cryptic titles. In the record in figure 3.1, the only field that would be a candidate for free text searching would be the title field; this work is a good example of one with a cryptic title that, by itself, does not reveal that this is the autobiography of the journalist and freelance writer Hunter S. Thompson.

A final problem with searches on free text data is that it is difficult to display the results effectively, because a heading display is not available. Because free text searches often pull up irrelevant material because of the homonym problem, the display problem causes real hardships for users, who cannot always easily tell why a given item was retrieved. (These display problems will be discussed in later chapters.) In contrast, the normalized subject fields (600 and 650 in the record in figure 3.1) contain headings that can be placed into a subject index together with *see* and *see also* references that can guide the user from narrower to broader terms, or from unused terms to used ones. In addition, the results of a user's search of the headings can be displayed much more concisely and are much easier to scan.

All of this should not be taken as an argument not to index free text fields at all, but rather a warning not to make such searches the primary or default search in a system. A better approach is to use free text searching as a backup when searching using normalized fields has failed.

The USMARC bibliographic record contains one more type of data: *coded data*. In fixed-length fields such as the 006, 007, and 008 fields can be found codes that identify an item as a serial or a monograph, a 16 mm. motion picture or a half-inch VHS videocassette, a color motion picture or a black-and-white motion picture, etc. There is a wealth of coded data in the average USMARC record, and most systems have only scratched the surface in making this data accessible and useful to catalog users. The 006 field is a recent development in the USMARC format, developed as part of an initiative known as *format integration*. Format integration was a response to the problem raised by the initial design of the USMARC format, which included a fair amount of cross-classification in its approach to different formats of material. For example, if one had a serial map, one had to decide to treat it as either a map or a serial; it was not possible to code and describe the various aspects of both. The 006 field was developed to hold the 008 field codes for a secondary aspect of an item. For example, a serial map would be coded as a map in the 008 field and as a serial in the 006 field. All system applications that check coded data in the USMARC format should be designed to check in both the 008 field and the 006 field if present.

The USMARC holdings format can also contain 006, 007, and 008 fields. All system applications, such as limiting (see chapter 12), that check coded data in the 007 field should be designed to check both bibliographic and holdings records for 007 codes.

Introduction to the USMARC Authority Record

An authority file is a file that records decisions made by catalogers about forms of name. It consists of authority records. An authority record represents a particular person, a particular corporate body, or a particular work. It contains the heading that catalogers have decided to use and *see* or *search under* references from any forms of name that they have decided not to use. In addition, it can contain *see also* references for related names, bodies, or works and various scope and history notes that indicate why certain decisions were made or that help explicate particularly complex bibliographic situations. The authority file can be an invaluable tool for users of the catalog, who benefit from its cross-reference structure and from its scope and history notes.[2] Figure 3.4 contains a portion of a USMARC authority record for an author. The 100 field contains the established form of name, and the 400 field contains a *see* reference from another name by which Hunter S. Thompson is known. The *see* reference can be used to help the user who searches under RAOUL DUKE instead of HUNTER S. THOMPSON. The 667 field contains a note that gives further information about the person represented in the heading. It can be very useful to display such information to users. The 670 fields are probably less useful for users, as they form a record for the cataloger of the forms of name that were observed in various sources as a justification for the decision about the form of name to use to identify this person and the various cross-references to make. Think of the 670 fields as being something like the citations to primary source materials found in footnotes in historical works.

The term *authority control* refers to an important way catalogers create order out of bibliographic chaos. One form of chaos occurs when two different people use the same name. When this happens, catalogers use birth and death dates, middle initials, middle names, or qualifiers of various kinds to differentiate between the two people (see figure 3.5). Another form of chaos occurs when one person uses more than one name. Catalog function 2.2 (a), to allow a user to ascertain which works by a particular author are in the library (see chapter 1), requires that a single form of name be chosen for entry and that *see* references be made from all unused forms of name (see figure 3.6). The Paris

---

100 10   ≠a Thompson, Hunter S.
400 10   ≠a Duke, Raoul
667 __   ≠a free-lance writer
670 __   ≠a Carroll, E.J. Hunter, c1993: ≠b CIP t.p. (Hunter)
670 __   ≠a Random House dict. of the Eng. lang., 2nd ed., 1988 ≠b (under def. for gonzo: Hunter S. Thompson, b. 1939)

Figure 3.4   A portion of a USMARC authority record for an author

---

An example of two people with the same name are the two Tristram Coffins. One is a novelist and peace activist; the other is a folklorist. In order to differentiate them, catalogers have added birth dates to both and a middle name to the folklorist. This allows the online catalog to offer the following display:

Coffin, Tristram, 1912-
   Mine eyes have seen the glory, a novel. 1964.
   Not to the swift, a novel. 1961.
   The passion of the Hawks; militarism in modern America. 1964.
   Senator Fulbright. 1967, c1966.
   The sex kick; eroticism in modern America. c1966.

Coffin, Tristram Potter, 1922-
   The British traditional ballad in North America. c1977.
   The female hero in folklore and legend. 1975.
   Folklore from the working folk of America. 1973.
   Folksong & folksong scholarship. 1964.
   Indian tales of North America; an anthology for the adult reader. 1961.
   Our living traditions; an introduction to American folklore. 1968.
   The proper book of sexual folklore. 1978.

Figure 3.5   An example of two people with the same name

Principles dictated that one form of name be chosen with *see* references from the others, in order to carry out catalog function 2.2 (a). The *Anglo-American Cataloguing Rules,* second edition, 1988 revision (AACR2R) has failed to follow these internationally adopted principles by allowing entry of works written under a pseudonym under the pseudonym, effectively allowing an author who has written under more than one pseudonym to be represented in the catalog under more than one form of name.[3] The argument used by the editors of AACR2R was that sometimes a person writes under more than one name, writing different kinds of works under each name. J.I.M. Stewart, for example, writes novels and literary criticism under his true name and murder mysteries under the pseudonym Michael Innes. When this occurs, the editors feel that Stewart has established two different *bibliographic identities* and therefore should be treated as if he were two different authors. This approach is now being applied to all contemporary authors who use pseudonyms; the distinctions among the kinds of works written by Victoria Holt, Jean Plaidy, and Philippa Carr (all pseudonyms for Eleanor Alice Burford Hibbert, 1906-1993) are less clear.

Under current practice, these various names for one person are linked by *see also* references (see figure 3.7). To ensure that the second objective is not impaired by this new cataloging practice, effective system design is necessary to use these *see also* references to alert users to the fact that the author they seek has written under more than one name. Unfortunately, system design will be hampered by the fact that such *see also* references are difficult to distinguish in the USMARC format from *see also* references that are made because catalogers were unable to break a conflict between a heading and what should have been a *see* reference (see figure 3.8). The 500 field by itself is not a predictor of the fact that this is a case of multiple pseudonyms. There

---

An example is Charlie Chaplin, whose name appears on his works as both *Charles Chaplin* and *Charlie Chaplin*, and may even appear as *Charlot* on French versions of his films. To ensure that all of his works come together in the catalog, catalogers have "established" his name as *Chaplin, Charlie, 1889-1977*, with *see* references from:

Charlot, 1889-1977
Chaplin, Charles, Sir, 1889-1977

Figure 3.6   An example of one person who used more than one name

---

The following is a USMARC authority record for a pseudonym that is being treated as if it were a different author from other pseudonyms used by the same person:

100 10 ≠a Stark, Richard
500 10 ≠a Westlake, Donald E. ≠w nnnc
663   ≠a Works by this author are entered under the name used in the item.
              For a listing of other names used by this author, search also under ≠b
              Westlake, Donald E.

Figure 3.7   A portion of a USMARC authority record for a pseudonym

Authority record for writer on crystals:

```
100 10 ≠a Hayes, William
400 10 ≠a Hayes, W.
670    ≠a Crystals with the fluorite structure, 1974.
```

Authority record for author of *Midnight express*:

```
100 10 ≠a Hayes, Billy
500 10 ≠a Hayes, William
670    ≠a Midnight express [MP] 1978: ≠b credits (based on the book by William
          Hayes)
670    ≠a LC in OCLC, 10-22-92 ≠b (hdg.: Hayes, Billy; usage, Billy Hayes)
```

Figure 3.8   **Portions of two USMARC authority records; the second record has a 500** *see
also* **reference that does not represent a pseudonym, but refers instead to the
different person represented by the first record**

are other legitimate uses of the 500 field that do not signal the existence of pseudonyms. In the example in figure 3.8, there really are two people, both of whom are
named William Hayes, one of whom wrote *Midnight Express*, and one of whom writes
on crystals; because dates are not available for distinguishing the two, and the writer
of *Midnight Express* actually uses Billy more frequently than William, the headings
were differentiated, but it was not possible to differentiate the *see* reference on one
record from the heading on the other, so the *see* reference was made into a *see also*
reference instead. The combination of the 663 field and the delimiter w nnnc subfield
in the 500 field in the pseudonym record must be used to signal the existence of the
pseudonym condition to enable the design of more effective displays to alert users.
Such displays will be discussed in chapter 6.

Though AACR2R defied the Paris Principles to enter one personal author under
more than one name when pseudonyms are used, AACR2R was actually mandated
by the Paris Principles to enter the same corporate body under several different names
in cases in which the corporate body has changed its name over time. For example,
in the early 1960s, the American Institute of Electrical Engineers changed its name
to the Institute of Electrical and Electronics Engineers. The Paris Principles were
influenced by Seymour Lubetzky's principle that a change of name is a change of
identity for corporate bodies; thus, works published before the name changed are entered under the earlier form of name (American Institute of Electrical Engineers), and
works published after the name changed are entered under the later form of name
(Institute of Electrical and Electronics Engineers). Because many users would actually
consider both names to refer to the same corporate body, it is important to provide
effective displays of authority records for corporate bodies to explain this cataloging
practice that may not correspond to users' mental models (see figure 3.9).

Subject headings are also represented by authority records. An authority record
for a subject heading records a decision made by a cataloger about what a particular
topic is commonly called by users; in addition, it records cross-references that can be
used to help users who have searched on synonyms or terms not used (sometimes

called *see references, search under references,* or *USE FOR references*); it also can contain cross-references to broader or narrower or related terms that might lead a user to works that might also contain useful information (sometimes called *see also references*); and finally, the authority record can contain scope notes that define the way in which the heading has been used in the catalog. Figure 3.10 contains a portion of a USMARC authority record for a subject heading.

Form and genre headings also have authority records. The established form of heading appears in the 155 field in these records. This is a relatively new development, and there are still some unresolved questions about how it will be applied to

---

110 20 ≠a American Institute of Electrical Engineers
410 20 ≠a AIEE
410 20 ≠a Instituto americano de ingenieros electricistas
410 20 ≠a Amerikanskoe obshchestvo inzhenerov-elektrikov
510 20 ≠a Institute of Electrical and Electronics Engineers ≠w b

The ≠w b in the 510 field means that the 510 field contains a later form of name. The subfield can be used to generate a display that explains the relationship between the name in the 110 field and the name in the 510 field. See chapter 6 for further discussion of possible displays enabled by this subfield code.

Figure 3.9 **A portion of a USMARC authority record for a corporate body that has changed its name**

---

150 _0 ≠a Magic
450 _0 ≠a Necromancy
450 _0 ≠a Sorcery
450 _0 ≠a Spells
550 _0 ≠a Occultism ≠w g
680 __ ≠i Here are entered works on the use of charms, spells, etc., believed to
          have supernatural power to produce or prevent a particular result considered
          unobtainable by natural means. Works on a type of entertainment in which
          a performer does tricks of so-called magic are entered under ≠a Conjuring.

The 150 field contains the established heading, MAGIC. The 450 fields contain *see* references to it. The 550 field is a *see also* reference, reminding the user that the broader term that encompasses *magic* and other related topics is *occultism* (the ≠w subfield contains code g, meaning *broader term*). This can remind the user that if he or she is interested in a broad search, a search on OCCULTISM might produce some more useful citations and might also guide him or her to other useful narrower terms encompassed by OCCULTISM. And, finally, the 680 field contains a scope note that could be very useful to the user who searched on the term MAGIC hoping to find books about magic tricks.

Figure 3.10 **A portion of a USMARC authority record for a subject heading**

LCSH headings that are form or genre headings rather than topical subject headings, e.g., WESTERN FILMS. The LC will probably make two authority records—one a 150 record for the heading's use as a topical subject heading (works about westerns) and the other a 155 record for the heading's use as a form/genre heading (the westerns themselves). Another recent development is the designation of delimiter v subfields to contain form and genre subdivisions, which up until now have never been distinguished from delimiter x subfield topical subdivisions in the USMARC format. It is still not known whether the LC will try to convert existing headings in the US-MARC database to the new subfield code once all the form and genre subdivisions have been identified as part of the project described above. Before 1996, the US-MARC bibliographic format contained a 755 field for indexing physical characteristics. This field has now become obsolete, although it still exists in many bibliographic records. Headings that would have been placed in a 755 field before 1996 are now placed in a 655 field; thus, it would be wise for systems to ignore the distinction between 755 and 655 in indexing and index them the same way (in the same indexes, using the same indexing algorithms, and making no distinctions between them on public display).[4] While it is likely that form and genre headings and subdivisions will undergo some type of massive cleanup in the next few years, at the current time they can still be found mixed in with topical headings and subdivisions.

Hierarchical Force in Authority Records

Like an author with pseudonyms, who can be represented by more than one record in the authority file, an author entered under a single form of name can also be represented by more than one record. There are many topical subdivisions that can be added to subject headings for authors to bring out the subject matter of books about the author. For example, all of the following headings may be represented in the authority file:

>Tchaikovsky, Peter Ilich, 1840-1893—Bibliography.
>
>Tchaikovsky, Peter Ilich, 1840-1893—Correspondence.
>
>Tchaikovsky, Peter Ilich, 1840-1893—Criticism and interpretation.
>
>Tchaikovsky, Peter Ilich, 1840-1893—Diaries.
>
>Tchaikovsky, Peter Ilich, 1840-1893—Discography.
>
>Tchaikovsky, Peter Ilich, 1840-1893—Friends and associates.
>
>Tchaikovsky, Peter Ilich, 1840-1893—Homes and haunts.
>
>Tchaikovsky, Peter Ilich, 1840-1893—Journeys.
>
>Tchaikovsky, Peter Ilich, 1840-1893—Manuscripts.
>
>Tchaikovsky, Peter Ilich, 1840-1893—Museums.
>
>Tchaikovsky, Peter Ilich, 1840-1893—Thematic catalogs.

It would be desirable for systems to be able to recognize the relationship between the authority records for the headings listed above and the authority record for Tchaikovsky without subdivisions. The authority record for Tchaikovsky without subdivisions should be held to have hierarchical force over authority records for the same heading with subdivisions. Whenever it is desirable to index the main heading, it should be considered whether it is also desirable to index records for the same heading with its subdivisions. Whenever it is desirable to display the main heading, it is highly likely that it is desirable to display the records for the same heading with subdivisions. Cross-references to the main heading should be held to apply to the main heading with subdivisions as well. In other words, if a user is interested in Tchaikovsky, she or he may very well find it helpful to be told about the bibliographies, thematic catalogs, etc. that are indexed under these headings and to be led to this display no matter what form of name she or he searches under.

Corporate bodies exhibit hierarchical force in yet another way. They, too, can have various topical subject and form subdivisions attached. In addition, however, because it is common for corporate bodies to be made up of various departments and divisions, a single corporate body may be represented by many different authority records for each separately established department or division of the body (see figure 3.11).

If works are represented in the authority file at all (and many are not), they are represented in a very complex way because a work with an author or creator is "named" using both its author and title. For example, see figure 3.12 for the authority

---

110 10 ≠a United States. ≠b Federal Bureau of Investigation
410 20 ≠a FBI
410 10 ≠a United States. ≠b Dept. of Justice. ≠b Federal Bureau of Investigation
410 20 ≠a Federal Bureau of Investigation (U.S.)
410 20 ≠a FBR
410 20 ≠a Federalnoe biuro rassledovanii
510 10 ≠a United States. ≠b Bureau of Criminal Identification
510 10 ≠a United States. ≠b Dept. of Justice. ≠b Division of Investigation ≠w a

The following is a portion of an authority record for a section of the FBI:

110 10 ≠a United States. ≠b Federal Bureau of Investigation. ≠b Uniform Crime
Reports Section

Note that the *see* reference from FBI to UNITED STATES. FEDERAL BUREAU OF INVESTIGATION occurs only on the first authority record above. It is not repeated on the second authority record. If a user were to search on FBI UNIFORM CRIME REPORTS SECTION, the search would fail unless the system were smart enough to recognize the hierarchical relationship between these two records.

Note also the cataloging practice of entering many federal agencies under the federal government. Thus, while the Uniform Crime Reports Section is a part of the FBI, the FBI itself is part of the Department of Justice, which, in turn, is part of the federal government of the United States (entered in the catalog as "United States"). The federal government of the United States is one of the largest and most complex corporate bodies in the world. Software design that recognizes hierarchical force in corporate names must allow the user to scan parts of the hierarchy without overwhelming them with the entire thing.

Figure 3.11   **Portions of USMARC authority records, one for the FBI and the other for a subdivision of the FBI**

Authority record for Tchaikovsky:

Heading used:

Tchaikovsky, Peter Ilich, 1840-1893

See references:

Ciaikovsky, Piotr Ilic, 1840-1893
Tchaikovski, P. (Piotr), 1840-1893
Tchaikowsky, Peter Ilich, 1840-1893
Chaikovskii, P. (Petr), 1840-1893
[etc.]

There are two more authority records for the *Nutcracker* and its suite, which look like this:

Authority record for the ballet The nutcracker:

Heading used:

Tchaikovsky, Peter Ilich, 1840-1893. Shchelkunchik

See references:

Tchaikovsky, Peter Ilich, 1840-1893. Casse-noisette
Tchaikovsky, Peter Ilich, 1840-1893. Nussknacker
Tchaikovsky, Peter Ilich, 1840-1893. Nutcracker
[etc.]

Authority record for the suite from the ballet:

Heading used:

Tchaikovsky, Peter Ilich, 1840-1893. Shchelkunchik. Suite

See references:

Tchaikovsky, Peter Ilich, 1840-1893. Shchelkunchik. Suite from the ballet The nutcracker
Tchaikovsky, Peter Ilich, 1840-1893. Shchelkunchik. Nussknacker-Suite
Tchaikovsky, Peter Ilich, 1840-1893. Shchelkunchik. Nutcracker suite
[etc.]

Figure 3.12 Authority records for a work by Tchaikovsky

records for a work by Tchaikovsky. If a user uses a variant form of Tchaikovsky's name, for example, TCHAIKOWSKY, along with a variant title, for example, NUTCRACKER SUITE, the search will only succeed in retrieving all versions of this work held if the search is matched against at least two of these authority records. If the search is matched only against the headings on bibliographic records, or only against individual authority records, it will retrieve nothing because of the variance in both composer's name and title. In other words, the work called the *Nutcracker Suite* is represented by a hierarchical group of records, and the ideal match for a search would be a within-group match that treated this group of records as a single record for matching purposes (see the next section in this chapter).

Subject headings, too, can exhibit hierarchical force. It is very common for subject headings of all kinds to have subdivisions added to them to divide a large topic up into manageable pieces, based on geographic coverage, form (such as dictionaries, indexes, etc.), chronology, and further topical division. Consider the example in figure 3.13, in which each line represents a separate authority record. Again, it would be desirable for systems to be able to recognize the relationship between the authority records for the headings listed in figure 3.13 and the authority record for WATER without subdivisions. The authority record for WATER without subdivisions should be held to have hierarchical force over authority records for the same heading with subdivisions. Whenever it is desirable to index the main heading, it should be considered whether it is also desirable to index records for the same heading with its subdivisions. Whenever it is desirable to display the main heading, it is highly likely that it is desirable to display the records for the same heading with subdivisions. In other words, if a user is interested in works about water, he or she may very well find it helpful to be told about the bibliographies, handbooks, etc. that are indexed under these headings.

Water.
Water—Abstracts.
Water—Aeration.
Water—Aeration—Congresses.
Water—Bibliography.
Water—Congresses.
Water—Dictionaries.
Water—Economic aspects.
Water—Handbooks, manuals, etc.
Water—Law and legislation—Italy.
Water—Pollution—Nevada.
Water—Study guides.
Water—California—Congresses.
Water—Great Lakes Region.
Water—United States—Congresses.

Figure 3.13   **Hierarchical relationship between a subject heading and its subdivisions**

Relationship between Authority Records and Bibliographic Records

It is important to notice that one authority record for a heading should link to that heading used in a number of different ways. For example, the authority record for SHAKESPEARE should link to his name whether it appears as a main entry (100), an added entry (700), a series added entry (800), or a subject heading on a work about Shakespeare or one of his works (600). This has important implications for system design. It means that the way a name is used in a bibliographic record is not recorded in the authority record. In the following chapters we will recommend displays that require information from both the authority record and the bibliographic record. For example, we will recommend a display that shows the user both the works by and the works about Shakespeare (in two sequences). The user should be able to see such displays as the result of a search on authority file headings. We will also recommend that a user be able to limit a search on authority file headings by date, language, etc. For these recommendations to be carried out, the link between the authority record and the bibliographic record must not preclude information for displays or search limiting being drawn from both the authority record and the bibliographic records linked to it.

How Computer Software Can Recognize All of the Records That Represent One Work; or, How Computer Software Can Recognize the Main Entry

Earlier in this chapter, we emphasized the fact that what OPAC users seek is usually represented by more than one record in the OPAC. Obviously, if the user is interested in a particular author, that author may have written more than one book; if the user is interested in a particular subject, there may be more than one book on that subject. The most complex case, however, is that of a particular work sought by the user. There are two main reasons for the complexity. One is that works are often identified by both author and title; thus, the "name" of the work, so to speak, is found in more than one field. The other is that works are not nearly as well managed by catalogers as are authors and subjects. There are many works that exist in more than one edition under more than one title and that have never been subjected to authority control. Ideally, each work is assigned a citation form, generally known as a *main entry*, which is used on all editions of the work, regardless of the titles that might appear on their title pages.

When a work has been subjected to authority control, an authority record for the work which contains either a 130 field or a 100, 110, or 111 field with a delimiter t subfield will be created. Whenever such an authority record exists, all bibliographic records that match it (i.e., that have a 245 or 130 with text that matches the text in a 130 field in an authority record or that have a 100/240 or 245, 110/240 or 245, or 111/240 or 245 or a 600, 610, 611, 700, 710, or 711 field with a delimiter t subfield that matches an equivalent authority record) can be safely assumed to represent the same work, works about the same work, or works related to the same work. 6XX fields indicate the work represented by the bibliographic record is about the work in question.

7XX fields indicate the work represented by the bibliographic record is either related to the work in question or contains the work in question (see figure 3.14).

Works that are entered under author (i.e., that have 100, 110, or 111 fields) can probably be safely identified by main entry (1XX field plus 24X field), even when there is no corresponding authority record. In other words, if two bibliographic records have identical 1XX and 24X fields, they can safely be assumed to be editions of the same work.

In an authority record for the work:

100 10 ≠a Twain, Mark, ≠d 1835-1910. ≠t Adventures of Huckleberry Finn.
400 10 ≠a Twain, Mark, ≠d 1835-1910. ≠t Adventures of Huckleberry Finn
    (Tom Sawyer's comrade)
400 10 ≠a Twain, Mark, ≠d 1835-1910. ≠t Huckleberry Finn

In a bibliographic record for an edition of the work itself:

100 1_ ≠a Twain, Mark, ≠d 1835-1910.
245 10 ≠a Adventures of Huckleberry Finn / ≠c Mark Twain ; illustrated by E.W.
    Kemble and John Harley ; edited by Walter Blair ... [et al.].
260 __ ≠a Berkeley : ≠b Published in cooperation with the University of Iowa by
    the University of California Press, ≠c 1988.
300 __ ≠a lxiv, 875 p. : ≠b ill. ; ≠c 24 cm.
490 1_ ≠a The works of Mark Twain ; ≠v 8

In a bibliographic record for a work containing the work:

100 1_ ≠a Twain, Mark, ≠d 1835-1910.
245 10 ≠a Tom Sawyer and Huckleberry Finn / ≠c Mark Twain.
260 __ ≠a New York : ≠b Knopf, ≠c 1991.
700 12 ≠a Twain, Mark, ≠d 1835-1910. ≠t Adventures of Huckleberry Finn.

In a bibliographic record for a work related to the work:

100 1_ ≠a Miller, Roger, ≠d 1936-
245 __ ≠a Big river : ≠b the adventures of Huckleberry Finn : a musical play /
    ≠c book by William Hauptman ; adapted from the novel by Mark Twain ;
    music and lyrics by Roger Miller.
260 __ ≠a New York : ≠b Grove Press, ≠c 1986.
700 1_ ≠a Twain, Mark, ≠d 1835-1910. ≠t Adventures of Huckleberry Finn.

In a bibliographic record for a work about the work:

245 00 ≠a Satire or evasion? : ≠b Black perspectives on Huckleberry Finn /
    ≠c edited by James S. Leonard, Thomas A. Tenney, Thadious M. Davis.
260 __ ≠a Durham : ≠b Duke University Press, ≠c 1992.
300 __ ≠a iv, 281 p. ; ≠c 22 cm.
600 10 ≠a Twain, Mark, ≠d 1835-1910. ≠t Adventures of Huckleberry Finn.

Figure 3.14 Various guises of the main entry for a work

However, many works entered under title have no corresponding authority records. In this situation, matching on main entries can be risky. If the work has a fairly distinctive title, and its editions have retained the distinctive title, the work can be defined for the computer as all bibliographic records that have the same character string in the 245 field. This will not work for works that lack distinctive titles; for example, many different works all have the title *Smoking*. Because this approach hinges on the distinctiveness of titles, something the computer software cannot determine for itself without human intervention, the safest approach is to avoid trying to identify works entered under title.

Note that because of the hierarchical force that applies to authority records, the main entry representing the ballet should be considered to include all authority records representing its parts, i.e., all authority records that begin with that main entry. Thus, the main entry representing the ballet the *Nutcracker* (TCHAIKOVSKY, PETER ILICH, 1840-1893. SHCHELKUNCHIK) should be held to include, for search matching and display purposes, the separate authority record representing the *Nutcracker Suite* (TCHAIKOVSKY, PETER ILICH, 1840-1893. SHCHELKUNCHIK. SUITE) and all bibliographic records attached to it. (See figure 3.12.)

Special Problems—Serial Records

Serial works have been treated differently from most monographic works in that the use of authority records to demonstrate complex relationships among serial works has been avoided, and instead the bibliographic records themselves are used to create links between related works. Whenever a serial changes its title, it is treated as if it were a new, related work; that is, a new record is made for the new title. The records for the related works are linked in a chain fashion, such that each title in a complex serial history is linked to the title immediately preceding it and the title immediately following it but not to any of the other titles the serial has borne (see figure 3.15). This means that the adequate demonstration of a serial history to a catalog user is dependent on a library holding all the links in the chain. If the library does not hold issues of the serial under all of its titles, the user will not be effectively led to all of the issues that are held.

Basic Types of Indexing Algorithms

System designers so far have tended to use at least four different types of indexing algorithms, which are not easily definable or necessarily mutually exclusive; that is, one system may use more than one type of indexing. The terms used to refer to these four types of indexing algorithms have not yet stabilized, but currently the most commonly used terminology seems to be as follows:

Keyword indexing

In this book, this term is used to mean the type of indexing in which indexed fields or headings are broken down into words (a *word* being operationalized as *a string of characters bounded by spaces*), each of which is separately indexed.

245 00　≠a Journal of library automation.
260 __　≠a Chicago, Ill. : ≠b American Library Association, ≠c c1968-c1981.
300 __　≠a 14 v. : ≠b ill. ; ≠c 26 cm.
310 __　≠a Quarterly.
362 0_　≠a Vol. 1, no. 1 (Mar. 1968)-v. 14, no. 4 (Dec. 1981).
550 __　≠a Official publication of the Information Science and Automation
　　　　Division of the American Library Association, 1968-1978; of the Library
　　　　and Information Technology Association of the ALA, 1979-1981.
650 _0　≠a Libraries ≠x Automation ≠x Periodicals.
710 2_　≠a American Library Association. ≠b Information Science and Automation
　　　　Division.
710 2_　≠a Library and Information Technology Association (U.S.)
780 05　≠t JOLA technical communications ≠g Mar. 1973 ≠x 0021-3748 ≠w (DLC)
　　　　74014019
785 00　≠t Information technology and libraries ≠x 0730-9295 ≠w (DLC) 82645170

The fields special to serials include the 362 field and the 780 and 785 fields. The 362 field gives the designation of the volumes as published (not as held in the library), including dates of publication, and volume designations. The 780 field gives, in this case, the title of a serial that was absorbed by this serial. The 785 field gives the title that succeeded this one in the history of the serial. In chapters 5 and 6, we will discuss effective ways to index and display this information.

Figure 3.15　An example of a portion of a USMARC record for a serial

Keyword indexing has been used in the literature to describe the following different situations:

1. word indexing (the only meaning used in this book);
2. free text subject indexing (i.e., indexing transcribed and composed fields rather than controlled vocabulary fields);
3. combination free text and controlled vocabulary subject indexing (i.e., indexing, transcribed, composed, *and* controlled vocabulary fields);
4. keyword browsing, with provision of an index of single words, stripped of context, sometimes with an indication of number of postings and an indication of the type of field in which the term appeared;
5. a direct cross-field search of terms in bibliographic records rather than a *browse* of the headings; and
6. indexing of all fields without regard to type of field, in a dictionary arrangement of all headings.

The lesson to be learned here is that the term *keyword indexing* should either be avoided or carefully defined henceforth. The definition should include

1. whether or not the fields indexed are implied (free text fields? controlled vocabulary fields? both?); in this book, we do not mean to imply any particular type of field to be indexed;
2. a type of indexing (word indexing rather than phrase indexing); this is the only meaning we wish the term to have in this book;

3. the types of records indexed (bibliographic records? authority records? both?); in our use of the term in this book, we do not mean to imply any particular type of record to be indexed;
4. the co-occurrence rules (two keywords must co-occur within a single field? within a particular group of fields? within a record?); in this book, we do not mean to imply any particular set of co-occurrence rules; and
5. the type of resultant display (headings? bibliographic records retrieved?); in this book, we do not mean to imply any particular resultant display.

To reiterate, in this book, we wish to use the term *keyword indexing* to mean word indexing.

Phrase indexing

A field or subfield is indexed as a whole, with order of terms preserved, such that subsequent matching of search arguments must match both terms and order of terms. (Also known as *direct field* indexing, *exact phrase* indexing, *character string match* indexing, or *left-to-right match* indexing.)

Search key indexing

A field or subfield is indexed as a whole, with order of terms preserved (as in phrase indexing), but only a fixed-length portion of each term is indexed, e.g., the first four letters of the first term, the first three letters of the second term, and the first letter of the third term.

Permuted indexing

A field or subfield is indexed as a whole, with order of terms preserved (as in phrase indexing), but the field is then rotated to bring each separate word in the field to the head of the field.[5]

To get around weaknesses in the nature of access provided by each of the above indexing approaches, system designers have employed additional techniques. For example:

Keyword indexing, because it tends to result in high recall and low precision, that is, lots of noise or false drops, may be supplemented by attaching locational data to each term indexed (pertaining to the term's location in a particular field and in a particular record) to allow the use of positional operators to specify how closely words need to occur to each other (sometimes known as *adjacency searching*).[6] Another way to correct for keyword indexing problems is to limit co-occurrence of terms (discussed shortly) to within-field matching, rather than within-multiple-field or within-record matching.

Phrase indexing, because it requires an exactitude of match not attainable by most users without extensive lookups before the search, tends to be supplemented with either explicit (voluntary) or implicit (automatic) truncation, allowing searches to match only the first part of the field or subfield indexed.

Search key indexing, because user-input search keys require a great deal of rule learning, may be accompanied by automatic search key formulation by the searching program prior to matching users' input against the index.

System designers have a number of co-occurrence options for the design of systems offering keyword access or for the design of other types of indexing systems that allow combination searches. *Co-occurrence* refers to the rules followed by the computer when looking for two or more keywords (or other types of input) in combination. Co-occurrence rules could tell the computer to look for two or more keywords to co-occur

1. within the same subfield;
2. within the same field;
3. within particular fields within the same bibliographic record (e.g., within the personal name fields);
4. within any field in the same bibliographic record;
5. within the same authority record;
6. within particular fields within the same bibliographic record and associated authority records linked to those fields; or
7. within a group of hierarchically related authority records (as in the *Nutcracker Suite* example described earlier in this chapter).

Examples of these different types of co-occurrence rules are shown in figure 3.16. We will be discussing below which of these options might be the best default for various types of searches.

It should be noted that the choice of indexing type has a profound effect on the overall design of the system. For example, systems offering keyword access usually allow cross-field searching, or searching for keywords across several different fields or headings. When a cross-field search is done, it may be difficult or impossible to arrange the results by the heading matched, because frequently more than one heading or field is matched. Thus, it can be very difficult to design effective displays of multiple records in keyword indexed systems. This lack of an effective display can be especially frustrating for users who retrieve many false drops, easy to do in keyword searchable systems. Also, keyword-indexed systems commonly offer users searches that bypass the authority file. Finally, most keyword systems have stop-lists, lists of words that cannot be searched because they retrieve so many records; it is not uncommon for users to be frustrated in attempting a search that consists entirely of stop-list words.

On the other hand, systems offering phrase indexing tend to assume that a search will match just one heading. If steps are not taken to get around this rigidity, a user who is looking for a known work, and who has both author words and title words, can be required to search *either* on the author words *or* on the title words. Systems offering phrase indexing also demand that the user know the beginning words in headings sought and can be intolerant of users who do not invert personal names or who input an article at the beginning of a title.

The term *browse* has been used to mean a search that results in a list of words or headings from which to choose. However, within that rather broad definition occur a number of different meanings:

1. a search of an index rather than of the bibliographic records, with types of indexes that might be searched including (a) the authority file (including cross-references); (b) all headings attached to bibliographic records; (c) all headings attached to bibliographic records, plus cross-references from the authority file; or (d) single words broken out of headings, titles, note fields, etc.;[7]

Keyword search for WASTE and FUEL (user is interested in the use of waste products for fuel):

(1) Within the same subfield:

650 _0 ≠a <u>Waste</u> products as <u>fuel</u> ≠x Abstracts.

(2) Within the same field:

650 _0 ≠a Reactor <u>fuel</u> processing ≠x <u>Waste</u> disposal.

(3) Within particular fields within the same bibliographic record (for example, within the subject heading fields):

245 10 ≠a United States waste trade with Mexico and Canada.
650 _0 ≠a Hazardous <u>waste</u> management industry ≠z United States.
650 _0 ≠a <u>Fuel</u> trade ≠z United States ≠x Corrupt practices.

(4) Within the same bibliographic record:

245 00 ≠a Disposal of radioactive <u>waste</u>.
260 __ ≠a Paris : ≠b Nuclear Energy Agency, Organisation for Economic Co-operation and Development, ≠c c1992.
505 0_ ≠a A comparison of sorption databases used in recent performance assessments / I.G. McKinley and A. Scholtis -- The selection and use of a sorption database for the geosphere model in the Canadian nuclear <u>fuel</u> waste management program / T.T. Vandergraaf, K.V. Ticknor and T.W. Melnyk ...

Keyword search for EXPROPRIATION OF LAND (in which "of" is a stop word):

(5) Within the same authority record:

150-0 _0≠a Eminent domain
450-3 _0≠a <u>Expropriation</u>
450-4 _0≠a <u>Land</u>, Condemnation of

Keyword search for AERODYNAMIC FORCES ON SWEEPBACK WINGS (in which "on" is a stop word):

(6) Within particular fields within the same bibliographic record and associated authority records linked to those fields:

Bibliographic record:

245 00 ≠a Methods of conducting a wind tunnel investigation of lift in roll at supersonic speeds.
650 _0 ≠a Airplanes ≠x <u>Wings</u>, Swept-back ≠x Testing.
650 _0 ≠a Lift (Aerodynamics).

Authority record 1:

150 _0 ≠a Airplanes ≠x <u>Wings</u>, Swept-back
450 _0 ≠a Airplanes ≠x <u>Sweepback</u>

Figure 3.16   Examples of various types of co-occurrence rules

Authority record 2:

150 _0 ≠a Lift (Aerodynamics)
450 _0 ≠a <u>Aerodynamic forces</u>

Keyword search for TCHAIKOWSKY NUTCRACKER SUITE

(7) Within a group of hierarchically related authority records (as in the *Nutcracker Suite* example):

Authority record 1:

100 10 ≠a Tchaikovsky, Peter Ilich, ≠d 1840-1893
400 10 ≠a <u>Tchaikowsky,</u> Peter Ilich, ≠d 1840-1893

Authority record 2:

100 10 ≠a Tchaikovsky, Peter Ilich, ≠d 1840-1893. ≠t Shchelkunchik. ≠p
<u>Suite</u>
100 10 ≠a Tchaikovsky, Peter Ilich, ≠d 1840-1893. ≠t Shchelkunchik. ≠p
<u>Suite</u> from the ballet The <u>nutcracker</u>

2. in keyword searching, co-occurrence of more than one keyword within a heading, rather than within a record;
3. placement in an index at the heading closest to the search done, even when no exact match was found;
4. a phrase index as opposed to a keyword index; or
5. a search of an index of headings unlinked to bibliographic records, as opposed to an index of headings linked to bibliographic records that enables a display that includes both headings and bibliographic titles under them.

In evaluating a so-called browse function, it is important to identify which one of the above meanings of *browse* is being used. It is important to note, too, whether the bibliographic records are linked to any headings or terms that might be displayed, so that users can go directly to bibliographic records rather than having to redo the search in another file. Because *browse* can have so many meanings, it would be helpful for users, if when *browse* is used to describe a function, it could be defined in functional terms in *HELP* screens, to help sophisticated users employ a given *browse* function more effectively. Now that the Internet is making multiple OPAC searching more and more common, system-to-system variations in definition of terms are likely to cause more and more problems for users. Because of the ambiguity of meaning described above, the terms *browse file* or *browse search* have been avoided in this book.

The various types of indexing offered by any given OPAC can be cryptic and confusing even to sophisticated users. One thing that might help would be better documentation in the form of *HELP* screens, as we have already mentioned. Another would be to work on better, more explanatory names for the types of indexing available. Some systems have already begun to try to do this. For example, Resource Librarian offers users the following choices: *"begins with," "equals,"* and *"contains."* [8] USCInfo offers the following choices on their form fill-in screen: *"Find all words above," "Find at least one of the words above,"* and *"Find the words above as a single phrase."* [9]

Notes

1. Gregory J. Wool, "Bibliographical Metadata; or, We Need a Client-Server Cataloging Code!" in *Finding Common Ground: Creating the Library of the Future without Diminishing the Library of the Past*, ed. Cheryl LaGuardia and Barbara A. Mitchell (New York: Neal-Schuman, 1998), p. 398–401.

2. Nicholson Baker, "Discards," *New Yorker*, April 4, 1994, p. 69, 74, 76.

3. *Anglo-American Cataloguing Rules*, 2nd ed., 1988 revision (Chicago: American Library Association, 1988).

4. For a discussion of the reasons that a distinction between intellectual and physical form is not useful, see Jackie M. Dooley and Helena Zinkham, "The Object as 'Subject': Providing Access to Genres, Forms of Material and Physical Characteristics," in *Beyond the Book: Extending MARC for Subject Access*, ed. Toni Petersen and Pat Molholt (Boston: G. K. Hall, 1990), p. 43–80.

5. An example of a system that employs this type of indexing is DOBIS; INNOPAC offers a type of permuted indexing as an option (see Walt Crawford, *The Online Catalog Book: Essays and Examples* [Boston: G. K. Hall, 1992], p. 224, 302).

6. The term *false drops* refers to documents that match the input search but are not in fact useful; an example would be a document about thin films in an engineering context retrieved by a user interested in motion pictures who used the term *films* in the search.

7. Systems that offer indexes of single words broken out of headings, titles, note fields, etc. include Catalog Plus (Crawford, *Online*, p. 179); InfoTRAX Scan (Crawford, *Online*, p. 269); LS/2000 (Crawford, *Online*, p. 342).

8. Crawford, *Online*, p. 448.

9. Ibid., p. 497.

Demonstration of Relationships— Authors and Works

In the next four chapters, we discuss the design decisions necessary to ensure that an OPAC carries out the cataloging objectives, that is, to ensure that an OPAC effectively demonstrates the relationships among all the works of a particular author and all the editions of a particular work. Note that this means that online catalog designers should assume that any given search ought to retrieve multiple records from multiple files. A search for a particular author ought to produce an authority record for that author as well as bibliographic records for all the editions of his or her works. A search for a particular work ought to produce authority records for the author(s) of the work as well as bibliographic records for all of its editions. Serial works can be particularly problematic for the system designer, because what most users might consider to be a single serial work is often represented in the catalog as if it were more than one work if the serial has changed its title. Serial records do contain information that could allow the system to link multiple serial records together, however.[1]

A number of design decisions affect how well the objectives are carried out. It is better for the user if only one file (or at least what appears to be one file to the user—a virtual single file) must be searched, rather than two files, in order to be sure one has seen all the works of a particular author or all the editions of a particular work. Thus, file structure must be effectively designed to achieve this objective. If from the user's point of view it appears that only one file is being searched, because records in many files are searched and all results are displayed in one alphabetic or classified order, the objective has been achieved. It does not matter to the user how many files there are underneath the interface, as long as knowledge of files is not required in order to search successfully.

The most difficult virtual single file to achieve is an integrated bibliographic and authority file. Many systems offer searches that do not search the authority file. Such systems do not offer the user a virtual single file. Many systems that do allow searching of the authority file do not integrate searches of the bibliographic records with authority file searches when necessary. For example, the OPAC with which the authors are most familiar, ORION, the UCLA Libraries' current online information system, separates the authority file from the bibliographic file for searching purposes; the BROWSE search searches headings and cross-references from authority records, while the FIND search searches bibliographic records; because of this partitioning, a BROWSE search cannot be limited by publication dates (e.g., "look for a writer who published in the 1840s"), and a FIND search does not search on cross-references. Obviously, the solution to this problem is not just to place all authority records and bibliographic records in a single file. However, part of the solution is to consider both sets of records to constitute a single virtual file, so that the goal becomes to make invisible to the user the complex linking between the two files that is necessary to allow complex searching and complex displays.

The term *file* is being used to mean a collection of records kept separate in some way from other collections of records. Common examples are monograph and serial files or bibliographic and authority files. In contrast, the term *index* is used for a collection of headings or entries. Common examples are subject and name indexes. A common hybrid of these two, a combination of both authority records and headings stripped from bibliographic records (when there is no corresponding authority record), is sometimes called an *index* and sometimes called a *file*.

It is better for the user if a single search retrieves all the works of an author and all the editions of a work, rather than several searches being necessary. Thus, effective indexing must be done to achieve this objective.

And finally, no matter how effectively the files have been designed and the indexing has been done, if the works of an author and editions of a work do not *display* together in a logical and useful array when the user is looking over everything retrieved by her or his search, the rest of the design work might as well not have been done.

Note

1. Melissa M. Bernhardt, "Dealing with Serial Title Changes: Some Theoretical Considerations," *Cataloging & Classification Quarterly* 9, no. 2 (1988): 25–39.

4

Demonstration of Relationships—Authors and Works—File and Index Structure Decisions

Relationship between the Authority File and the Bibliographic File

One of the great unsolved problems of online catalog design is how to ensure that *every* user's search is matched against our cross-reference structure (see figure 4.1). The value of integrating the authority file into all available searches is particularly clear when you consider names that are well known to English-speaking users in their English forms but have been established in non-English forms to facilitate international cooperative cataloging and internationally useful catalogs. (See figure 4.2.) In the card catalog, where cross-references were interfiled with bibliographic records, and what was essentially phrase or left-to-right searching was the only option, the problem of ensuring that *every* user's search is matched against cross-references was readily solved. It is not solved so easily in keyword-searchable online catalogs. Until it is, online catalogs will not work as well as card catalogs in this fundamental respect: one search will never be enough to be sure you have found all you are looking for. What we need is a single search guaranteed to match all variant forms of author name and all variant forms of title known to exist, so that the search can retrieve all editions of a work.[1] Because the solution to this problem involves both file design and indexing decisions, it will be discussed further in chapter 5.

In creating the links between the authority file and the bibliographic file, the problem (discussed in chapter 3) of information stored partially in the authority record and partially in the bibliographic record should not be forgotten. For example, there is nothing in the authority record to enable a display that distinguishes between the works by a person and the works about a person—it is the 600 tag in the bibliographic record that distinguishes the works *about* from the works *by*. Also, allowing users to limit authority file searches by date or language will require drawing information from bibliographic records.

There has been some discussion in the cataloging literature of how frequently authority records really do help users find things they would not otherwise have found. Shore (p. 4-5) found that 51 percent to 59 percent of the names examined had entries (authority controlled headings) that were the same as their transcribed (title page) forms; this was not a study in actual title page variation, however. Fuller (p. 16) found that 84 percent of personal names in the catalog need no cross-references, i.e., the author's name does not vary from title page to title page; in fact, most of these nonvarying authors are one-work authors. However, Taylor (p. 13) found that 43 percent of failed author searches were for authors that had name authority records with cross-references. This would seem to indicate that the authors that users are most interested in tend to be prolific authors with frequent name variations across the title pages of their multiple works and across citations to their work. Thomas (p. 396) found that 47 percent of references on LC authority records for authors would be unnecessary in a keyword-searchable system; the implication is that they *are* useful in phrase-indexing systems or functions. Watson and Taylor (p. 15) found that 41.5 percent of personal name cross-references and 21.9 percent of corporate name cross-references would be unnecessary in an "automatic right-hand truncation and keyword searching environment"; however, these cross-references would still be useful in a phrase-searchable system and in large displays. Jamieson, Dolan, and Declerck (p. 279) found that 46 percent of the cross-references leading to headings on a sample of bibliographic records would be unnecessary if keyword searching of each record was allowed; however, they fail to point out the following problems: (1) if the library does not have a book using the form that a user has used in his or her search, the user's search will fail; (2) in a cross-field keyword search, no headings are available for display, so the user whose search matches more than one author can have a difficult time sorting through the results; and (3) a search that matches a cross-reference form retrieves only books with that form on the title page, missing books by the same author with other forms on the title page.

Full citations for user studies are found in the bibliography of user studies in appendix A.

Figure 4.1   Studies of the usefulness of name-title cross-references

The corporate body commonly known in English as:
  PLO
is entered in the catalog as:
  Munazzmat Al-Tahrir Al-Filastiniyah.
The musical work commonly known in English as:
  The nutcracker suite
is entered in the catalog as:
  Tchaikovsky, Peter Ilich, 1840-1893.
    Shchelkunchik. Suite.

Figure 4.2   Examples of a corporate body and a musical work well known in the United States in English, established in languages other than English

Name-Title Search

Some systems do not allow the user to search more than one file or index in a single search. This tends to happen in systems that are fundamentally based on phrase or left-to-right match indexes. Michael Berger actually counted as suboptimal an exact title search on the MELVYL system that also included the author's name.[2] It hardly seems friendly to penalize the user for having too much information about the work sought. This limitation of searches to one file or index can make life difficult not only for the user who is looking for a particular work and who knows both the author and the title but also for the user who does not know whether the elements of her or his citation represent author or title information, a common problem with users who seek works that emanate from corporate bodies. A search using both the author and the title can be much more precise than one that must be for either the author (especially if it is a prolific author) or the title (especially if it is a common title) (see figure 4.3). It may be essential to success, if the user's citation consists of only partial information about author and title, e.g., *"Smith's Manual."* The title index should *never* be the default for a known work search.

Music librarians, who routinely deal with prolific authors (i.e., composers) and nondistinctive titles, have required that a name-title search be available for an online public access catalog to serve music users.[3] Users of what used to be called "works of corporate authorship," especially conference proceedings, benefit if a name-title search is available in which names need not be differentiated from titles; with citations to conference proceedings, for example, it is often difficult to predict which elements will form part of a title and which part of the conference name (see figure 4.4). On the other hand, if the search is designed so that those users who *can* do so have the *option* of indicating which portions of the search are specifications of the title, and which are specifications of the author, this can help the search algorithms search name and title indexes more effectively in those cases, producing more precise results with less noise.

One possible solution to the problem of providing adequate support for users who are looking for a particular work, using both author name and title, might be a name-title index that includes the following:

1. every name-title main entry (in USMARC format terms, every 1XX field in a bibliographic record, with the 240 field following it, if present; otherwise, the 245 field following it up to the delimiter c subfield);
2. every name-title added entry (in USMARC format terms, every 6XX and 7XX field with a delimiter t subfield);

Consider the example of Beethoven's *5th Symphony.* When an author search (FIND PA BEETHOVEN) is done on the MELVYL system, the very large online union catalog containing everything held by the University of California, more than 7,000 records are retrieved. When a title search (FIND TW 5TH SYMPHONY) is done, more than 1,200 records are retrieved. However, when a search is done combining both the composer and the title of the work, fewer than 200 records are retrieved.

Figure 4.3   An example of a nondistinctive title of a work by a prolific composer

Consider the following example. A user comes to the library with the following citation:

3rd International Conf on Solidification Processing, Sheffield, England, Sep 21-23, 1987.

Unbeknownst to the user, the title page of the publication sought reads as follows:

Solidification
Processing
1987

Proceedings of the
Third International Conference,
organised by the Department of Metallurgy,
University of Sheffield, and held at
Ranmoor House, Sheffield, on
21-24 September 1987

This title page presentation forced the cataloger to consider this an unnamed conference and catalog it as follows:

245 00 ≠a Solidification processing 1987 : ≠b proceedings of the third international conference / ≠c organised by the Department of Metallurgy, University of Sheffield, and held at Ranmoor House, Sheffield, on 21-24 September 1987.

In other words, this cataloging record will have no entry for the conference as a name, and only if the search the user does includes a search of both title and statement of responsibility subfields will the search be successful. A search done only on X11 fields in the USMARC formats would fail.

Figure 4.4   An example of a conference citation

3. every name-title authority record, together with its cross-references (in USMARC format terms, every authority record with a delimiter t subfield);
4. every title field (in USMARC format terms, bibliographic record: 24X fields, 4XX fields, 630, 730, 740, and 830 fields; authority record: 130 authority records with all cross-references); and
5. every name cross-reference; ideally, a smart program would recognize the relationship between name cross-references referring to the main heading and that main heading used as part of a name-title uniform title (see the Tchaikovsky example in chapter 3).

Other Combination (Cross-File and Cross-Index) Searches

A system that allows inclusion of author and subject terms, or title and subject terms, or all three in the same search can be very useful for the user who has a fragmented or garbled citation to a known work of which the subject is known or a citation to such a work that includes many nondistinctive or stop-list words.[4] Unfortunately, systems that offer cross-file searches often do not ensure that such searches also search cross-references, and this can occasionally lead to failed searches. This is part of the larger problem of designing systems that ensure that all searches are matched against cross-references.

Title Heading Index

Titles are particularly difficult to provide access to in online catalogs, because while some types of titles usually are under authority control (serial uniform titles, series, titles of anonymous classics, musical works, and works of prolific authors, such as Shakespeare), the majority of titles are not. Titles can pose particular problems for users; their citations may be to variant titles that have been treated as subtitles, parallel titles (i.e., the title in another language that is not chosen as the first title in the record), or title added entries in our cataloging records (see figure 4.5). Or their citations may be to titles of series or serials, or to individual monographs in monographic series, and a series or serial may be treated differently in different libraries (see figure 4.6).[5] Some libraries may make only one record for a series or serial as a whole. Other libraries may make individual records for items in a series or serial (analytics when they all have the same classification number or "cat-as-sep"s when they are given different classification numbers). It is unfair to expect the user to know whether a given title should be sought for as a series title or as the title proper of a serial record, especially because one library frequently makes a different decision from another in this regard. Indeed, Berger found that users of the MELVYL system were having major problems finding serials because serials are not currently indexed with monographs in the MELVYL system, and looking for serials requires that the user specify a search of the serial file.[6] He also includes an example of a series search on the MELVYL system that failed but would have retrieved one record if it had been done as a journal search instead.[7] This illustrates the danger of providing separate indexes for series and for serials rather than a general title index that includes everything. Instead, systems should ensure that title searches are matched against *all* title fields, including serial title and series title fields and all types of title added entries and title cross-references. One way to help the hapless user is to provide a title heading index that lists all title fields in alphabetical order (see figure 4.7).

For example, a user may have a citation to a work by Carl B. Smith entitled *Volunteer Programs That Work*. Only on searching the OPAC will the user discover that the citation is actually to the following:

Smith, Carl B.
   Getting people to read : volunteer programs that
work / Carl B. Smith and Leo C. Fay.

Of course, the user will only discover this record if the OPAC indexes and displays subtitles adequately.

Figure 4.5   An example of a citation to a subtitle

For example, a user might come in with a citation to a work entitled *Social Aspects of AIDS,* by Cindy Patton. Only on searching the OPAC can it be discovered that the book the user is looking for is

> Patton, Cindy, 1956-
>   Last served? : gendering the HIV pandemic.
>   London ; Bristol, PA : Taylor & Francis, 1994.
>   (Social aspects of AIDS)

In other words, unknown to the user, what she or he thought was the title was actually the title of a monographic series. The OPAC could only solve this problem if the series was indexed in the title index used in this user's name-title search.

Figure 4.6   An example of a citation to a series title

Title fields include all title fields and subfields in title authority records (130 and 1XX ≠t) and titles from bibliographic fields, including 130, 210, 211, 212, 214, 222, 24X, 440, 6XX ≠t, 7XX ≠t, 730, 740, 830, and 8XX ≠t fields and subfields in the USMARC format. If subfield coding for titles in contents notes becomes common practice, it may be possible to list those titles as well someday. Beware of indexing 490 fields; the 490 field contains either a series that catalogers have decided not to invest any effort in placing under authority control due to their judgment that few users will need access to it or a series traced differently in an 8XX field; a 490 field in the latter case would actually conflict with *see* references in the authority file.

Figure 4.7   Title fields in the USMARC formats

Linking Transcribed Fields to the Authority File

Most existing systems do not have very elegant displays of the works of prolific authors and the editions of multiple-edition works. This is because certain title fields, notably the 245 and the 440 fields, serve double duty as heading fields and transcribed fields (see chapter 3 for the previous discussion of this problem). A particular work with an author may be represented by an author field (normalized and linked to an authority record) and the title proper (transcribed from the item);[8] or it may be represented by an author field and a uniform title (both normalized);[9] or it may be represented by an author-title added entry (normalized).[10]

If these combinations of headings, each of which represents a work, are not displayed together effectively, the catalog is not meeting the second cataloging objective, 2.2 (b). Consider, for example, the display in figure 4.8, typical of current online public access catalogs. The user in search of *As You Like It* would be forgiven for thinking that

1	400 Shakespeare, William, 1564-1616.
2	14 Shakespeare, William, 1564-1616. All's well that ends well.
3	34 Shakespeare, William, 1564-1616. Antony and Cleopatra.
4	40 Shakespeare, William, 1564-1616. As you like it.
...	

Figure 4.8   Typical flawed display of a work in a current online public access catalog

his or her search was over when line 4 was chosen.[11] However, most editions of *As You Like It,* indeed, all those represented by Shakespeare in the 100 field and *As you like it* in the 245 field (title on item), are found at line 1. Line 4 contains only those records with *As you like it* in other fields and subfields besides the 245.[12] The reason for this is that line 1 represents those records that have the uniform title in a transcribed field, which most existing systems are not willing to link to the authority file, because they would be vulnerable to change on dynamic updating (the type of editing in which a cataloger changes a heading in an authority record, and the system then changes the heading in all bibliographic records that are linked to that authority record). A better display would put all editions of *As You Like It,* as well as all works about it, together at line 4. In addition, it would compress headings for the works of Shakespeare and, when one particular work was chosen, list editions of the work itself first, then works about it, then related works.[13] (See figure 4.9.)

What is probably needed to obtain displays that combine normalized and transcribed fields effectively is a system that is smart enough to link transcribed fields to authority records yet remember that they are transcribed fields and as such should be protected from dynamic update (i.e., automatic change by the computer). Instead of simply changing the fields in the bibliographic records when the authority record is changed, the smart system would leave the transcribed fields as is but add a normalized field containing the new form. (See figure 4.10.) It can be seen that the proposed solution to this problem is very complex and requires cooperation between the cataloger and the machine. The proposal should at least give designers an idea of the nature of the problem and its potential solution. Perhaps there are clever designers who can think of even better solutions.

Shakespeare, William, 1564-1616.
1. All's well that ends well.
2. Antony and Cleopatra.
3. As you like it.
4. Comedy of errors.
5. Coriolanus.
6. Cymbeline.
7. Hamlet.
8. Henry V.
9. Henry VI.

When the user chooses line 3, for As You Like It, the following display could result:

Shakespeare, William, 1564-1616. As you like it.

1. Editions of As you like it.
2. Works about As you like it.*
3. Other works related to As you like it.†

When the user chooses line 1, for editions of As You Like It, the following display could result:

1 As you like it / by William Shakespeare ; translated into modern English with analysis and commentary by Gary S. Michael. 1991.
2 As you like it / literary consultant, John Wilders. 1978.
3 As you like it / edited by Richard Knowles ; with a survey of criticism by Evelyn Joseph Mattern. 1977.
4 As you like it / William Shakespeare ; edited by Agnes Latham. 1975.
5 As you like it : an old-spelling and old-meaning edition, prepared by Christine Trautvetter. 1972.
6 As you like it / edited by Arthur Quiller-Couch & John Dover Wilson. 1957.
7 As you like it / by William Shakespeare ; a facsimile of the first folio text, with an introduction by J. Dover Wilson, and a list of modern readings. 1929.
8 As you like it : a comedy / by Mr. William Shakespear. 1734.

********French & English:
9 Comme il vous plaira = As you like it / Shakespeare ; introd. traduction et notes par J.-J. Mayoux. 1956.
********Frisian:
10 As jiemme it lije meie : in blijspul / uut it Ingels fen William Shakspeare [sic] ; forfryske in mei forkleerjende noten forsjoen troch R. Posthumus. 1842.
********German:
11 Wie es euch gefaellt / William Shakespeare ; Deutsch von Elisabeth Plessen ; Regie Peter Zadek. [1986?]

---

*In the USMARC bibliographic format, 6XX fields contain subject added entries for the work.

†In the USMARC bibliographic format, added entries for the work with second indicator 1 (now obsolete) or blank.

Figure 4.9   Ideal display of a work in an online public access catalog

The problem

There are two types of titles used as headings that occur in transcribed fields and that therefore need to be protected from global update. One is the uniform title and the other is the series. Uniform titles and series are in transcribed fields when the normalized form actually occurs on the title page equivalent of the item cataloged; when that happens, catalogers do not add a normalized field that simply duplicates what appears in the transcribed field.

EXAMPLES

Example of uniform title in normalized field:

100 1_ ≠a Shakespeare, William, ≠d 1564-1616.
240 10 ≠a Hamlet
245 14 ≠a The three-text Hamlet : ≠b parallel texts of the first and second quartos and first folio / ≠c edited by Paul Bertram and Bernice W. Kliman.
260 __ ≠a New York : ≠b AMS Press, ≠c c1991.

Example of uniform title in transcribed field:

100 1_ ≠a Shakespeare, William, ≠d 1564-1616.
245 10 ≠a Hamlet / ≠c edited by G.R. Hibbard.
260 __ ≠a Oxford ; New York : ≠b Oxford University Press, ≠c 1994, c1987.

Example of uniform title in normalized fields with no corresponding transcribed fields:

600 10 ≠a Shakespeare, William, ≠d 1564-1616. ≠t Hamlet.
         [for a work about Hamlet]
700 10 ≠a Shakespeare, William, ≠d 1564-1616. ≠t Hamlet.
         [for a work related to Hamlet in some way, e.g., an adaptation]

Example of series title in normalized field:

490 1_ ≠a Bibliographies of modern authors, ≠x 0749-470X ; ≠v no. 21
830 _0 ≠a Bibliographies of modern authors (San Bernardino, Calif.) ; ≠v no. 21.

Example of series title in transcribed field:

440 _0 ≠a Social aspects of AIDS

Example of series title in normalized field with no corresponding transcribed field:

630 00 ≠a Bibliographies of modern authors (San Bernardino, Calif.)
         [for a work about the series]

(Continued)

Figure 4.10 **Draft of specifications for a programming module to allow transcribed fields to be linked to authority records**

Desired results

1. Uniform titles and series titles that occur in transcribed fields should link with authority records for those uniform titles and series titles for display purposes. This would allow the following display, for example:

Screen 1:
> Shakespeare, William, 1564-1616.
>> 1. All's well that ends well.
>> 2. Antony and Cleopatra.
>> 3. As you like it.
>> 4. Hamlet.
>> 5. Henry V.

Screen 2 (after line 4 above is chosen):
> Shakespeare, William, 1564-1616.
>> 1. Editions of Hamlet
>> 2. Works about Hamlet
>> 3. Works related to Hamlet

Screen 3 (after line 1 above is chosen):
> Shakespeare, William, 1564-1616.
>> Editions of Hamlet:
>> 1. Hamlet. The three-text Hamlet : parallel texts of the first and second quartos and first folio / edited by Paul Bertram and Bernice W. Kliman. c1991.
>> 2. Hamlet / edited by G.R. Hibbard. 1994, c1987.

Example of a bad current display that needs this solution for correction:

> R1 339 Shakespeare, William, 1564-1616.
> *[Note: Most Editions of Hamlet Are Here at Line R1 Because the Uniform Title Occurs in the 245 Field!]*
> R2　17 Shakespeare, William, 1564-1616. All's well that ends well.
> R3　42 Shakespeare, William, 1564-1616. Antony and Cleopatra.
> R4　26 Shakespeare, William, 1564-1616. As you like it.
> R5 321 Shakespeare, William, 1564-1616. Hamlet.
> *[Note: Only Editions of Hamlet with the Uniform Title in a Normalized Field, e.g., 1XX/240, 600, or 700 Field, Are Here.]*

2. Uniform titles and series titles that occur in transcribed fields should link with authority records for those uniform titles and series titles for global update purposes in such a way that the transcription is never changed by the computer but instead is superseded by the correct heading field. (Type 1 below)

3. It should also be possible to do efficient global changes to uniform titles and series titles that do *not* occur in transcribed fields but need to be changed to the forms that *do* occur in transcribed fields. (Type 2 below)

Figure 4.10—Continued

4. It should also be possible to do efficient global changes to uniform titles and series titles that do *not* occur in transcribed fields and are being changed to new forms that also do *not* occur in transcribed fields. (Type 3 below)

5. It should be possible to do efficient global changes to uniform titles and series titles in normalized fields that have no corresponding transcribed fields (e.g., subject and related work added entries). (Type 4 below)

Summary of types of global changes

Type 1: Old form is in transcribed field; new form needs to be in a normalized field that supersedes the transcribed field. Editing by the cataloger of the transcribed field to adjust indicators is required.

Type 2: Old form is in a normalized field; new form already occurs in transcribed field; deletion of normalized field and editing by the cataloger of the transcribed field to adjust indicators is required.

Type 3: Old form is in a normalized field; new form will continue to be in a normalized field; no editing of the transcribed field is required.

Type 4: Old form is in a normalized field that has no corresponding transcribed field (e.g., subject and related work added entries).

Note: All four types could potentially occur in the process of doing a global change on a single uniform title or series title.

Assumptions made Concerning following proposed algorithms

1. The program can be assumed to "know" whether the old form is linked to a transcribed field, as opposed to a normalized field.

2. The program can be assumed to "know" whether the old form occurs in the type of field that can be expected to occur in normalized/transcribed pairs or not; i.e., the program can differentiate between Type 3 and Type 4 changes.

3. The program can't be made "smart" enough to:
   a. use character string matching to discover whether the new form is already present in a transcribed field
   b. "know" all articles in all languages so as to be able to set nonfiling indicators accurately in all cases
   c. "know" how to tell when a transcribed form is so similar to a normalized one that there is no reason to "trace" it

Because of the latter assumption, the following algorithms build in a stage for cataloger confirmation and partial editing, if necessary.

(Continued)

I. Proposed algorithm for a smart global change program to carry out Type 1 global changes:

I.A. Uniform titles

I.A.1. Specification for display to the catalog editor:

Display the following fields (if present) in MARC format form:
130
100,110,111
240
245

I.A.2. Specification for global change algorithm:

Each record linked to the authority record that needs to be changed should be shown to the catalog editor using the above display.

The cataloger should be allowed to input the authority record for the new form for the uniform title, so that the program can supply the new form at the appropriate places below.

1. The catalog editor should be prompted with the following question:
   Add 240 field with new form in it? Y/N
2. If the cataloger answers yes, the system should supply the following:
   240 10 ≠a [text of changed title]
3. Next, the system should prompt the cataloger with the following question:
   Trace title on item? Y/N
4. If the answer is yes, the system should change the first indicator in the 245 field to 1.

I.B.   Series

I.B.1. Specification for display to the catalog editor:

Display the following fields in MARC format form:
440 field that matches the authority record being changed
All 490 fields
830 field that matches the authority record being changed

I.B.2. Specification for global change algorithm:

Each record linked to the authority record that needs to be changed should be shown to the catalog editor using the above display.

The cataloger should be allowed to input the authority record for the new form for the series, complete with indicators and subfield codes. The program should be smart enough to know from this the correct tags, indicators, and subfield codes for the new heading in the bibliographic record(s). New forms could follow input conventions for any one of the following USMARC bibliographic fields or combinations of fields:
440
490/830
490/800
490/810
490/811

Figure 4.10—Continued

1. The tag of the 440 field should be changed to 490, first indicator 1, and the data in the field should be maintained as is.

2. Based on the new form in the new authority record already input by the cataloger, the computer should supply the new form in the appropriate 8XX field (830, 800, 810, or 811).

II. Proposed algorithm for a smart global change program to carry out Type 2 and Type 3 global changes:

II.A. Uniform titles

II.A.1. Specification for display to the catalog editor:

Display the following fields (if present) in MARC format form:

      130
      100,110,111
      240
      245

II.A.2. Specification for global change algorithm:

The cataloger should be allowed to input the authority record for the new form for the uniform title, so that the program can supply the new form at the appropriate places below.

When the authority record (old form) is linked to a 1XX/240 combination of fields:

1. The catalog editor should be prompted with the following question:
   Delete 240 field? Y/N/escape (The escape option is necessary for cases in which the cataloger needs to leave some records as is and work on others because two different works have mistakenly been represented as one in the catalog.)
2. If the cataloger answers yes, the system should:
   Delete the 240 field.
3. If the answer is no, the 240 field should be retained and changed to the new form.
4. Next, the system should prompt the cataloger with the following question:
   Trace title on item? Y/N
5. If the answer is yes, the system should change the first indicator in the 245 field to 1. (If no, first indicator should be 0.)

When the authority record (old form) is linked to a 130 field:

1. The catalog editor should be prompted with the following question:
   Delete 130 field? Y/N
2. If the cataloger answers yes, the system should:
   Delete the 130 field.
3. If the cataloger answers no, the system should place the new form into the 130 field.
4. If the 130 field has been deleted, the system should check the first indicator in the 245 field, and if it is a 1, the system should change it to a 0.

(Continued)

II.B. Series

II.B.1. Specification for display to the catalog editor:

Display the following fields in MARC format form:

440 field that matches the authority record being changed
All 490 fields
830 field that matches the authority record being changed

II.B.2. Specification for global change algorithm:

The cataloger should be allowed to input the authority record for the new form for the series, complete with indicators and subfield codes. The program should be smart enough to know from this the correct tags, indicators, and subfield codes for the new heading in the bibliographic record(s). New forms could follow input conventions for any one of the following USMARC bibliographic fields or combinations of fields:

440
490/830
490/800
490/810
490/811

The cataloger should be allowed to indicate which 4XX/8XX combination should be worked on whenever the record contains more than one.

1. The catalog editor should be prompted with the following question:
   Delete 8XX field? Y/N
2. If the cataloger answers yes, the system should:
   Delete the 8XX field.
3. If the cataloger answers no, the new form should be placed in the appropriate 8XX field.
4. If the 8XX field was deleted in step 2, the system should prompt the cataloger with the following question:
   Trace series title on item? Y/N
5. If the answer is yes, the system should change the 490 field designated by the cataloger to a 440 field.
6. The cataloger should be prompted to set the second indicator based on the number of nonfiling characters that are present in the series title.
7. If the answer in question 4 is no, the first indicator in the 490 field should be set to 0.

III. Proposed algorithm for a smart global change program to carry out Type 4 global changes:

These global changes can be carried out in the usual way without cataloger intervention.

Figure 4.10—Continued

Naming the File(s)

Some of the other design decisions that must be made in the process of designing an online public access catalog that demonstrates author and work relationships are as follows. First, will you have several different indexes, and if so, what will you name them? Requiring users to specify an index (such as AUTHOR or SUBJECT) adds to the complexity of the procedures a user must learn in order to use the catalog effectively (see figure 4.11).[14] The value of increasing the efficiency of searching by the use of specific indexes should be balanced against this increased complexity for the user. If the system can possibly afford to do so, a general search not limited to particular indexes could be quite helpful as a default search for the novice user or for the user with an ambiguous or garbled citation (see figure 4.12). See figure 2.1 for a version of a form fill-in designed for such a system. Sorting and labeling the results of such a search will enable the user to see the range of possibilities and how they are defined by the library, which may enable her or him to refine or improve her or his search and future searches. For an example of a labeled display, see figure 4.13.

Ballard and Smith, p. 65:
    8% of zero-hit searches in author searching
Dickson, p. 28, 32:
    3% of all title searches
    3% of all author searches
Ferl and Millsap, p. 87:
    28% of all subject searches
Hunter, p. 400:
    4% of all title searches
    2% of all author searches
    1% of all subject searches
Peters, p. 270:
    1% of all title searches
    3% of all subject searches
Sinnott, p. 97:
    1% of all author searches (5.5% of zero-hit searches)
Taylor, p. 8:
    1% of all searches (8% of zero-hit searches)

Berger ("Information-Seeking") also found that specification of the wrong index was a frequent cause of error on the part of MELVYL searchers, but he did not give percentages of failed searches because of this problem (p. 83–90, unsuccessful known-item searches; p. 111–112, 114–118, unsuccessful periodical title searches; p. 125–129, title word searches that would have retrieved more if converted to subject searches; p. 138, invalid index specification [keyword index not available on the MELVYL system]).

Full citations for user studies are found in the bibliography of user studies in appendix A.

Figure 4.11   **User studies that have analyzed the reasons for zero-hit searches and have determined that specification of the wrong index is a significant cause of search failure**

AUTOGRAPHICS (Walt Crawford, *The Online Catalog Book: Essays and Examples* [Boston: G. K. Hall, 1992], p. 255)

CARL Everybody's Catalog

Geac Advance and Geocat

LIAS

NLS (Dennis Auburn Hill, *User's Guide to the Library Computer Catalog: Network Library System (NLS) Catalog User's Guide*, 4th ed. [Madison: University of Wisconsin-Madison, 1993])

PALS, which has a "TE" (general term) search (Crawford, *Online*, p. 410)

Phoenix, which has an "S" (term) search (Ibid., p. 422)

Unicorn, which has a "word or phrase" search (Ibid., p. 480)

USCInfo, which has a "full record" search (Ibid., p. 497)

Figure 4.12   Some systems that provide a general search

(1)	The parachute	(title)
(2)	Parachute Club of America	(organization)
(3)	Parachutes	(title)
(4)	Parachutes	(subject)
(5)	Parachutes—Handbooks, manuals, etc.	(subject)
(6)	Parachutes—History	(subject)
(7)	Parachuting	(title)
(8)	Parachuting	(subject)
(9)	Parachuting—History	(subject)
(10)	Parachuting for sport	(subject)
(11)	Parachutist	(title)

Figure 4.13   An example of a labeled display, result of a general search

Note that labels (as seen in figure 4.13) will need to be carefully designed to be explanatory and comprehensible to users and also to be consistent with the terminology used in naming files and indexes for searches of particular files or indexes. Some decision making will be involved concerning how finely to divide categories; for example, will you want to list series titles separately from other titles? Will you want to list conferences separately from organizations? Some of this decision making may hinge on whether you think your users always know when they are dealing with a series or a conference name and whether you have the option of offering both broadly defined and narrowly defined searches, e.g., a general title search and a series search.

Whether you require the user to specify a particular file or index, or whether you just offer such specification as an option, the decision as to what to call the file or index is an important one. If the file contains both names and titles, it is important to call it something that makes that clear to the user, e.g., NAME AND TITLE SEARCH. Calling the file or index AUTHOR can be misleading for users, who may not think of an actor, or an artist, or a musician, or a defendant in a court case as an author, yet all these are tagged indistinguishably from authors in the USMARC format. You would probably also include conferences and other corporate bodies in the AUTHOR INDEX, and not all users may realize that that is where corporate names are to be found. On the other hand, calling the index the NAME INDEX can also be misleading, because many proper names, e.g., the Greek god Zeus, are indexed as topical subject headings[15] rather than as names.[16] Also, users seeking a journal title may consider that title to be the *name* of the journal.

Very specialized systems might be able to offer more specific names for their indexes; for example, the ILLINET online music subsystem has composer/performer indexes. Even here, though, the user interested in Irving Berlin or another songwriter might find the term *composer* confusing. Actually, this difficult naming problem makes it that much more desirable to have a general index that includes everything, as well as form fill-in screens for general searches, so novice users need not specify indexes. This is also an area where careful documentation, shared with users in the form of *HELP* screens, can help clear up much confusion; for example, users should be warned if the NAME or AUTHOR file contains some titles, but not all titles, as is the case if it consists only of authority records, because only some titles have authority records.

Conclusion

One of the most intractable problems that remains unsolved in OPAC design is that of facilitating the user's search for a known work using both the author's name and the title of the work. Better integration of authority files and bibliographic files could help users with their known-work searches, probably still the most common type of search done on OPACs in large research libraries. Better integration of all files in OPACs would enable users to formulate complex searches limited by date and format, without losing access to syndetic structure contained in the authority file.

Notes

1. OPAC (NLS) users interviewed by Johnson and Connaway complained that a lack of cross-references in the catalog made foreign names difficult to search (Debra Wilcox Johnson and Lynn Silipigni Connaway, "Use of Online Catalogs: A Report of Results of Focus Group Interviews," typescript [Feb. 1992]: p. 10, 19).

2. Michael Berger, *The User Meets the MELVYL System: An Analysis of User Transactions*, Technical Report no. 7 (Oakland, Calif.: Division of Library Automation, University of California, 1996), appendix, p. 7.

3. Lenore Coral, Ivy Anderson, Keiko Cho, et al., "Automation Requirements for Music Information," *MLA Notes* 43 (Sept. 1986): 14–18. (A report of the Subcommittee on Music Automation of the Music Library Association.)

4. OPAC (NLS) users interviewed by Johnson and Connaway specifically requested the ability to combine searches (Johnson and Connaway, "Use of Online Catalogs," p. 28).

5. Catherine M. Dwyer, Eleanor A. Gossen, and Lynne M. Martin, "Known-Item Search Failure in an OPAC," *RQ* 31 (winter 1991): 228–236.

6. Michael George Berger, "Information-Seeking in the Online Bibliographic System: An Exploratory Study" (Ph.D. diss., UC Berkeley, 1994), p. 111–112, 114–118.

7. Berger, *The User Meets,* appendix, p. 7.

8. In the USMARC format, tags 1XX and 245 delimiter a.

9. In the USMARC format, tags 1XX and 240.

10. In the USMARC format, tag 7XX or 6XX (for works about the work) with a delimiter t subfield.

11. Note that this smart user knows that it is wiser in most systems to search for a known work under author, rather than under title, because the author is more likely to be the main entry and therefore may lead to a larger number of relevant records.

12. Such as a delimiter t subfield after a 600 or 700 field for Shakespeare.

13. The display can be based on USMARC tags in the bibliographic record. The work itself could be represented by the following tags or combinations of tags: 100, 110, or 111, plus 240 or 245; 130; 700, 710, or 711, plus delimiter t; 730. Note that for such displays to work, catalogers must be using uniform titles to bring together all the editions of a work, regardless of title changes; unfortunately, these rules are optional in AACR2R.

14. Martha M. Yee and Raymond Soto, "User Problems with Access to Fictional Characters and Personal Names in Online Public Access Catalogs," *Information Technology and Libraries* 10 (March 1991): 3–13. See also Nicholson Baker, "Discards," *New Yorker,* April 4, 1994, p. 81.

15. 650 fields in the USMARC format.

16. X00 or X10 fields in the USMARC format.

5

Demonstration of Relationships—Authors and Works—Indexing Decisions

In this chapter we examine ways to improve the chances of success for a user who is looking for the works of an author or for a particular work. We make recommendations for the default author search, and for the default work search, and we examine ways that systems could compensate for common user errors and citation variations. System designers should remember the latter in particular when designing default searches; there is no guarantee that a user's citation is going to match the way the work sought has been cataloged. Thus, it behooves systems to be as flexible as possible in matching a user's search terms to terms in the records in the system.

Entry Terms and Order of Terms

A phrase or search key index requires that the user know entry terms, just as the user needed to do in card catalogs. Users must invert names in author searches; for title searches, the initial article cannot be typed in, so the person looking for the film *La Strada* must type in the title as *Strada* or the search will fail. In phrase-indexed systems or phrase-indexed searches that require knowledge of entry terms, failure to invert personal names or drop an initial article is a frequent source of failed searches (see figure 5.1). While users of a card catalog could notice right away that all names are inverted and look under surname, the users of computer systems, who are confronted with a blank screen on which they must type their searches, may very well not expect to have to invert names or drop articles from titles. Phrase-indexing systems or functions that search names in both direct and inverted forms and recognize articles and skip over them to begin the matching process are a real help to users. If this approach is used, it is highly recommended that USMARC filing indicators be used to indicate which words are articles to be skipped, rather than giving the computer a list of articles to skip. Many articles are used in other ways as well, and when not used as articles, they should not be skipped. See examples in figure 5.2.

User studies that have analyzed zero-hit searches and have found that the requirement to drop the article in front of a title in phrase-indexed systems is a significant source of search failure

Dickson, p. 28:	10% of all title searches
Hunter, p. 400:	6% of all title searches

The requirement that users invert personal names in phrase-indexed systems is also a significant source of search failure:

Ballard and Smith, p. 65:	18% of zero-hit searches
Dickson, p. 32:	13% of all author searches
Hunter, p. 400:	6% of all author searches
Janosky, Smith, and Hildreth, p. 580:	25% of users doing assigned searches failed to invert author names
Peters, p. 270:	2% of all author searches
Taylor, p. 8:	4% of all author searches (17% of zero-hit searches)

Full citations for user studies are found in the bibliography of user studies in appendix A.

Figure 5.1   Examples of failure to match on entry terms in phrase-indexed systems

A la carte (title of a journal)
El Cid (name of a historical figure)
El Segundo (name of a city)
A (film title)

Figure 5.2   Examples of articles that should not be ignored in sorting

Having to know entry terms can be a real hardship for a user whose title citation, unbeknownst to him or her, is to the subtitle or the parallel title, not the title proper of the work sought (see figure 5.3). Having to know entry terms can also be a hardship for a user looking for works of corporate bodies, such as conference proceedings, as citations are frequently garbled or abbreviated (see figure 5.4).

On the other hand, if the user does know the entry term, she or he should have the option of using it to make the search more precise. In pure keyword searching, the user is not allowed to specify that a particular word should occur at the beginning of a field. For example, a user interested in an author named Frederick Lewis might also have to retrieve authors named Lewis Frederick. The user interested in the photographer Robert Frank would have to browse through all of the authors with the forenames Robert Frank. Some systems that began as keyword access systems, such as the MELVYL system, have added a few exact searches, using phrase indexing, to allow users to specify that they want a particular string of words to occur at the beginning of a field. This is especially important for finding one-word titles using common words, such as the journal title *Science*. In any case, the user should be told when correct order is essential, and the user should be allowed to decide whether or not to do a search in which order must be specified. If our recommendation is followed, and the keyword-within-heading search is made the default, and if a search retrieves many hits, perhaps the user could be offered a LOOK HARDER command that would perform a left-to-right match; of course, the user should be consulted about the proper order of terms if the original search had more than one keyword in it.

A user may have a citation to a work by Carl B. Smith entitled *Volunteer Programs That Work*. However, the citation is actually to the subtitle of a work with a title proper of *Getting People to Read:*

Smith, Carl B.
 Getting people to read : volunteer programs that
work / Carl B. Smith and Leo C. Fay.

In a phrase-indexed system, or a phrase-index search, the user's search will fail (unless the cataloger has made an added entry for the subtitle, of course; but this is rarely done). However, a keyword search that required a match within a title field (with the title field defined as USMARC 245 field, ≠a and ≠b subfields) and produced a display of headings matched (including both the ≠a and ≠b subfields in the display) would allow the user's search to succeed.

Berger reports a similar problem that a user had with a parallel title. The user did a left-to-right matching title search on *Veterinary Multilingual Thesaurus* that failed because that title was a parallel title on a work with a first title of *Veterinarwissenschaft Mehrsprachiger Thesaurus.**

---

*Michael Berger, *The User Meets the MELVYL System: An Analysis of User Transactions*, Technical Report no. 7 (Oakland, Calif.: Division of Library Automation, University of California, 1996), appendix, p. 11.

Figure 5.3   Examples of subtitle and parallel title citations

---

A user may have a citation to a conference on chaos and order. Unbeknownst to the user, it was actually called *International Conference on Order in Chaos*. Thus, if the user began browsing in the catalog through headings beginning CONFERENCE ON, he or she would probably never find the desired conference. A keyword-within-heading search, e.g., FND KW CHAOS ORDER, would do the trick in this case.

Figure 5.4   An example of a garbled citation for a conference publication

Search key-indexing systems, or phrase-indexing systems without implicit truncation, require that the user know the correct order of all input terms. Users of catalogs frequently have inexact or faulty citations to the works they seek (see figure 5.5). The requirement that users not only have the exact words in a title spelled exactly as they are on the title page but also that they know the order in which the words occur on the title page may be so rigorous that a search that might succeed in a keyword-indexing system would fail in a phrase-indexing system.

The requirement that a user's searches match headings exactly is particularly unfortunate when the user is seeking a heading to which catalogers have added a parenthetical qualifier. Examples of such headings are: ABBA (MUSICAL GROUP); INTERNATIONAL CONGRESS ON GLASS (10TH . . .). Indexing software that required users to include MUSICAL GROUP or 10TH in their searches in order to retrieve these headings would be very unfriendly software indeed. Indexing software ought to be made "smart" enough to recognize the parentheses and ignore their content in matching users' searches against fields that contain authority controlled headings.

Another problem can occur when the user's citation has an abbreviated title that leaves out prepositions. Loanne Snavely and Katie Clark give the example of a user with a citation to *J Am Soc Hort Sci*. A phrase-indexing system or function demands that the user correctly guess the prepositions in this title. If the user guesses that the title is *Journal of the American Society of Horticulture Science*, the search is likely to fail in such a system, as the title is actually *Journal of the American Society for Horticulture Science*. As the authors point out, "In a large research library, there are so many entries that start with 'Journal of the American Society' that the two would not be near enough for someone to find them when an exact title search is conducted."[1]

For these reasons, our recommendation is to make the keyword-within-heading (or -within-authority-record) search, with a resulting default display of headings matched, the default, so that users are not required to know entry terms in order to conduct a successful search.

On the other hand, if the user does know the correct order of terms, he or she should have the option of using this knowledge to make the search more precise. In pure keyword access systems, the user is not allowed to specify order. Some systems that began as keyword access systems, such as the MELVYL system, have added a few exact searches, using phrase indexing, to allow users to specify order, when known. If our recommendation is followed, and the keyword-within-heading search is made the default, and if a search retrieves many hits, perhaps the user could be offered a LOOK HARDER command that would do a left-to-right match; of course, the user should be consulted about the proper order of terms if the original search had more than one keyword in it.

Note that both the phrase-index search and the keyword-within-heading search on an author's name will retrieve that author's name with any subject subdivisions that might have been added to the name.

Normalization

Computer algorithms for matching users' search terms to terms on records in the catalog should take a very liberal approach to normalization. All of the following should be ignored in matching search to records: diacritics, punctuation, subfield

Ayres, German, Loukes, et al., p. 269:	Author is correct 75% of the time. Title is correct 90% of the time.
Dwyer, Gossen, and Martin, p. 232:	22% of ILL requests for items owned are due to incorrect citations.
Lipetz, p. 4:	6% of failures were due to faulty citations.
Seymour and Schofield, p. 18:	Reasons for search failure: Incorrect surname 28% of failures Incorrect forename 4-6% of failures Incorrect title 8-12% of failures
Specht, p. 339:	6% of failures due to faulty citations. 7% of faulty citations due to incorrect surname. 4% of faulty citations due to incorrect title.
Tagliacozzo, Rosenberg, and Kochen, p. 235, 239:	30% of known-item searches had incorrect titles. 31% of known-item searches had incorrect authors.
Tate, p. 185:	78% of titles in a sample of published citations match catalog entries (i.e., 22% do not). 69% of authorship elements in a sample of published citations match catalog entries (i.e., 31% do not).

Berger (*The User Meets,* appendix, p. 10–11) gives a number of actual searches that failed because of inaccurate title citations:

Correct title:
The Decline and Fall of the Roman Empire

Title searched:
Rise and Decline of the Roman Empire

Correct title:
Every War Must End

Title searched:
Why Every War Must End

Correct title:
Complete Desk Reference of Veterinary Pharmaceuticals and Biologicals

Title searched:
Comprehensive Desk Reference of Veterinary Pharmaceuticals and Biologicals

---

Full citations for user studies are found in the bibliography of user studies in appendix A.

Figure 5.5   **User studies that address the question of the reliability of users' citations**

codes in the USMARC format, and capitalization. Note, however, that this liberal approach should be taken only in the searching context. In chapter 6, we will be urging that a conservative approach be taken to normalization in the context of display algorithms.

Default Searches

Author/name Search

Figure 5.6 lists the USMARC fields that contain personal name headings. In the card catalog, across-field keyword searches were not possible at all; in gaining this new power, we have lost much of our previous power to guide the user to those authorized forms of name and title that have the ability to retrieve *all* the editions of a sought work and *all* the works of a desired author. Online catalogs that offer users only left-to-right phrase indexing retain the power to guide users to authorized forms in this way but lose the power of keyword across-field searching, including the ability to search using both an author's name and a title.

One keyword-searchable catalog that has tried to solve the problem of ensuring that *every* user's search is matched against cross-references is the MELVYL online catalog, which matches a user's author search terms against both authority records and bibliographic records, performing a keyword search across all name fields in both sets of records and retrieving all bibliographic records that have the headings in the retrieved authority records.

In the USMARC format, personal names are found in the following fields in the bibliographic and authority formats:

Bibliographic record:
    100
    400
    600
    700
    800

Authority record:
    100
    400
    500

All names in bibliographic records should be represented by an authority record, even if it may be nothing more than a heading (lacking cross-references and notes). Thus, searching authority records should be enough. However, authority records should be linked to the fields in bibliographic records listed above to deliver optimal results.

Figure 5.6   USMARC fields containing personal name headings

It should be noted, however, that matching every search against authority records as well as bibliographic records is currently feasible only in those systems that, like the MELVYL system, limit searches to relatively specific keyword indexes. For example, the MELVYL system offers, among other specific keyword indexes, personal author, corporate author, and subject, and searches of these indexes can easily be matched against just those authority records appropriate to the search. A personal author keyword search in the MELVYL system can be limited to personal name fields in bibliographic records and personal author authority records. By contrast, the ORION system, which offers users broadly specified keyword indexes such as NT (Names and Titles) and KW (Names, Titles, Subjects, Note fields), has no way for the system to know that some keywords should be searched, for example, against personal author authority records and others should be searched against subject authority or uniform title authority records.[2]

The MELVYL approach makes it more likely that a user who has a citation with an author name that varies from those found on the title pages of the items in the collection will be led to the desired work. However, in MELVYL the link between authority records and bibliographic records is completely transparent, so the user may be confused as to why certain records were retrieved. For example, the user who does the search F PA HUNTER THOMPSON (i.e., FIND PERSONAL AUTHOR HUNTER THOMPSON) is presented with a list of 114 bibliographic records retrieved. One of the records retrieved is the following:

> Dunn, Seamus, 1939- Protestant alienation in Northern Ireland : a preliminary survey / by Seamus Dunn and Valerie Morgan. Coleraine : Centre for the Study of Conflict, University of Ulster, 1994.

The reason it is retrieved is apparent only when a search is done of the authority file. There, the vigilant searcher will find that there is an authority record for Lauran Paine that has references from the following three names (all pseudonyms used by Lauran Paine): Liggett, Hunter; Morgan, Valerie; and Thompson, Russ.[3] By way of a within-record keyword search of this authority record, the MELVYL system has linked the name Valerie Morgan to the name Hunter S. Thompson.

An improvement on the MELVYL solution, as yet untried as far as is known, is to have the searching software do keyword-within-record searches of authority records and then display all matched headings. Thus, in the above example, instead of immediately displaying bibliographic records, the interim display would consist of name headings, including the heading for Lauran Paine, so that the user could reject Lauran Paine and choose Hunter S. Thompson. What would be missed in such a solution would be transcribed fields (title on item and contents notes) that might have different forms of a name, but ideally these different forms would occur in cross-references in the authority records as well. In this new solution, the authority records would be linked to bibliographic records, so that a user selecting either a heading or a cross-reference from the list would be able to retrieve all bibliographic records linked to the authority record from which the heading or cross-reference was taken. In this way, the user would be able to benefit from the cross-reference structure and at the same time have more control over the process than is provided by the MELVYL system approach. Having the default co-occurrence rule be within a single authority record would prevent false drops caused by the matching of a search that includes forename and surname of a sought author with the forename of one author and the surname of another on the same bibliographic record; for example, a cross-field search

Ballard and Smith, p. 65:	8% of zero-hit searches were due to this problem.
Jones, p. 7:	20% of author searches on Okapi were of this type; this figure may reflect a higher incidence of works by two or more authors of interest to students pursuing professional studies at the Polytechnic of Central London, now University of Westminster, where Okapi was installed.

Full citations for user studies are found in the bibliography of user studies in appendix A.

Figure 5.7　**Error analysis user studies that have noted that users' searches can fail when two authors' names are typed in at the same time**

on James Stewart could retrieve a film with an actor named James and a screenwriter named Stewart.

It is probably more common for users, at least in general libraries, to be looking for the works of a particular author than it is for a user to be looking for the work of several authors together (see figure 5.7), although searches for the works of two authors do occur; they may occur more often in certain types of libraries, such as science libraries or libraries with performing arts collections. However, it does happen that a particular search is for the work of two people working together. For example, a user may wish to see the works of Gilbert and Sullivan. Another user may wish to see all the Cukor films starring Katharine Hepburn. Leslie Troutman points out the usefulness of allowing music users to find all the performances of the work of a particular composer by a particular performer.[4] Therefore, it is useful to offer a search across multiple author fields as an option. Note also that effective form fill-in design could help software tell when a search is for more than one author (assuming the user knows this, of course). In making decisions about defaults for your institution, you might find it helpful to examine transaction logs to see how frequently users search using the names of more than one author; the incidence may be much higher in certain types of special libraries than it is in general public or academic libraries.

Author/name and Topic Search

Karen Drabenstott and Marjorie Weller give a number of examples of users' searches that failed at least in part because the user included both a personal name and a topical term or two in a search. (See figure 5.8.) If a form fill-in approach has been used, and the user can indicate which terms are personal name terms and which terms are topical, it would be useful to display to the user the personal name(s) matched and all subject subdivisions attached, regardless of whether any of them match the topical terms input by the user. Once the user sees how the works by and about the person of interest are in fact organized in the catalog, she or he can either browse through those works to find the specific works of interest or more easily modify the search. Even if a form fill-in approach is not available, it is possible that an intelligent fuzzy matching algorithm could be developed that could recognize that portions of the

keyenesian economics (sic)
the hapsburg monarchy
notions of buddha
myers-briggs type indicator
hannibal and the battle of carthage
ras tafari (sic)
clinton and poverty
freud and aggression
religion tolstoy
chaucer criticism
delacroix and colr (sic)
skinner and sibling\s
foreign policy of roosevelt theodore
the life of william faulkner
descartes' future prediction
paintings of pollock/pollack (sic)
clarence darrow's relegious views (sic)
greek mythology's influence on shakespeare*

---

*Karen M. Drabenstott and Marjorie S. Weller, "Improving Personal-Name Searching in Online Catalogs," *Information Technology and Libraries* 15 (1996): 140.

Figure 5.8   Examples of failed searches using personal name and topical term

search match a heading or reference in the name authority file; if there is such a match, the algorithm could display the heading matched, ignoring the topical terms.

It should be noted, by the way, that subject subdivisions attached to personal names do exist to cover some of the topics sought in figure 5.8. For example, the following are valid LCSH headings:

Freud, Sigmund, 1856-1939—Views on aggression.

Chaucer, Geoffrey, d. 1400—Criticism and interpretation.

Darrow, Clarence, 1857-1938—Religion.

However, the subdivisions in the preceding list are all free-floating subdivisions. This means that they do not appear in LCSH itself. It also means that, currently, authority records do not exist for them that could lead users from their terms to these. For that reason, some version of fuzzy matching, as described above, may currently be the only option to ensure that users' terms are matched to the terms used in the catalog. Another caveat is that the—VIEWS ON subdivision is applied only to works by others discussing the person's views; the heading above would not be applied to a work on aggression by Freud himself, for example. Probably most of the works desired by the users whose searches are listed in figure 5.8 are found directly under the person's name. For example, biographies, such as the life of Hunter S. Thompson, as we have seen in chapter 3, are given a 600 field for Hunter S. Thompson but no form subdivision under his name indicating that the work is a biography, perhaps because works about people are commonly biographical.

Corporate Body Search

Frequently users of works produced by corporate bodies have no idea what the title pages of the works look like and therefore how they were cataloged. The words in a citation may appear to be the name of a conference, for example, but appear only in the title on the item sought, or vice versa (see figure 5.9). For corporate body searches, within-record keyword searches of corporate name authority records, or, if possible, within-hierarchically-related-group searches, may be the best default, but it might be helpful to offer as a backup search a cross-field keyword search across title and corporate name fields in bibliographic records for cases in which a user thinks a corporate body is named, but the cataloging rules do not lead to its being named. This situation may be most common with conferences, however, and the separate conference index displayed in figure 5.12 might take care of the problem more efficiently.

See chapter 3 for a discussion of the various options for co-occurrence rules for keyword searches. Briefly, a within-record search looks for two or more search terms input by the user to occur anywhere within a single record. A within-hierarchically-

---

Let us again consider the example we looked at in chapter 4. A user comes to the library with the following citation:

3rd International Conf on Solidification Processing, Sheffield, England, Sep 21-23, 1987.

Unbeknownst to the user, the title page of the publication sought reads as follows:

Solidification
Processing
1987

Proceedings of the
Third International Conference,
organised by the Department of Metallurgy,
University of Sheffield, and held at
Ranmoor House, Sheffield, on
21-24 September 1987

This title page presentation forced the cataloger to consider this an unnamed conference and catalog it as follows:

245 00 ≠a Solidification processing 1987 : ≠b proceedings of the third international conference / ≠c organised by the Department of Metallurgy, University of Sheffield, and held at Ranmoor House, Sheffield, on 21-24 September 1987.

In other words, this cataloging record will have no entry for the conference as a name, and only if the search the user does includes a search of both title and statement of responsibility subfields will the search be successful. A search done only on X11 fields in the USMARC format would fail. See also figure 5.12 for a suggested default search for conference publications.

Figure 5.9   An example of a conference citation

related-group search looks for search terms to occur within a group of records recognized by the computer program to be hierarchically related, such as records for a corporate body and its corporate subdivisions. A cross-field search looks for search terms to occur within a designated set of fields in bibliographic records, such as all of the fields containing titles. Figure 5.10 shows the USMARC fields containing names of corporate bodies.

The within-hierarchically-related-group matching mentioned above may require some experimentation, as the most difficult type of hierarchical relationship to deal with is that among corporate name authority records. The U.S. federal government is an example of an extremely complex corporate body with many subbodies; it would be unreasonable and unhelpful to match any search on a U.S. government agency against all authority records for all federal agencies. Perhaps it would be worthwhile to experiment with clumping authority records based on the segments that actually appear in main heading and cross-references on a given authority record. Consider, for example, the authority records for the FBI and one of its sections that we looked at in chapter 3 (see also figure 5.11). Perhaps it would be useful to cluster together (for keyword co-occurrence matching purposes) the authority records for UNITED STATES. FEDERAL BUREAU OF INVESTIGATION and UNITED STATES and search them all as a group representing possible keywords that could be used in a search for the FBI. That group plus the authority record for the UNIFORM CRIME REPORTS SECTION could be clustered together for the section. It might be necessary to experiment with automatic clumping rules, or even some human intervention, to achieve optimal results.

In the USMARC format, corporate names, including conference names, are found in the following fields and subfields:

Bibliographic record:
  110
  111
  410
  411
  610
  611
  710
  711
  810
  811

Authority record:
  110
  111
  410
  411
  510
  511

Figure 5.10   **USMARC fields containing corporate name headings**

---

110 10 ≠a United States. ≠b Federal Bureau of Investigation
410 20 ≠a FBI
410 10 ≠a United States. ≠b Dept. of Justice. ≠b Federal Bureau of Investigation
410 20 ≠a Federal Bureau of Investigation (U.S.)
410 20 ≠a FBR
410 20 ≠a Federalnoe biuro rassledovanii
510 10 ≠a United States. ≠b Bureau of Criminal Identification
510 10 ≠a United States. ≠b Dept. of Justice. ≠b Division of Investigation ≠w a

The authority record for a section of the FBI:

110 10 ≠a United States. ≠b Federal Bureau of Investigation. ≠b Uniform Crime
        Reports Section

Figure 5.11   Portions of USMARC authority records for the FBI and one of its sections

---

A conference index might usefully search the following fields:

(*Note:* This index should be limited to records coded as conference publications [code 1 in byte 29 in the 008 field]; this does assume accurate coding of such publications on the part of catalogers.)

    111
    110
    245, ≠a, ≠b, ≠c
    247
    500
    610
    611
    710
    711

Note that because some of the fields searched are not heading fields, the display of records retrieved would probably have to be a bibliographic record display in main entry order.

Figure 5.12   A suggested conference index

This type of indexing should be accompanied with displays of all headings matched to allow the user to participate as much as possible in the selection process before presenting the user with bibliographic record displays.

In a library that serves many users that need conference publications, a separate conference index might be useful. (See figure 5.12.)

Known-Work Search

Research has shown that one of the most common searches done by our users is a *known-item search* (actually, a search for a particular work, or a *known-work search*). As we have already noted in chapter 3, a particular work is rarely represented by an authority record standing for the work, and when it is, the authority record will contain variants of the title but only the authorized form of an author's name. Thus, a keyword search on authority records that included a variant of an author's name in addition to a title word would fail, even if an authority record for the work existed. In this case, in current systems, the searcher would have to realize that she must do an authority search on the author, in case she needs a *see* reference from the author in her citation to the form used in the catalog; then she must do another search using the authorized form of the author's name together with the title that she is seeking. It is a rare user who is knowledgeable enough to carry out these steps. Most users probably do just one search and if the work they want does not turn up, they conclude the library doesn't have it; or, if at least one edition turns up, they assume that they are seeing all available choices, while missing others that might be better for their purposes.

Unfortunately, at this point in the development of OPACs, most keyword searches do not search the fields in authority records at all but search only the bibliographic records. This means that the searcher who includes a variant form of name or title in her or his search may retrieve nothing at all, or only those records in which the variant appears; for example, a keyword search using the words JACK KENNEDY would retrieve only those records where JACK and KENNEDY appear in the bibliographic record and none of the records in which the only appearance of the former president's name was in the authorized form of KENNEDY, JOHN F. (JOHN FITZGERALD), 1917-1963 (see figure 5.13).

Phrase searches, or any search in which terms must match within a single field in a record, are more apt to be matched against the authority file and then to retrieve bibliographic records that are linked to retrieved authority records. This is, of course, preferable to phrase searches that retrieve either authority records or bibliographic records and do not link the two kinds of records. However, phrase searching does not solve the problem of the user whose search contains terms found in more than one field, as is the case in any known-work search done using both author and title words.

Many systems provide both keyword searches (in which the authority file is *not* searched) and phrase searches (in which the authority file *is* searched). While this offers flexibility to the user, it also requires a level of understanding of the nature of

---

If the user does a keyword-within-record search on JACK KENNEDY, he or she might retrieve the following bibliographic record:

Parmet, Herbert S.
  Jack : the struggles of John F. Kennedy
  New York : Dial Press, 1980.

However, the user would miss this more current biography:

Hamilton, Nigel.
  JFK, reckless youth
  New York : Random House, c1992.

Figure 5.13 **An example of a keyword-in-bibliographic-record search using a variant personal name**

keyword searching, of phrase searching, and of authority records that one suspects many intelligent users, including some librarians, do not have.

If we could use techniques such as form fill-in interfaces to get users to identify which keywords in their searches identify personal authors, which identify corporate authors, and which identify works, perhaps we could develop better indexing that would allow the user to search using any variant of the author's name and any variant of the title of a sought work and still retrieve all editions of the work, all related works, and all works about the work sought. A form-fill-in approach that allowed users to supply subject terms might be useful for extremely garbled or incomplete citations to nonfiction works of which the subject is known. Rebecca Denning and Philip Smith describe a system (ELSA) that shows the user lists of authorized headings in a window next to a form fill-in window, prompting the user to choose authorized forms for each box filled in on the form.[5] Screens are getting so large that perhaps it would be practical now to provide such a window to the authority file for each box the user fills in.

Consider the following indexing algorithm for a known-work search:

1. for personal author words, look for one of the following co-occurrence matches: either (a) within-record match on a personal author authority record, retrieving bibliographic records linked to the authority record; or (b) within-record cross-field match on personal author fields in a bibliographic record if more than one author (see figure 5.6 for fields to index);
2. for corporate author words, look for a co-occurrence match within a hierarchically related group of authority records;
3. for title words, look for the following co-occurrence matches: either (a) within-heading match on all title fields and subfields in a bibliographic record; or (b) within-hierarchically-related-group match of title subfields in authority records (see figure 5.14 for title index fields); and
4. if the user has provided subject words, look for a within-heading match of headings in the subject authority file.

A user seeking a work by two authors and using both names in the search has special problems (see figure 5.7 and accompanying discussion earlier in this chapter); indeed, some works are commonly identified by the names of two or more authors. The classic example of a work generally identified by the names of two authors is Masters and Johnson. If the system looks for co-occurrence of two elements of an author name within the same field, a search for Masters and Johnson will fail, because Masters is in one field and Johnson in another. Again, as noted earlier, effective form fill-in design could help software tell when a search is for more than one author (assuming the user knows this, of course). Another option would be to do a cross-field search as a backup.

The within-hierarchically-related-group matching, mentioned previously in the discussion of corporate bodies and title words, may require some explanation. In chapter 3, we described occasional complex relationships among work authority records. The example we used was that of the three authority records that contain references useful for guiding the user to the *Nutcracker Suite*: the one for TCHAIKOVSKY, the one for NUTCRACKER, and the one for its SUITE. This type of complex relationship should occur relatively infrequently, and the clumps should never be very large; they should be recognizable based on simple string matching: if two authority records have one or more of the same initial subfields, they are hierarchically related. One caveat: Because uniform titles are still optional in standard cataloging practice, and therefore

In the USMARC format, titles are found in the following fields:

Bibliographic record:

  130
  210
  222
  240
  242
  243
  245 (all subfields *except* the ≠c)
  246 (all subfields *except* the ≠i)
  247
  400 ≠t
  410 ≠t
  411 ≠t
  440
  600 ≠t
  610 ≠t
  611 ≠t
  630
  700 ≠t
  710 ≠t
  711 ≠t
  730
  740
  800 ≠t
  810 ≠t
  811 ≠t
  830
  840 (an obsolete field, but should be indexed if still found in records in the database)

Authority record:

  100 ≠t
  110 ≠t
  111 ≠t
  130
  400 ≠t
  410 ≠t
  411 ≠t
  430
  500 ≠t
  510 ≠t
  511 ≠t
  530

Figure 5.14 Title heading fields in the USMARC format

titles are so poorly controlled, the surest way to search for a particular work is still going to be to read through all the records under the author's name.

Series Search

It can sometimes be useful to provide a search that looks for a particular kind of known work. Such a search would be a subset of the known-work search just described. A series search is an example of such a search; it would provide better precision for someone who knows he or she is looking for a series. In designing a series search, it is important to remember that a series can be manifested in two different ways, even within the same catalog. A user cannot predict, when he or she comes to the catalog, whether the library has treated a series as a single bibliographic entity, that is, cataloged it as a serial, or as several bibliographic entities, that is, cataloged the series as multiple monographs, each with a series added entry. The library may even have treated the series in both ways, that is, cataloged it as a serial and provided what are usually called *analytic monograph records* for some or all items comprising the series. Because of these difficulties in predicting whether a series has been treated as a serial or as a monograph, it is important to include in a series search some author and title fields from serial records as well as series title fields from monograph records. The ideal series search should integrate the authority file with the bibliographic file, and perhaps even use serial records as a kind of authority record, with author and title added entries from the serial record being used to create cross-references that would lead the user not only to the serial record but to any monograph records in the series. In this ideal search, a user looking for a series but using a title other than the established title (i.e., a title that would appear as a 430 field in a series authority record or as a 246 field in a serial record) would be directed to all records, whether monograph or serial, representing the series (see figure 5.15).

Typographical Errors, Misspellings, and Variant Spellings and Forms

We know that typographical errors and misspellings are one of the most common reasons for search failure (see figure 5.16). One of the hardest adjustments card catalog users had to make in the transition to the online public access catalog was in learning how to type.[6] In the past, typing was not a skill that many people needed to learn. Spelling may be a skill that is dying out just when we need it the most! Even those who know how to type and spell will have problems with certain types of names. It is not unknown for a user's citation to read MACKENZIE when the author's name is McKenzie or DE GRASSE when the author's name is DeGrasse. Citations to authors can easily vary in fullness from the established forms (see figure 5.17).[7] For example, Jonathan Martin Jones, J. M. Jones, and Jon Jones could all be the same person, and a user's search on any one form would retrieve the others in the ideal system. The ideal algorithm would allow input of any of the following forms: Jones, Jonathan M.; Jones, Jon M.; Jones, J M; Jones, JM; Jones, J. Martin; Jones, Jon Martin; and Jones, Jonathan Martin. In response to the input of any one of the above forms, the ideal algorithm would retrieve *all* of the following: Jones, Jonathan M., 1926-; Jones, Jon M., 1931-; Jones, J. M., 1830-1900; Jones, J. Martin, 1848-1910; Jones, Jon Martin, 1972-; and Jones, Jonathan Martin, 1947-.

The following USMARC fields would be indexed as headings:

Series authority records:

    100
    110
    111
    130
    500
    510
    511
    530

Serial bibliographic records:

    100
    110
    111
    130
    240
    245 ≠a, ≠n, ≠p (if 130 and 240 absent)
    247

The following USMARC fields would be used to create cross-references:

Series authority records:

    400
    410
    411
    430

Serial bibliographic records:

    245 ≠a, ≠n, ≠p (if 130 or 240 present)
    246
    700
    710
    711

Figure 5.15 Fields to include in an ideal series search

Methods to get around the problem of typographical errors, misspellings, and variant spellings and forms include truncation, displaying search terms in a list of alphabetically close authors or titles, menu choice rather than typing, stemming algorithms, synonym dictionaries, and a smart approach to diacritics.

Truncation

In systems offering phrase indexing, implicit truncation is commonly used; in other words, the user's search is automatically truncated at a particular point, and the user is shown an alphabetical display of headings that match the initial part of his or her

Ballard and Smith, p. 65, 66:	18% of zero-hit author searches were misspelled. 20% of zero-hit title searches were misspelled.
Dickson, p. 28, 32:	21% of all title searches had typos and misspellings. 17% of all author searches had typos and misspellings.
Hunter, p. 400:	7% of all author searches had typos. 2% of all author searches had misspellings. 12% of all title searches had typos. 1% of all title searches had misspellings.
Jones, p. 7:	4% of all author searches had misspellings.
Peters, p. 270:	1% of all author searches had typos. 2% of all author searches had misspellings. 2% of all title searches had typos. 2% of all title searches had misspellings.
Sinnott, p. 97:	1% of all author searches had typos (= 5.5% of author search failures). 2% of all author searches had misspellings (= 7% of author search failures).
Taylor, p. 8:	1% of all author searches had typos (= 6% of author search failures). 5% of all author searches had misspellings (= 21% of author search failures).

Full citations for user studies are found in the bibliography of user studies in appendix A.

Figure 5.16   **Error analysis user studies that address the question of how often users make typographical and spelling errors in name-title searches**

search. One decision that has to be made is whether implicit truncation should occur at a point determined by the system or whether it should occur wherever the user ceases to input. The latter gives the user more power. The former might be useful as a backup if the initial search fails. Explicit truncation, available in most systems offering keyword access, requires the user to diagnose the problem and is little used even when available.[8]

Alphabetically Close Authors or Titles

Consider displaying a list of alphabetically close authors or titles derived from an authority file or index when a search results in no hits. Note that if the user has input more than one term, one must be chosen to begin the display of alphabetically close authors or titles. For this reason, this approach is probably most appropriate in a phrase-indexed system in which users have indicated the entry term they desire by typing it in first and in which they expect to match only a single field or heading.

Ballard and Smith, p. 65, 66:	2% of zero-hit author searches were because of misuse of initials and abbreviations
Dickson, p. 32:	10% of all author searches have forename fullness problems.
Hunter, p. 400:	2% of all author searches have forename fullness problems.
Peters, p. 270:	3% of all author searches have forename fullness problems.
Sinnott, p. 97:	2% of zero-hit author searches are because the middle initial stops truncation (in a phrase-indexing system) (e.g., Price, H. H.; Price, Henry Habberly).
	1% of zero-hit author searches are because "too much of the name was put in" (e.g., Jung, Carl; Jung, C. G.).
	2% of zero-hit author searches are because "middle word missing" (e.g., Mech, David; Mech, L. David).
Taylor, p. 10–11:	6% of zero-hit author searches are because the middle initial stops truncation (in a phrase-indexing system).
	2% of zero-hit author searches are because "too much of the name was put in" (e.g., Jung, Carl; Jung, C. G.).
	1% of zero-hit author searches are due to "middle word missing."

Berger also found that users of the MELVYL system were having forename fullness problems, but did not calculate the percentages of search failures due to this cause ("Information-Seeking," p. 100–102).

Full citations for user studies are found in the bibliography of user studies in appendix A.

Figure 5.17   **Failure analysis user studies that have revealed users' problems with forename fullness**

Menu Choice Rather than Typing

Touch-screen and point-and-click systems have been extensively developed to try to allow the user to recognize the author, work, or subject sought, rather than having to specify it ahead of time by typing a description, which can introduce many kinds of errors. Touch-screen and point-and-click systems are essentially menu-based systems, which, as we discussed in chapter 2, can be very slow and cumbersome but do have the advantage of requiring minimal typing and spelling skills of catalog users. Users must know entry terms to succeed, but including cross-references (derived from authority records) can increase users' chances for success.

Stemming Algorithms

Stemming algorithms are rules for complex truncation and other kinds of less-than-exact matching that computer software can use to find more matches; for example, a stemming algorithm might recognize that the letter *s* is commonly used to pluralize in English, so it might match a search term ending in *s* against that character string with and without the *s*. Weak stemming, which conflates singular and plural endings and removes possessive endings and the *-ing* suffix, can be quite helpful in accommodating variations in title citations. However, even weak stemming can introduce quite a lot of unwanted noise, equating *right* and *rights*, *house* and *housing*, etc., and strong stemming almost inevitably does so. An example of strong stemming used by Stephen Walker is that of stemming back to the string *organ*, which would retrieve all of the following: organ, organist, organic, organism, organization.[9]

Another variant on stemming is to bring up as a match anything that matches all letters but one or anything that matches all letters but not necessarily in order. This kind of matching can help correct typographical errors but, of course, can also inflict a great deal of noise on the user who can type correctly. For example, the user interested in *causal relationships* is probably not interested in *casual relationships*. Stephen Walker and Richard Jones provide a good review of stemming algorithms.[10]

If we could get novice users to use form fill-ins, and experienced users (who have bypassed form fill-ins) to enter surname and forename in inverted order, using a comma to separate surname from forename to indicate forenames and surnames of authors, we might be able to use more complex stemming algorithms on the forenames, so that JONATHAN MARTIN also retrieves "J. M.," as in the example used above. An algorithm that retrieved surnames beginning with "Mc" even when the search was for a surname beginning with "Mac," and vice versa, could also be useful.[11] Another useful algorithm might be one that recognized De Grasse, DeGrasse, and Grasse as all being potential matches for De Grasse, DeGrasse, or Grasse in a user's search. In general, smart algorithms designed to recognize common patterns found in personal names could hold great promise for improving success rates in OPACs.

Synonym Dictionaries

Borgman and Siegfried suggest the use of nickname dictionaries that could collect common variants, such as Bob and Robert, so that if either one were input it could automatically match on the other. They also describe various methods of grouping common surname variants.[12] Another application that might be worth exploring would be the use of synonym dictionaries to match names expressed in the various transliteration schemes available for languages such as Chinese and Russian. This might have helped the user studied by Berger whose MELVYL search failed because she or he searched for a Chinese author using a name spelled in the search as KO rather than KUO, as it was spelled in the desired record.[13] Synonym dictionaries could also be quite helpful for title matching, allowing matching on both American and English spellings, such as *color* and *colour*; on both *&* and *and*; hyphenated and nonhyphenated word forms; singular and plural forms that are more complicated than just additions of *s*; and numeric and alphabetic forms of numbers.[14]

The main danger in any automatic method to broaden a search, such as stemming or truncation or use of synonym dictionaries, is the introduction of more noise. The use of such algorithms usually removes some degree of control of the search from the user. Such algorithms are always unpredictable by the user; they are mechanical, not intelligent. They are invisible to the user and therefore somewhat mysterious, so they can make the user feel confused and out of control. And, finally, most are very costly in processing time. It might be wise to use these algorithms only as a backup search when the initial search fails.

Smart Approach to Diacritics

A common matching problem users have is caused by the variability in the use of diacritics by publishers and creators of citations. A German writer named Hermann Müller could be cited or searched as Müller, Mueller, or Muller. The ideal system would allow a user to search under any of the above three forms and would retrieve the name in any of the three forms.

Fuzzy Match

Fuzzy matching refers to various algorithms that look for a less-than-exact match with a user's search. A common approach is to match on some of the terms input in the user's search, but not all. One might also conceptualize such an approach as an implicit Boolean OR search. Because such an approach may increase the possibility of bringing up materials that are not relevant, it should be left to the user's discretion whether it is applied to any given search. For example, USCInfo (the OPAC at the University of Southern California) gives users a form fill-in screen and then offers users, as one of several options, "Find at least one of the words above."[15] However, as long as it is left to the user's discretion because of the potential for retrieval of irrelevant materials, such an approach might be helpfully suggested to users when initial searches fail. A display that then listed all matched headings might help the user figure out where the problem lay in his or her initial search. For example, an actual search on the MELVYL system reported by Berger was for a title given by the user as *Why Every War Must End*. Berger found that the title on the item was *Every War Must End*. In other words, the user's search failed because of the inclusion of the word *Why*, which did not actually occur in the title.[16] This user would have been helped by a fuzzy match search. A user doing a known-work search with both author and title might benefit from a LOOK HARDER command that displayed all matching authors and allowed the user to browse through their works, because the user's title citation may be inaccurate; even better would be a search that displayed all works with an author match and a title match on at least one keyword.

Some keyword-searchable systems give the postings for all terms searched, even on nonfuzzy match searches, so that users can see how many items each term would retrieve and which terms would retrieve materials and which would not.

Stop Words

Keyword systems frequently find it necessary to maintain *stop-lists* consisting of words such as articles and prepositions that are so common that a search using one of them overloads the system. These stop-lists can contain words, such as *United States*, that can be critical for the success of some searches. It is not uncommon for someone's entire search to consist of stop words; a notorious example is the journal entitled *And*.[17]

If the user inputs a search using a stop word, the system should not reject the whole search but should simply ignore the stop word, conduct the search, and inform the user of the stop word(s) ignored. Ideally a system should permit a search that consists entirely of stop words. Such a search capability would not necessarily require the indexing of all stop words. Some alternatives might be to

1. allow catalogers to designate headings that consist only of stop words, so that these only could be indexed;
2. index any heading that consists entirely of stop words; or
3. exclude controlled vocabulary and authorized headings from application of the stop word algorithm; in other words, put *United States* on the stop word list for free text searches but not for corporate names, titles, or subject headings.

Any of these approaches might actually be better for the user than indexing all stop words for the occasional search that needs them to be indexed: the user's search under any of the approaches described above would retrieve a more manageable number of hits than would be retrieved on a comprehensive stop word search.

Karen Drabenstott and Marjorie Weller noticed that some users' searches on personal names failed because they used terms of address and other appendages to names such as *Dr.*, *Senator*, *Sir*, and *Jr.* It should be noted here that cataloging practice is generally not to use such terms in headings; the reasoning is that some can vary throughout a person's life. However, this practice probably does not correspond to users' expectations. Thus, Drabenstott and Weller noted two users whose searches failed because they searched under DR MARTIN LUTHER KING JR and SENATOR LLOYD BENTSEN.[18] If use of stop words could be limited to personal name searches only, a possible solution to this problem might be to add such terms associated with names to a stop-list. You certainly would not want to have them on a general stop-list, however, as many might be used legitimately in titles. Unfortunately, some words that are usually terms of address may occasionally be true forenames or surnames, e.g., a person who is actually named *Major* or whose last name is actually *Doctor*. You might want to provide an option for turning off the stop-list for names of this nature.

Implicit Boolean Operators

Should we assume that a user always needs to have two terms ANDed rather than ORed? Many keyword-searchable systems make this assumption. It has the advantage of saving the user keystrokes (and possible typographic errors) in the course of typing in the explicit operators. It also protects the user from having to know how to use Boolean operators. Some systems assume an adjacency operator between two keywords without an explicit Boolean operator; for example, a search for FOSTER CARE would be taken to mean *foster* must occur next to *care*. This may be doing too much on the user's behalf without letting the user in on how the search is being defined.

If a given operator is implicit when two or more keywords are entered in a search, it might be desirable, when the results of the search are displayed, to make the implicit operator explicit and offer alternatives, e.g., FOSTER AND CARE; FOSTER ADJ CARE; or FOSTER OR CARE.

Keyword Searches That Limit the User to One Term

When phrase-indexed systems add on so-called keyword access, the keyword access can be somewhat restricted compared to the keyword access offered on systems that were originally designed for keyword access. Some phrase-indexed systems limit the user to a single keyword in a keyword search.[19] If possible, the user should be allowed to formulate searches using two or more keywords.

Conclusion

Effective indexing decisions balance the need to allow for user or citation error and confusion against the need to avoid frustrating users who have exact and accurate information. In the next chapter, we will discuss the design of effective displays to help users make sense of the large retrievals that are inevitable when the user is either searching in a large database or looking for prolific authors or multiple-edition works.

Notes

1. Loanne Snavely and Katie Clark, "What Users Really Think: How They See and Find Serials in the Arts and Sciences," *Library Resources & Technical Services* 40 (Jan. 1996): 51.

2. A thought from one of the authors: it might be possible to write a sophisticated searching algorithm that would create sets of bibliographic records based on independently matching each keyword in a search against all appropriate authority records and bibliographic fields. These sets of records would then be matched against each other, and the records common to all the sets would represent the retrieval. Such an algorithm would take, for example, each keyword in a name-title search and use it to create a set of bibliographic records that either contained the keyword in name or title fields or that were linked with name or title authority records containing that keyword. The algorithm would then compare the resulting sets of bibliographic records (Boolean AND the sets together), and present to the catalog user just those records that appeared in every retrieved set. Using this algorithm, the search FIND NAME TITLE STRAVINSKI FIREBIRD would retrieve those bibliographic records that were either linked to authority records containing the keyword STRAVINSKI (e.g., bibliographic records linked to the authority record for Igor Stravinsky) or had the keyword STRAVINSKI in a name or title field *and* were either linked to authority records containing the keyword FIREBIRD (e.g., bibliographic records linked

to the authority record for [established title]) or had the keyword FIREBIRD in a name or title field.

3. By the way, the authority record matched on the MELVYL system has *see* references from the various pseudonyms used by Lauran Paine; current practice would call for these to be *see also* references.

4. Leslie Troutman, "The Online Public Access Catalog and Music Materials: Issues for System and Interface Design," *Advances in Online Public Access Catalogs* 1 (1992): 17.

5. Rebecca Denning and Philip J. Smith, "Interface Design Concepts in the Development of ELSA, an Intelligent Electronic Library Search Assistant," *Information Technology and Libraries* 13 (June 1994): 133–147.

6. Nicholson Baker, "Discards," *New Yorker*, April 4, 1994, p. 80.

7. A thorough review of existing systems for matching varying personal name forms can be found in Christine L. Borgman and Susan L. Siegfried, "Getty's Synoname and Its Cousins: A Survey of Applications of Personal Name-Matching Algorithms," *Journal of the American Society for Information Science* 43 (Aug. 1992): 459–476.

8. Stephen Walker and Richard M. Jones, *Improving Subject Retrieval in Online Catalogues. 1, Stemming, Automatic Spelling Correction and Cross-Reference Tables* (London: British Library, 1987), p. 12.

9. Stephen Walker, "The Okapi Online Catalogue Research Projects," in *The Online Catalogue: Developments and Directions*, ed. Charles Hildreth (London: Library Association, 1989), p. 91.

10. Walker and Jones, *Improving*, p. 21–28.

11. OCLC's search key for names beginning with either "Mc" or "Mac" reduces either to "M," so that "McKay" would be searched as MKAY; MKAY will retrieve either "MacKay" or "McKay" but will not retrieve "Mackay"; in other words, it looks for a capital letter in the middle of the name to recognize which names to compress. This reliance on capital letters is hazardous in a database that contains many typographical errors. However, in general the search key is very useful.

12. Borgman and Siegfried, "Getty's Synoname," p. 467–473.

13. Michael Berger, *The User Meets the MELVYL System: An Analysis of User Transactions*, Technical Report no. 7 (Oakland, Calif.: Division of Library Automation, University of California, 1996), appendix, p. 12.

14. Apparently the INNOPAC system does provide some synonym control, according to Walt Crawford, *The Online Catalog Book: Essays and Examples* (Boston: G. K. Hall, 1992), p. 295. OPAC users interviewed by Johnson and Connaway specifically requested that English and American spellings be linked (Debra Wilcox Johnson and Lynn Silipigni Connaway, "Use of Online Catalogs: A Report of Results of Focus Group Interviews," typescript [Feb. 1992], p. 14).

15. Crawford, *Online*, p. 497.

16. Michael Berger and Mary Jean Moore, "The User Meets the MELVYL System," *DLA Bulletin* 16, no. 1 (fall 1996): 16.

17. There has not been too much research on the question of how frequently stop-lists cause users' searches to fail. However, Gouke and Pease included two titles that consisted of nothing but stop words, and half of the searches for those titles failed; eleven of their titles had stop-list words in them, and nine out of twenty-two searches for those titles failed (Mary Noel Gouke and Sue Pease, "Title Searches in an Online Catalog and a Card Catalog: A Comparative Study of Patron Success in Two Libraries," *Journal of Academic Librarianship* 8 [July 1982]: 140).

18. Karen M. Drabenstott and Marjorie S. Weller, "Improving Personal-Name Searching in Online Catalogs," *Information Technology and Libraries* 15 (1996): 140–141.

19. Walker and Jones, *Improving*, p. 12.

6

Demonstration of Relationships—Authors and Works—Display Decisions

When making display decisions, the catalog designer should assume multiple-record retrievals as the norm. Remember that the most popular works go into multiple editions, and the most popular authors are the most often published. Also, remember (from chapter 3) that one author, corporate body, or work may be completely represented only by a group of authority records, including authority records for various pseudonyms, authority records that include various subject subdivisions, authority records for various changes in corporate name, authority records for various corporate subdivisions (parts of the main body), and authority records for the various changes in the title of a serial work.

Ineffective displays can render useless all of the expensive work done by catalogers and system designers to demonstrate relationships in the catalog. If two records representing the same work are buried screens apart in an incoherent display, the relationship between them is not being demonstrated to the user. If the author or the corporate body or the serial the user seeks is thirteen screens away from where the user expects to find it, it has been effectively lost, and the library might just as well not have purchased the material in the first place, because few will be able to find it to use it.

Some research indicates that users are having a great deal of difficulty browsing through large retrievals and that large retrievals are not uncommon (see figure 6.1). One only has to consider the size of the files under Mozart, Shakespeare, or the *Bible* to realize why this might be. Anyone doing research in the humanities, or in the history of the sciences, is likely to encounter prolific authors and multiple-edition works.

Display commands have added a layer of complexity to catalog searching that was completely absent in the card catalog, in which the user could flip cards or walk to another drawer in order to move about. It is frustrating for users now to have to learn how to tell a computer to move about on one's behalf. For example, Beverly Janosky, Philip Smith, and Charles Hildreth found that five out of twenty-eight people given an assigned author search failed to complete it successfully because of failure to master display commands.[1] Display commands should be carefully designed to be as simple and intuitive as possible; for example, use of the enter key for moving forward in a list seems fairly easy to remember. Make sure that the user can move backward or

Anderson, Reich, Wagner, et al., p. 12.

Berger, "Information-Seeking," p. 60–61:

Keyword searches generate 92% of long search conditions (note that on the MELVYL system, the system studied by Berger, these are keyword-within-record searches, making a heading display impossible). Berger went so far as to count any search for a voluminous author on the MELVYL system a suboptimal search (Berger, *The User Meets*, appendix, p. 7)!

Drabenstott and Vizine-Goetz, p. 158:

Initial access points retrieved an average of:

200 bibliographic records on SULIRS (Syracuse University Library Information Retrieval System)

350 headings on ORION.

Graham, p. 27:

37% of single keyword searches on MOPAC developed by GEAC Computers, Inc. resulted in 100 or more hits.

Kaske and Sanders, p. 40.

Kern-Simirenko, p. 32.

Lynch, p. 112:

The average search on the MELVYL system retrieved 118 records.

Malinconico, 1979:

The average retrieval on the MELVYL system was 97-125 records per search.

Martin, Wyman, and Madhok, p. 3.

Matthews, Lawrence, and Ferguson, p. 124:

In the CLR study, 27% of users checked this problem, making it the 8th ranked.

Pease and Gouke, "Patterns of Use," p. 288:

17% of those who had changed from online catalog use to card catalog use switched because they had retrieved too many hits online.

Wiberley, Daugherty, and Danowski, 1995, p. 247:

26% of questionnaire respondents reported experiencing postings overload on LUIS (Library User Information Service) (both subject and known-work searching and including keyword-within-record searches).

Wyly, p. 229:

Author searchers on MILO (Mainframe Interface to Libraries Online) retrieved an average of 62 hits (probably bibliographic records, rather than headings, but this is not completely clear).

Corporate author searchers on MILO retrieved an average of 247 hits.

Series title searchers on MILO retrieved an average of 91 hits.

Title keyword searchers on MILO retrieved an average of 117 hits.

Note: Research that did not distinguish between author/work and subject searching is included here as well.

Full citations for user studies are found in the bibliography of user studies in appendix A.

Figure 6.1 **User studies that have reported user problems with reducing results of author or work searches**

forward in a list, and up and down in a hierarchy, at any time. Make sure it is possible to jump many records or headings forward and backward, if so desired. There is nothing more frustrating than viewing a large retrieval in a system that allows you to view just one record at a time. Never require the user to return to the summary display in order to move on to the next record. Whenever possible, assign permanent unique line numbers and allow their use from anywhere.

Display and Arrangement of Multiple Headings

In the following section, we discuss

1. why it is important for systems to provide headings displays as a default whenever a user's search matches more than one heading;
2. the best ways to arrange multiple headings on a screen in a headings display;
3. the value of a conservative approach toward normalization in the display context;
4. a smarter approach toward diacritics;
5. the value of compressing headings displays in order to summarize a retrieval for the user;
6. deduping of displays of headings;
7. the value of placing the user into the context of an A to Z list of headings, including headings not matched by the initial search;
8. the display of cross-references;
9. the display of relationships among serials;
10. the display of relator terms; and
11. the display of postings, or number of records, in summaries of headings or index entries retrieved.

Need for Headings Displays

If a search matches more than one heading, or a heading with subdivisions, the results should be displayed as a list of matched headings rather than matched bibliographic records. (See chapter 5 for a discussion of the desirability of making a keyword-within-heading search the default.) Displaying matched headings permits the user to make an informed choice. To display bibliographic records at this point, before allowing the user to make a decision about which author or work is desired when more than one has been retrieved, is to present the user with what may well be a baffling display. Compare the two possible results of an author search on Tristram Coffin shown in figure 6.2 (remember from chapter 3 that there are two persons named Tristram Coffin: one is a novelist and peace activist; the other is a folklorist). Bypassing an initial headings display can be particularly frustrating for the user who is interested in an author with a rather common name. Consider, for example, the user interested in browsing through the library's holdings of the works of e.e. cummings. Bypassing an initial headings display in displaying the results of a search on CUMMINGS E# would result in the first display in figure 6.3 (in a system that arranges brief displays by title). Displaying brief titles under authors' names, as seen in the second display in figure 6.3, clearly distinguishes the works of e.e. cummings from those of others with the same name.

Immediate display of bibliographic records, bypassing heading display (in a system that arranges brief displays by title):

> The British traditional ballad in North America. c1977.
> The female hero in folklore and legend. 1975.
> Folklore from the working folk of America. 1973.
> Folksong & folksong scholarship. 1964.
> Indian tales of North America; an anthology for the adult reader. 1961.
> Mine eyes have seen the glory, a novel. 1964.
> Not to the swift, a novel. 1961.
> Our living traditions; an introduction to American folklore. 1968.
> The passion of the Hawks; militarism in modern America. 1964.
> The proper book of sexual folklore. 1978.
> Senator Fulbright. 1967, c1966.
> The sex kick; eroticism in modern America. c1966.

Display by headings matched:

> Coffin, Tristram, 1912-
>> Mine eyes have seen the glory, a novel. 1964.
>> Not to the swift, a novel. 1961.
>> The passion of the Hawks; militarism in modern America. 1964.
>> Senator Fulbright. 1967, c1966.
>> The sex kick; eroticism in modern America. c1966.

> Coffin, Tristram Potter, 1922-
>> The British traditional ballad in North America. c1977.
>> The female hero in folklore and legend. 1975.
>> Folklore from the working folk of America. 1973.
>> Folksong & folksong scholarship. 1964.
>> Indian tales of North America; an anthology for the adult reader. 1961.
>> Our living traditions; an introduction to American folklore. 1968.
>> The proper book of sexual folklore. 1978.*

---

*In most systems, this display would probably actually take place in two stages, with the headings being displayed first and the bibliographic records being displayed only after a particular heading was selected. Note the usefulness of the illustrated one-stage approach to display, however, for a user who is not sure which Coffin is the one he or she is looking for. The one-stage display shows the types of work each Coffin writes in the initial display. The one-stage display would not be ideal for displaying thousands of records retrieved, but it might be a useful option for a smaller retrieval.

Figure 6.2   Two ways to display the works of two different authors with the same name

Immediate display of bibliographic records, bypassing headings display:

1 x 1. 1944.
The companion to St. Paul's Cathedral. 1869.
Complete poems, 1913-1962. 1981.
Eimi. 1933.
Guidelines for consulting with the Department of Fish and Game on projects subject
   to CEQA that may affect endangered and threatened species. 1986.
Him. 1927.
No thanks. 1935.
Pots, pans and millions: a study of woman's right to be in business. 1929.
Puella mea. 1923.
Soil survey of Clay County, Florida. 1989.
Tom. 1935.

Displaying first by headings matched produces clearly superior results:

Cummings, E. E. (Edward Estlin), 1894-1962.
   1 x 1. 1944.
   Complete poems, 1913-1962. 1981.
   Eimi. 1933.
   Him. 1927.
   No thanks. 1935.
   Puella mea. 1923.
   Tom. 1935.
Cummings, E. M.
   The companion to St. Paul's Cathedral. 1869.
Cummings, Earle W.
   Guidelines for consulting with the Department of Fish and Game on projects
   subject to CEQA that may affect endangered and threatened species. 1986.
Cummings, Eddie.
   Soil survey of Clay County, Florida. 1989.
Cummings, Edith Mae Cunliffe, b. 1888.
   Pots, pans and millions: a study of woman's right to be in business. 1929.

Figure 6.3   Two ways to display the works of several authors named Cummings

A headings display is also superior to a title display when searching for conference publications. Consider a search for conference proceedings using the keyword
INTELLIGENT in a keyword-within-heading corporate name search (see figure 6.4).

Michael Berger notes that display by heading matched could have helped users
with many of the suboptimal and failed searches he studied on the MELVYL system.[2]
Most MELVYL searches result in immediate display in main entry order of all bibliographic records matched, even when many different headings were matched. If the
headings were displayed instead, the user could reject those that are not of interest
and choose only those that are in fact what she or he is looking for.

Immediate display of bibliographic records, bypassing heading display (in a system that arranges brief displays by title):

ANZIIS 94. c1994.
Conference on Intelligent Robotics in Field, Factory, Service, and Space (CIRFFSS '94). 1994.
First International Conference on Intelligent Systems Engineering, 19-21 August 1992. c1992.
First International Conference on Intelligent Systems in Process Engineering, proceedings of the Conference held at Snowmass, Colorado, July 9-14, 1995. c1996.
Foundations of intelligent systems. c1996.
Intelligent Network '96. c1996.
Methodologies for intelligent systems. c1994.
MFI '94. c1994.
NAFIPS/IFIS/NASA '94. c1994.
Proceedings. c1991.
Proceedings. c1993.
Proceedings. c1993.
Proceedings. c1995.
Proceedings of the 1993 International Workshop on Intelligent User Interfaces, January 4-7, 1993, Orlando, Florida. c1992.
Proceedings of the 1994 IEEE International Symposium on Intelligent Control, 16-18 August 1994, Holiday Inn Crowne Plaza, Columbus, Ohio, USA. c1994.
Proceedings of the 1995 IEEE International Symposium on Intelligent Control, August 27-29, 1995, Monterey Marriott Hotel, Monterey, California, 93940, USA. c1995.
Proceedings of the 1996 IEEE International Symposium on Intelligent Control. c1996.
Proceedings of the second World Congress on Intelligent Transport Systems. 1995.
Safety, reliability, and applications of emerging intelligent control technologies. 1995.
Second International Conference on "Intelligent Systems Engineering," 5-9 September 1994, venue, Technical University of Hamburg—Harburg, Germany. c1994.
Third International Conference on Intelligent Materials, Third European Conference on Smart Structures and Materials, Lyon, 3-4-5 June 1996, Center of Congress "L'Espace tete d'or." c1996.

Displaying first by headings matched again produces clearly superior results:

Australian and New Zealand Conference on Intelligent Information Systems (2nd : 1994 : Brisbane, Qld.)
    ANZIIS 94. c1994.
Conference on Intelligent Robotic Systems for Space Exploration (3rd : 1991 : Rensselaer Polytechnic Institute)
    Proceedings. c1991.
Conference on Intelligent Robotics in Field, Factory, Service, and Space (1st : 1994 : Houston, Tex.)
    Conference on Intelligent Robotics in Field, Factory, Service, and Space (CIRFFSS '94). 1994

Figure 6.4   **Two ways to display the results of a keyword-within-heading search for a conference**

IEEE Intelligent Network Workshop (1996 : Melbourne, Australia)
Intelligent Network '96. c1996.
IEEE International Conference on Multisensor Fusion and Integration for Intelligent
Systems (1994 : Las Vegas, Nev.)
MFI '94. c1994.
IEEE International Symposium on Intelligent Control (1993 : Chicago, Ill.)
Proceedings. c1993.
IEEE International Symposium on Intelligent Control (1994 : Columbus, Ohio)
Proceedings of the 1994 IEEE International Symposium on Intelligent Control,
16-18 August 1994, Holiday Inn Crowne Plaza, Columbus, Ohio, USA. c1994.
IEEE International Symposium on Intelligent Control (1995 : Monterey, Calif.)
Proceedings of the 1995 IEEE International Symposium on Intelligent Control,
August 27-29, 1995, Monterey Marriott Hotel, Monterey, California, 93940,
USA. c1995.
IEEE International Symposium on Intelligent Control (1996 : Dearborn, Mich.)
Proceedings of the 1996 IEEE International Symposium on Intelligent Control.
c1996.
IFAC Workshop on Safety, Reliability, and Applications of Emerging Intelligent
Control Technologies (1994 : Hong Kong)
Safety, reliability, and applications of emerging intelligent control technologies.
1995.
International Conference on Intelligent and Cooperative Information Systems
(1993 : Rotterdam, Netherlands)
Proceedings. c1993.
International Conference on Intelligent Manufacturing (1995 : Wu-han shih, China)
Proceedings. c1995.
International Conference on Intelligent Materials (3rd : 1996 : Lyon, France)
Third International Conference on Intelligent Materials, Third European
Conference on Smart Structures and Materials, Lyon, 3-4-5 June 1996, Center
of Congress "L'Espace tete d'or." c1996.
International Conference on Intelligent Systems Engineering (1st : 1992 : Heriot-
Watt University)
First International Conference on Intelligent Systems Engineering, 19-21 August
1992. c1992.
International Conference on Intelligent Systems Engineering (2nd : 1994 : Technical
University of Hamburg-Harburg)
Second International Conference on "Intelligent Systems Engineering," 5-9
September 1994, venue, Technical University of Hamburg-Harburg, Germany.
c1994.
International Conference on Intelligent Systems in Process Engineering (1995 :
Snowmass, Colo.)
First International Conference on Intelligent Systems in Process Engineering,
proceedings of the Conference held at Snowmass, Colorado, July 9-14, 1995.
c1996.
International Symposium on Methodologies for Intelligent Systems (8th : 1994 :
Charlotte, N.C.)
Methodologies for intelligent systems. c1994.

(Continued)

International Symposium on Methodologies for Intelligent Systems (9th : 1996 : Zakopane, Poland)
  Foundations of intelligent systems. c1996.
International Workshop on Intelligent User Interfaces (1993 : Orlando, Fla.)
  Proceedings of the 1993 International Workshop on Intelligent User Interfaces, January 4-7, 1993, Orlando, Florida. c1992.
North American Fuzzy Information Processing Society. Conference (1994 : San Antonio, Tex.)
  NAFIPS/IFIS/NASA '94. c1994.
World Congress on Intelligent Transport Systems (2nd : 1995 : Yokohama, Japan)
  Proceedings of the second World Congress on Intelligent Transport Systems. 1995.

Figure 6.4—Continued

Note that when the search is a title search, rather than an author search, the initial display ought to be a list of all titles matched, including titles in added entry fields and, ideally, titles in authority records. A list of bibliographic records in main entry order produced in response to a title search is much more difficult to scan, because many titles matched may not even appear in summary displays; for example, titles in 246 fields in the MARC format will probably not appear in summary displays.

Try to avoid truncation of headings or titles in even the briefest displays; too often the distinctive words in long headings or titles occur on the second or third line of the display, and a truncated summary display in such cases is worthless to the hapless user.

Arrangement of Headings

Arrangement of multiple headings in a display can be a very important factor in the success or failure of a user's search. However, there is evidence that very few current systems succeed in consistently displaying together the works of a particular author, or the editions of a work.[3]

If the headings matched have parenthetical qualifiers (e.g., serial uniform titles), or subdivisions (e.g., subdivisions such as —DRAMA under personal names), or if more than one author or work begins with the same initial term, the search/display software can produce an elegant and useful display if the principle of filing elements, discussed in the LC filing rules, is followed.[4] According to this principle, headings are divided into filing elements. In the heading LINCOLN, ABRAHAM, 1809-1865—DRAMA, the first filing element is LINCOLN, the second is ABRAHAM, the third is 1809-1865, and the fourth is DRAMA. In the serial title HEALTH ADVOCATE, the title proper from beginning to end constitutes one filing element. In the serial uniform title HEALTH (SAN FRANCISCO, CALIF.), the first filing element is HEALTH, the title of the journal, and the second is (SAN FRANCISCO, CALIF.), the latter being a parenthetical qualifier added by the cataloger to differentiate this journal from other journals with the same title. According to the principle of filing elements, the computer would first arrange the heading in alphabetical order using just the first element. If there are no other headings beginning with that element, the computer would stop there. If there are, the computer would then arrange those headings using just the second element, etc. (See figure 6.5.)

Display of headings retrieved on a keyword search of HOMER, following the principle of filing elements:	Display that does not follow the principle of filing elements:
Homer.	Homer, Anne.
Carmina minora.	Homer. Carmina minora.
Iliad.	Homer, Davis A.
Odyssey.	Homer-Dixon, Thomas F.
Homer, Anne.	Homer, Frederic A.
Homer, Davis A.	Homer. Iliad.
Homer, Frederic A.	Homer, Joy, 1915-
Homer, Joy, 1915-	Homer. Odyssey.
Homer, Winslow, 1836-1910.	Homer, Winslow, 1836-1910.
Homer-Dixon, Thomas F.	

Display of serial titles following the principle of filing elements:	Display that does not follow the principle of filing elements:
Health (Canberra, A.C.T.)	Health advocate.
Health (Chicago, Ill.)	Health alert.
Health (New York, N.Y. : 1981)	Health (Canberra, Australia)
Health (San Francisco, Calif.)	Health care costs.
Health advocate.	Health care management review.
Health alert.	Health (Chicago, Ill.)
Health care costs.	Health cost review.
Health care management review.	Health (New York, N.Y. : 1981)
Health cost review.	Health news.
Health news.	Health reports.
Health reports.	Health (San Francisco, Calif.)

Figure 6.5   **Displays following the principle of filing elements contrasted with those that do not**

It can be seen from the examples in figure 6.5 that filing following the principle of filing elements has the effect of not requiring users to know about additions to headings made by catalogers in order to disambiguate homonyms and in order to subdivide large files and make them easier to scan. If the principle of filing elements is not followed, and a mechanical alphabetical arrangement that ignores punctuation is used, the user must know about these additions in order to find the headings in what can be multiscreen displays. If you searched on the title word HEALTH in a system of any size, you would get many more titles than those listed above, and the journals called *Health* would be separated from each other by multiple screens. What user, looking for the journal *Health*, published in San Francisco, Calif., would think to look for it on the sixth screen, when the first screen begins with HEALTH ADVOCATE? A user with any sense would conclude the library did not own the sought journal.

Normalization

As a corollary to the above comments on the ideal arrangements of headings, it is essential that normalization algorithms not be allowed to undermine effective arrangements. To this end, normalization algorithms should be extremely conservative in the display context. Ideally, none of the following would be normalized prior to application of the display algorithms. Another way to say this is that all of the following should be available to be used in display algorithms: diacritics, commas, periods, colons, dashes, parentheses, hyphens, USMARC subfield codes, and capitalization.

A Smarter Approach to Diacritics

Smart software that could recognize diacritic equivalents in arrangements could be very helpful to users. For example, a user's citation may include the author's name Mueller, while the catalog record sought may contain the name in the variant form of Müller, or vice versa. If both forms of the name Müller arrange in the same place in the display, the user will not have to suffer for having a variant citation.

Compression

An even better display would summarize or compress all headings with the same initial filing element and differentiate them only for users that chose a further display of those headings. Perhaps the compressed display could be offered only when the display otherwise would go onto more than one screen. Consider the example in figure 6.6. This type of compressed display could help users scan quickly through quite large retrievals.[5]

1	4	Health.
2	1	Health advocate.
3	1	Health alert.
4	1	Health care costs.
5	1	Health care management review.
6	1	Health cost review.
7	3	Health news.
8	5	Health reports.

The user who chose to look at line 1 would then see the following display:

Health (Canberra, A.C.T.)
Health (Chicago, Ill.)
Health (New York, N.Y. : 1981)
Health (San Francisco, Calif.)

Figure 6.6   An example of a compressed display of titles

Deduping the Displays of Headings

Usually catalogers will not have added the same heading more than once to a particular bibliographic record, so it will not be necessary to dedupe displays, that is, to check for multiple occurrences of the same bibliographic record attached to the same heading and, when they occur, display the bibliographic record only once.

Placing the User in an A to Z List of Headings

It is possible to design displays that put a user's search in an alphabetic context surrounded by other headings or terms, not just those matched by the search; this has been done by some systems. (Note, however, that this is only possible in phrase-indexing systems and in keyword-searching systems that have searches in which the co-occurrence rules are for more than one keyword to occur within a single heading or authority record; in keyword systems that allow co-occurrence across more than one heading or field, a search does not result in a single heading that could be put into context.) The user can be allowed to scan up and down and reach headings or terms that did not match the search query. This can be very helpful to users with inexact citations to particular authors and works. It is easier to put a user's search in context when the user's search is matched against the file or index using a left-to-right match, but one can imagine ways to do this in keyword-matching systems as well. The context could be based on the first keyword input, or the user could be provided with several contexts in windows, one context for each keyword input.

The following options may be useful for putting the search in a context provided by other terms or headings: (1) authority file (authorized headings and cross-references, with authorized headings linked to bibliographic records); or (2) dictionary file consisting of authorized headings and cross-references from the authority file, and all title headings on bibliographic records (based, for example, on the name-title index described in chapter 4).

If the user's search is one that can be matched using co-occurrence within a single authority record, the best context in which to put it would be the authority file, including both authorized headings and cross-references in the display. This would be the best default for an author search.

For a known-work search, the best context would be a dictionary file, which could be the display resulting from the name-title index described in chapter 4. Unfortunately, this would be a rather complex file to build and probably is not available on existing systems. Known-work searches, among the most common searches done, are the hardest for which to design online catalogs, because works are partly represented by authority controlled fields and partly represented by fields that are not under authority control (notably the 245 field in the USMARC bibliographic format). Complex relationships among works also create difficulties. The problems that result from keyword indexing across fields, including the inability for systems to guarantee that every search is matched against cross-references, make it difficult to index known works effectively (as discussed in chapters 3, 4, and 5) and especially difficult to display them in a meaningful order.

If the user is scanning through the headings from the authority file, it should be possible simply to select any heading of interest and see the bibliographic records attached. This is only possible in systems that link the authority file to the bibliographic records. It should be remembered that headings may be retrieved through the use of a keyword search as well as through the use of a phrase search. When headings are retrieved through the use of a keyword search on a single term, it might be helpful if the default initial display, from which the user could scan up and down, showed the headings, if any, that *begin* with that keyword.

Display of Cross-References

Some systems automatically match on *see* references and do not tell the user that items are being retrieved that do not match the initial search; such systems are sometimes known as *transparent systems*. In order to give the user more control, it may be better to tell the user when a search has matched a *see* reference and to give him or her the opportunity to choose whether or not to continue; after all, the *see* reference hit may *not* lead to the author or work desired by the user (cf. the earlier example in chapter 5 of a search for Hunter S. Thompson that retrieved works by Lauran Paine). Many systems that tell a user when a search has matched a *see* reference, however, make the user retype her or his search. It can save the user some keying to display the *see* reference as a choice that can be selected in order to retrieve records attached to the used term, if the user so desires (see figure 6.7). Perhaps even better is a system that permits the user to select a *see* reference without rekeying and then takes the user not directly to bibliographic records but to the established heading with its accompanying cross-references and subdivisions, which might prove serendipitous (see figure 6.8).

Effective displays of authority records for authors who use pseudonyms could help our catalogs reimplement the second cataloging objective of retrieving *all* the works of an author, despite the fact that this objective has been undermined, or at least rendered more complex to achieve, by AACR2 and AACR2R, which treat different pseudonyms used by the same person as different "bibliographic identities" and thus, essentially, as different authors (see figure 6.9).

The approach of always showing a heading in the context of its syndetic structure, before displaying bibliographic records, might also be a useful option for a user doing comprehensive historical research on a corporate body, when displaying corporate names with complex histories of name changes. This display might not be a good default display for all corporate searches, however, because the screen also needs to hold all of the corporate subdivisions for the body under each name. Perhaps it would be helpful to do some research on actual corporate name searches to see how often complex displays would result from this approach and how often they might be helpful (see figure 6.10).

Your search, FNA MALCOLM LITTLE, retrieved:

Line no. for selection:		No. of records:
1	Arnold, Malcolm. Little suite, brass band, no. 3, op. 131	1
2	Little, Ian Malcolm David.	18
3	Little, Malcolm, 1925-1965 (form of name used in this catalog: X, Malcolm, 1925-1965)	45

Figure 6.7   An example of a selectable *see* reference

When line 3 in the display in figure 6.7 is chosen:

Line no. for selection:		No. of records:
1	X, Malcolm, 1925-1965. USED FOR: Little, Malcolm, 1925-1965	25
2	X, Malcolm, 1925-1965—Assassination.	5
3	X, Malcolm, 1925-1965—Bibliography.	2
4	X, Malcolm, 1925-1965—Drama.	6
5	X, Malcolm, 1925-1965—Influence.	1
6	X, Malcolm, 1925-1965—Juvenile literature.	4
7	X, Malcolm, 1925-1965—Philosophy.	1
8	X, Malcolm, 1925-1965—Pictorial works.	1

Figure 6.8   An example of an intervening display that might suggest other headings of interest

Your search, FNA ED MCBAIN, retrieved:

Line no. for selection:		No. of records:
1	McBain, Ed, 1926- For works of this author written under pseudonyms, search also under:*	18
2	Hunter, Evan, 1926-	15
3	Marsten, Richard, 1926-	4
4	ALL OF THE ABOVE	37

*This text is derived from a 663 field in the USMARC authorities format.

Figure 6.9   An example of a display of an author who has used pseudonyms

Your search, FNA INSTITUTE OF ELECTRICAL AND ELECTRONICS ENGINEERS, retrieved:

Line no. for selection:		No. of records:
1	Institute of Electrical and Electronics Engineers For works of this corporate body issued under its earlier names, search also under:	452
2	Institute of Radio Engineers	42
3	American Institute of Electrical Engineers	51
4	ALL OF THE ABOVE	545

Figure 6.10   An example of a display to inform users about changes in corporate name

Display of Relationships among Serials

Another useful way to display relationships among multiple records would be to devise methods to link together the records for serials that have changed their titles. It may not be that easy to carry this out, as the records themselves may not always carry all of the needed information. In a 1993 study of Cooperative Online Serials Program (CONSER) records on OCLC, Robert Alan found that only 71 percent of title-change record sets could be linked using numbers such as OCLC control numbers, International Standard Serial Numbers (ISSNs), or Library of Congress Card Numbers (LCCNs) in linking fields.[6] Title main entries would also be unreliable for linking with older records. It may be, however, that most currently published titles are in better shape than older ceased titles, which may be less in demand by users anyway. Also, if systems made better use of linking fields, institutions might have more incentive to maintain these fields in bibliographic records. Another problem arises in a given library that may not have a complete run of a given journal. If the pieces of the run that represent a particular title are not owned by the library, the catalog may not contain all of the records necessary to explain the complete history of the serial to the user.

Even if not all serials that have changed titles can be linked, it is probably worth it to link those that can be linked. For example, users could be offered the display shown in figure 6.11. Sometimes a journal can have a very complex history, with many mergers, splits, and continuations. Serials catalogers often diagram these histories in the process of working out all of these relationships. If the OPAC would support graphical relationships between records, it could allow serials catalogers to pass on these graphical histories to confused users instead of limiting them to textual

---

Your search, FTI JOURNAL OF LIBRARY AUTOMATION, retrieved:

Line no. for selection:		No. of records:
1	Journal of library automation* (1968-1981)	1
2	*Absorbed:* JOLA technical communications (1969-1972)	1
3	*Continued by:* Information technology and libraries (1982-)	1

*This display would have to be generated from the 008, bytes 7-10 (date 1) and 11-14 (date 2), 780, and 785 fields in the bibliographic record for the *Journal of library automation*, as well as the 008 (bytes 7-10 and 11-14) fields found in the bibliographic records for *JOLA technical communications* and *Information technology and libraries* (found via the links in the 780 and 785 fields in *Journal of library automation*). See chapter 3 for further information.

Figure 6.11   An example of a serial title display indicating the serial's history

explanations carried in multiple bibliographic records that may be imperfectly linked. Ideally, perhaps portions of the graphical representation standing for parts of the run not held by the library could result in a display of a message to that effect.

See figure 6.12 for a list of the display constants called for by USMARC for the serials linking fields.

Display of Relator Terms

Many older USMARC records have delimiter e subfields added to 700 personal name added entries, with abbreviated terms, known as *relator terms*, that indicate specific

Field in USMARC bibliographic record with indicators:	Display constant:
760 0_	Main series:
	or
	Subseries of:
762 0_	Has subseries:
765 0_	Translation of:
767 0_	Translated as:
770 0_	Has supplement:
772 0_	Supplement to:
772 00	Parent:
775 0_	Other editions available:
776 0_	Issued in other form:
777 0_	Issued with:
780 00	Continues:
780 01	Continues in part:
780 02	Supersedes:
780 03	Supersedes in part:
780 04	Formed by the union of ... and ...
780 05	Absorbed:
780 06	Absorbed in part:
780 07	Separated from:
785 00	Continued by:
785 01	Continued in part by:
785 02	Superseded by:
785 03	Superseded in part by:
785 04	Absorbed by:
785 05	Absorbed in part by:
785 06	Split into ... and ...
785 07	Merged with ... to form ...
785 08	Changed back to:

Figure 6.12 Display constants called for by USMARC for the serials linking fields

Sturges, Preston.
   direction:
      Christmas in July. 1940.
      The Palm Beach story. 1942.
   writing:
      Christmas in July. 1940.
      Easy living. 1937.
      The Palm Beach story. 1942.
      The power and the glory. 1933.

Figure 6.13   An example of a display using relator terms

subsidiary functions carried out by the person named in the field, e.g., *illus.* for an illustrator or *ed.* for an editor. This practice is now obsolete for standard book cataloging, so the subfield should perhaps not display in summary displays of headings derived from standard monograph records, because it is not consistently used and could mislead people or, worse, lead to collocation problems if it actually affects the order of display; in other words, it could lead to the works of an editor being displayed in two alphabets, one under the heading without a relator and one under the heading with a relator.

However, in certain specialized fields, these relator terms are being added consistently to all records and could be used to produce elegant displays. For example, there is a list of relator terms for filmmakers that distinguishes screenwriters from production designers and directors, etc.[7] If users were given the option of arranging displays using these relator terms, it could offer the possibility of providing the display in figure 6.13. Note that this display would probably require a solution to the problem (discussed in chapters 3 and 4) caused by the fact that you want to let users reach this display by searching the authority file, but some of the information in the display must be drawn from the bibliographic record, in this case, the relator terms.

Display of Postings

Displaying the number of postings, or the number of records associated with each line of a display of headings or index terms, can help the user in decision making about the next step in searching; for example, a large posting might lead the user to try to think of ways to narrow the search. If the number of postings continues to appear on the screen after the user chooses to scan through the bibliographic records under a particular heading, it can give the user a sense of how far she or he has gone and how far she or he still has to go.

Display and Arrangement of Multiple Bibliographic Records

This section will deal with the display of multiple bibliographic records. This is the obvious next display when a user's search has matched only one heading or when a user has selected a heading from a previous summary display of headings. However, it is also the easiest display to offer to searchers who have used co-occurrence rules that are across multiple fields within a bibliographic record.

Records Retrieved by Matches on More than One Heading or Field

Once co-occurrence of keywords across multiple fields is allowed, the option of displaying single headings is more problematic, because the keyword search could easily match one word in one heading and a second word in a note field with no corresponding heading. The easiest option is simply to display the bibliographic records retrieved. If the records are arranged by main entry, the editions of multiple-edition works will tend to come together, and the user who has searched for the works of a particular author will be able to distinguish between the works of which the sought author was the primary author and the works of which the sought author was a secondary author. Some systems may arrange these records by title or by date; the latter options work against the second cataloging objective, 22 (b), of displaying all the editions of a work (see chapter 1). For this reason, main entry order would be the best default. Some systems offer sort options to the user, such as author/title, title/author, date, or call number.[8] This approach at least gives the user the option to ask for other arrangements for particular searches or even to view the same search several different ways. If in the single record display the keywords matched are highlighted, the user can quickly see why a particular record was retrieved; this highlighting can allow the user to scan through multiple records quickly.[9]

Another option for the display of records retrieved on cross-field searches that might be explored is that of displaying only the fields matched. When the fields matched are long note fields, this would make it difficult to compress long displays; perhaps sentences matched, rather than fields matched, could be tried. When two different headings are matched, the display could use the terms *paired with* to link the two headings (see figure 6.14).

Your search, FNA MASTERS AND JOHNSON, retrieved:

Line no. for selection:		No. of records:
3	Johnson, Virginia E. paired with: Masters, William H.*	15

---

*This suggestion was made by Jo Crawford at the University of Wisconsin-Madison in a personal communication in September 1994.

Figure 6.14   An example of a possible cross-field match display

Summary Displays of Multiple Bibliographic Records

Bibliographic records in summary displays should be kept brief, so that as many records as possible can fit on the screen at one time. On the other hand, these records should not be so cryptic that they are unusable. If, in addition to the main entry, title proper only is displayed, more records can fit on the screen; however, including the subtitle can explain cryptic or nonexpressive titles (see figure 6.15). Including the call numbers, or other location devices, in the summary display of bibliographic records can save steps for the user who can recognize the particular edition or the particular work sought from title alone. We suggest that you strongly consider including, at a minimum, the main entry, the title and subtitle, and the date.[10] Compression of all records with the same main entry could help to make a long display easier to scan. Note that even in a display of records that has been retrieved by selecting on a name/ author heading, there may be records with main entries that are different from the heading selected; e.g., the author selected may be the second author, an editor, etc. (see figure 6.16). The main entry characterizes the work in important ways and pulls together the editions of a work; it can be quite important for identifying and characterizing works with nondistinctive titles, such as *Poems, Papers,* or *Annual Report.* Compare, for example, the two displays in figure 6.17. In the field of music, in which composition is considered primary authorship and performance is considered secondary authorship, the main entry display can differentiate between the works that a person composed and the works that the same person merely performed. Consider the differences between the two displays of works of Leonard Bernstein in figure 6.18, for example. In the display by main entry, you can see much more clearly which works Bernstein conducted and which he composed.

The following three works all have the same cryptic title, but each has a subtitle that explains more fully what the work is about. Including the subtitle on summary displays would allow users to make decisions from that display more often rather than having to go into the full bibliographic record in order to decide which work was desired.

Eckhardt, Linda West, 1939- Satisfaction guaranteed : simply sumptuous mail-order foods with recipes and menus for fast and fabulous meals. 1986.

Herndon, Booton. Satisfaction guaranteed : an unconventional report to today's consumers. 1972.

Strasser, Susan, 1948- Satisfaction guaranteed : the making of the mass market. 1989.

Figure 6.15   Examples of works with cryptic titles

Cummings, E. E. (Edward Estlin), 1894-1962.
  Aragon, 1897- The red front. c1933.
  Armitage, Merle, 1893-1975. The poetry of e.e. cummings. 1957.
  Bergsma, William, 1921- [Songs] Six songs, to poems by E.E.
    Cummings, for voice and piano.
  Blitzstein, Marc. [Vocal music. Selections] Zipperfly & other songs [sound recording].
    p1991.
  Cage, John. Forever and sunsmell : song with percussion duet. 1960.
  Cummings, E. E. (Edward Estlin), 1894-1962. Complete poems, 1913-1962. 1981.
  —— Eimi. 1933.
  —— Him. 1927.
  —— No thanks. 1935.
  —— Puella mea. 1923.
  —— Tom. 1935. [... etc.]

The —— substituted for the same main entry repeated over and over might make for a
more scannable and more compact display.

Figure 6.16   An example of added entries and main entries displayed under one heading

Title display of two records in response to a search on Ulysses S. Grant:

[Papers].
[Papers].

Main entry display of two records in response to the same search:

Grant, Ulysses S., 1822-1885. [Papers]
Lincoln, Abraham, 1809-1865. [Papers].
[Grant is an added entry on the second record.]

**Figure 6.17   Two possible partial displays under Ulysses S. Grant, one using the main
entry and one not**

Items in a Series

It is very helpful to allow users the option of displaying the items in a series either
in volume number order or by main entry (see figure 6.19).

Subarrangements of Records within One Heading

In chapter 4, in the section on linking transcribed fields to the authority file, we
discussed a problem that results in most existing systems lacking elegant displays of
the works of prolific authors and the editions of multiple-edition works. Here, we
reiterate our recommendation for the ideal display of the works of an author and the

Display by title:

Bernstein, Leonard, 1918-

Age of anxiety. 1993, c1977.
Candide, c1994.
Chichester psalms. 1991, c1965.
Concertos, harpsichord, string orchestra, BWV 1052, D minor. 1957.
Concertos, piano. 1966.
Concertos, violin, orchestra, op. 14. 1965.
Halil. c1981.
Rhapsodies, violin, orchestra. 1962.

Display by main entry:

Bernstein, Leonard, 1918-

Bach, Johann Sebastian, 1685-1750. Concertos, harpsichord, string orchestra, BWV 1052, D minor. 1957.
Barber, Samuel, 1910- Concertos, violin, orchestra, op. 14. 1965.
Bartok, Bela, 1881-1945. Rhapsodies, violin, orchestra. 1962.
Beethoven, Ludwig van, 1770-1827. Concertos, piano. 1966.
Bernstein, Leonard, 1918-
——— Age of anxiety. 1993, c1977.
——— Candide, c1994.
——— Chichester psalms. 1991, c1965.
——— Halil. c1981.

Figure 6.18   Two possible displays of the works of Leonard Bernstein, one using the main entry and one not

In volume number order:

International series in experimental social psychology:

v. 1. Cultures in contact. 1982
v. 2. Howitt, Dennis. The mass media and social problems. 1982
v. 3. Pearce, Philip L. The social psychology of tourist behaviour. 1982
v. 4. Colman, Andrew M. Game theory and experimental games. 1982
v. 5. Genius and eminence. 1983

In main entry order:

International series in experimental social psychology:

Colman, Andrew M. Game theory and experimental games. 1982
Cultures in contact. 1982
Genius and eminence. 1983
Howitt, Dennis. The mass media and social problems. 1982
Pearce, Philip L. The social psychology of tourist behaviour. 1982

Figure 6.19   Two options for displaying the items in a series

editions of a work. A helpful display could compress headings for the works of Shakespeare and, when one particular work was chosen, list editions of the work itself first, then works about it, then related works (see figure 6.20).[11] Note that this display would probably require a solution to the problem (discussed in chapters 3 and 4) caused by the fact that you want to let users reach this display by searching the authority file, but some of the information in the display must be drawn from the bibliographic record, in this case, the tags (600 for works about) and indicators (e.g., second indicator 2 for works contained).

As shown in the display in figure 6.20, a chronological arrangement of the editions of a work can be quite helpful. Notice, by the way, how the inclusion of the statement of responsibility subfield identifies particular editions in the summary display.[12] While a chronological arrangement may be helpful under a single heading, i.e., once a particular work has been chosen from a summary display, it can be unhelpful prior to that. Some systems arrange chronologically all works retrieved on a search (which may match many different authors and works). This might be acceptable as an option for the knowledgeable user, but it may not be a wise default arrangement, as it has the effect of separating the editions of a work.

Display of a Single Record

Most systems have a default single record display that leaves out some fields.[13] Research that questions how much of the bibliographic record users really need has suffered from faulty research design. The approach taken by Alan Seal et al. was to replace a full entry microfiche catalog with a short entry microfiche catalog and then, in interviews, to ask users of the short entry catalog whether they had "found what they wanted to know from the catalogue." Using this methodology, only 1 percent to 3 percent of searches were reported by users to have failed because of lack of bibliographic description.[14] However, this study does not take into account the possibility that the users did not know ahead of time what they might learn from the catalog. One of the major factors to take into account in designing all catalog-use research is that users come to the catalog in search of information they do not yet have. If they miss something that might have been useful, they may not know they have missed it, and thus they may not be able to report the fact that they have missed it.

In a Council on Library Resources (CLR) survey, among the questions asked users about their most recent searches was one asking them what they had been trying to find.[15] This was the question used to determine how many users sought known items and how many sought works on a subject. Among the possibilities offered was "Information such as publisher, date, spelling of a name, etc." The fact that very few users checked the latter possibility has been used by some reporters of CLR findings to argue that "Most users do not express a need for detailed bibliographic information."[16] These researchers seem to have lost sight of the fact that "detailed bibliographic information" has many more functions than just verification of publisher and date for a citation. The principal function of the descriptive part of the cataloging record has never been primarily to aid in bibliographic verification, but rather to identify or distinguish among various works, and editions of works, and to characterize them to aid the user in choosing among them.

Shakespeare, William, 1564-1616.
1. All's well that ends well.
2. Antony and Cleopatra.
3. As you like it.
4. Comedy of errors.
5. Coriolanus.
6. Cymbeline.
7. Hamlet.
8. Henry V.
9. Henry VI.

When the user chooses line 3, for *As You Like It,* the following display could result:

Shakespeare, William, 1564-1616. As you like it.

1. Editions of As you like it.
2. Works about As you like it.*
3. Other works related to As you like it.†

When the user chooses line 1, for *As You Like It,* the following display could result:

1 As you like it / by William Shakespeare ; translated into modern English with analysis and commentary by Gary S. Michael. 1991.
2 As you like it / literary consultant, John Wilders. 1978.
3 As you like it / edited by Richard Knowles ; with a survey of criticism by Evelyn Joseph Mattern. 1977.
4 As you like it / William Shakespeare ; edited by Agnes Latham. 1975.
5 As you like it : an old-spelling and old-meaning edition, prepared by Christine Trautvetter. 1972.
6 As you like it / edited by Arthur Quiller-Couch & John Dover Wilson. 1957.
7 As you like it / by William Shakespeare ; a facsimile of the first folio text, with an introduction by J. Dover Wilson, and a list of modern readings. 1929.
8 As you like it : a comedy / by Mr. William Shakespear. 1734.

********French & English:
9 Comme il vous plaira = As you like it / Shakespeare ; introd. traduction et notes par J.-J. Mayoux. 1956.

********Frisian:
10 As jiemme it lije meie : in blijspul / uut it Ingels fen William Shakspeare [sic] ; forfryske in mei forkleerjende noten forsjoen troch R. Posthumus. 1842.
********German:
11 Wie es euch gefaellt / William Shakespeare ; Deutsch von Elisabeth Plessen ; Regie Peter Zadek. [1986?]

---

*In the USMARC bibliographic format, 6XX fields contain subject added entries for the work.

†In the USMARC bibliographic format, added entries for the work with second indicator 1 (now obsolete) or blank.

Figure 6.20   **Ideal display of the works of an author and the editions of a work**

It is likely that users make use of all fields in the bibliographic record from time to time, depending on the circumstances, and that they are not able to articulate their use of these fields very well. The most common fields to be left out in or buried at the bottom of default single record displays are the note fields.[17] The notes frequently contain information essential for carrying out the second objective of the catalog, 2.2 (b); for example, although a new, revised edition of a work that has changed its title may have a note indicating the title of the earlier edition, the user who doesn't realize there is a newer edition, and has a citation to the earlier title, may not recognize the later edition if that note does not display. According to current cataloging practice, however, an added entry should link the later edition to the earlier (although this has not always been the case), but the records for the two editions may display far apart in a multiple-record retrieval, and only the note will tell the user looking at the record for the later edition that it is indeed an edition of the work sought (see figure 6.21).

For many nonbook materials, the most critical information appears in the notes. A nonbook record without its notes can be so cryptic as to be incomprehensible. Compare the displays of a record for a German newsreel with and without its notes shown in figure 6.22.

The user is looking for the latest edition of Guyton's *Basic Human Physiology* and does a name-title keyword search on ARTHUR GUYTON HUMAN, retrieving the following results:

Guyton, Arthur C.
    Basic human physiology. 1971.
    Basic human physiology. 1977.
    Function of the human body. 1964.
    Function of the human body. 1969.
    Function of the human body. 1974.
    Human physiology and mechanisms of disease. 1982.
    Human physiology and mechanisms of disease. 1987.
    Human physiology and mechanisms of disease. 1992.
    Human physiology and mechanisms of disease. 1997.

Only if the bibliographic records display the notes (and only if the user is suspicious and checks the full bibliographic record display for every item retrieved above) will the user discover, on looking at the 1982 edition of *Human Physiology and Mechanisms of Disease*, that this text changed its title between 1977 and 1982:

Guyton, Arthur C.
    Human physiology and mechanisms of disease / Arthur C. Guyton. -- 3rd ed. -- Philadelphia : Saunders, 1982.

    x, 709 p. : col. ill. ; 28 cm.

    Rev. ed. of: Basic human physiology. 2nd ed. 1977.
    Includes bibliographies and index.

1. Human physiology. 2. Physiology, Pathological.

Figure 6.21   **An example of the value of including notes in the default single record display**

Without notes:

Die Deutsche Wochenschau. [Nr. 511]. -- Germany : [s.n.], 1940[-06 or 1940-07]

With notes:

Die Deutsche Wochenschau. [Nr. 511]. -- Germany : [s.n.], 1940[-06 or 1940-07]
Newsreel.
SUMMARY: Battle of France: air bombing of strategic sites prepares the way for troops. The right wing of the Army launches its offensive from Amiens to Rouen and LeHavre; the infantry spreads out, passing fires set by the retreating French; soldiers stop to milk abandoned cows. Cavalry advances quickly in the Somme region; artillery pounds the Weygand line; fresh reserves arrive for the push to the coast; General von Kluge leads the Army in Rouen, where soldiers fight fire in the historic cathedral. Germans feed residents of occupied towns; work crews begin clean-up efforts; Hitler pays them a surprise visit; the central Army offensive aims at Paris; resisters are disarmed and many prisoners taken at Noyon.

Figure 6.22   Displays of a record for a newsreel with and without its notes

Another field often left out of the display of a record is the uniform title.[18] The uniform title is there to bring together all of the editions of a work; it should, therefore, be determining the arrangement of one record vis-à-vis others. If the uniform title is not displayed, the user may be confused as to why a record has come up at a particular point (see figure 6.23).

Including a list of all the access points on the record (i.e., the tracings) as well can help users formulate new searches or, if navigating is allowed (discussed in chapter 1), can allow the user to select a new search without typing it in (see figure 6.24). Some systems leave out the statement of responsibility subfield after the title.[19] This subfield often contains statements of subsidiary authorship, concerning translators, illustrators, writers of commentaries, etc. that can be critical in aiding a user in deciding whether to choose a particular edition of a sought work. (See the Shakespeare example in figure 6.20 for a display that makes use of statements of subsidiary authorship to differentiate among different editions and facilitate choice.)

Another field commonly left out of displays is the field that contains an untraced series or a series traced differently (the 490 field in the USMARC bibliographic format).[20] Sometimes this field contains a series that the library has decided not to trace at all.[21] However, the series statement does appear on the title page of the edition of the work cataloged. If it is not shown to the user, there are times when this might lead the user to misidentify a sought edition. There are times when an untraced series could still characterize a particular edition and help the user decide whether or not to choose it. Displaying a series that has been traced differently may be less useful for most library users, but it is important for the use of cataloging staff, who need to know how the series actually appeared on the title page of the item.[22] Make sure the display distinguishes between transcribed forms (which should appear only in the body of the description) and normalized forms (which should appear only in the tracings). See chapter 3 for a discussion of the importance of distinguishing between these two kinds of data. Note that the 246 field in the USMARC bibliographic format presents a special case in this regard. The 246 field is currently designed so that it can function as both a note and as an added entry. As such, it should sometimes display *twice*, once with the

The user is browsing through the works of Oscar Wilde. The initial display looks like this:

Wilde, Oscar, 1854-1900.
1. The happy prince.
2. The importance of being earnest.
3. Lady Windermere's fan.
4. The nightingale and the rose.
5. The selfish giant.

The user decides to look at the editions of *The Selfish Giant*, and chooses line 5. The summary screen looks like this:

Wilde, Oscar, 1854-1900.
1. The selfish giant. 1911.
2. The selfish giant. 1932.
3. The selfish giant. 1945.
4. The selfish giant. c1954.
5. Selfish giant. Portuguese. O gigante egoista. c1982.

If the user chooses line 5, the display without a uniform title would look like this:

Wilde, Oscar, 1854-1900.
O gigante egoista / Oscar Wilde ; illustrado por Joana Isles. -- Lisboa: Difusao Verbo, c1982.

However, if the uniform title is included, the display clearly indicates where the user is in the display of Wilde's works, and why this record is placed at this spot:

Wilde, Oscar, 1854-1900.
[Selfish giant. Portuguese]
O gigante egoista / Oscar Wilde ; illustrado por Joana Isles. -- Lisboa: Difusao Verbo, c1982.

Figure 6.23   Single record displays including the uniform title

note fields (together with the display constants in figure 6.25 that are associated with the second indicator or with the text found in the delimiter i subfield) and once with the added entries.[23]

In summary, we strongly recommend that the complete record be the default display for a single record to help the novice user who might not know that he or she is viewing a shortened version of the record, much less realize that he or she can ask for a full version (or know how to do so). More sophisticated users can be given lots of options to shorten the records on command. In fact, some might even benefit from being allowed to ask for display of any combination of USMARC tags.

There is some disagreement about the value of labeling the fields of an individual bibliographic record. Walt Crawford, Lennie Stovel, and Kathy Bales advocate labeled displays and give lots of examples.[24] However, the only user study that addressed this issue had serious design flaws. Benjamin Fryser and Keith Stirling conducted a timing and user preference study comparing LC card format display of bibliographic records with a display with fields labeled. They found that 83 percent preferred the labeled display. However, their methodology casts serious doubt on the findings; users were first instructed to identify a predetermined bibliographic field as quickly as possible; presumably, the instructions to the users employed the same terms as were used in the labels on the labeled displays. Then the users were asked their preferences. Predictably, they tended to prefer the format that had just allowed them to be tested most successfully. (For some reason, the figures on how long it took users to identify particular fields were not directly reported.)[25]

A user interested in scholarly works on Native American costumes and textiles finds the following book on a subject search under the subject heading TEXTILE FABRICS—GUATEMALA. If the display includes a list of other added entries on this record, she or he may be stimulated to find more books of interest by searching under the HEARD MUSEUM OF ANTHROPOLOGY AND PRIMITIVE ART or, if the system allows this, by navigating from this display to the entries under the museum:

Dieterich, Mary G.
   Guatemalan costumes : the Heard Museum collection / text
by Mary G. Dieterich, Jon T. Erickson, Erin Younger ; prepared
in coordination with an exhibition by the Heard Museum, April 28,
1979. -- Phoenix, Ariz. (22 E. Monte Vista Rd., Phoenix 85004) :
The Museum, c1979

95 p. : ill. (some col.) ; 28 cm.

Bibliography: p. 94-95

1. Costume--Guatemala--Exhibitions. 2. Textile fabrics--Guatemala--
Exhibitions. 3. Decoration and ornament--Guatemala--Exhibitions.
4. Erickson, Jon T. 5. Younger, Erin. 6. Heard Museum of
Anthropology and Primitive Art.

Figure 6.24   An example demonstrating the value of displaying tracings

---

ƀ   [no display constant; use contents of ≠i subfield instead]
0   [no note generated]
1   [no note generated]
2   Distinctive title:
3   Other title:
4   Cover title:
5   Added title page title:
6   Caption title:
7   Running title:
8   Spine title:

Figure 6.25   Display constants associated with the 246 field second indicator

Although it is popular nowadays to scoff at the use of the card format in online displays, the card format was originally designed to deal with a problem that does not go away with the advent of online catalogs—a shortage of space in which to convey information about the particular edition of a work.[26] Computer screens do not offer unlimited space either. Crawford, Stovel, and Bales report 30 percent of records investigated on RLIN required a second screen using a cardlike display, 84 percent when using a labeled display.[27] Also, note that the card format sets off information by means of paragraphing and indentation, rather than by labeling, not just to save space but so as to avoid the imposition of more arcane bibliographic vocabulary on users. How many users would understand the terms *material, other entries,* and *corporate author,* for example? These were all terms used in labeled displays by Crawford, Stovel, and Bales.[28] A little experience on a reference desk is enough to lead one to observe that users are not always articulate about bibliographic matters; any user who has ever created a footnote can recognize *Houghton Mifflin* as a publisher's name but may not know the term *imprint;* users who are not interested in the publisher can just skip over that line of the display. If, in fact, users have no names for bibliographic fields in their common vocabulary, it is possible that labels of bibliographic fields would cause more problems than they would solve, resulting in a longer and more confusing display.

Labels carry with them another problem: often there is no term available that briefly, clearly, and accurately summarizes the types of data that might occur in a particular field. The field labeled *Author* in many OPAC displays is a good case in point. In the *Author* field can be found, for example, painters, actors, musicians, conferences, and defendants in court cases, yet the term *author* has a relatively narrow meaning to most users. Thus we end up with amusing displays such as the one in figure 6.26.

Some systems may force you to use labels, however, and some of you may have to design labels because of decisions made by your institution. If you must display labels, try to choose as general a term as possible, so as to ensure that it covers every type of data that might occur in the field or area being labeled. Oddly enough, in the example shown in figure 6.26, the most accurate label for Lizzie Borden would probably be *Main entry;* of course, that term will probably not be familiar or helpful to most users. It is probably impossible to find vocabulary that is both accurate and recognizable by the public. See figure 6.27 for some ideas about possible labels.

Although we recommend against system-supplied labels, we strongly recommend that systems be designed to display all the display constants called for by the US-MARC format. These constitute a national standard that should be followed by all catalog systems. When catalogers create national-level standard records, they assume that USMARC display constants will be displayed, so as to make many fields comprehensible to users. If these display constants do not display, the records may be

Author: Borden, Lizzie, 1860-1927, defendant.
Title: Trial of Lizzie Borden / edited, with a history of the case, by Edmund Pearson.

Figure 6.26   An example of poorly functioning field labels in a single record display

AACR2R and USMARC terminology is probably the most accurate expression of the kind of data to be found in the relevant fields.

Labels based on AACR2R terminology:

1XX	Headings
	Access points
245	Title and statement of responsibility area
245 ≠a	Title proper
245 ≠b	Parallel titles and other title information
245 ≠c	Statements of responsibility
250	Edition area
254-257	Material (or type of publication) specific details area
260	Publication, distribution, etc., area
260 ≠a	Place of publication, distribution, etc.
260 ≠b	Name of publisher, distributor, etc.
260 ≠c	Date of publication, distribution, etc.
300	Physical description area
4XX	Series area
5XX	Note area
7XX	Added entries

Labels based on USMARC format terminology:

1XX	Main entry
245	Title statement
245 ≠a	Title
245 ≠b	Remainder of title
245 ≠c	Remainder of title page transcription/statement of responsibility
250	Edition statement
254	Musical presentation statement
255	Cartographic mathematical data
256	Computer file characteristics
257	Country of producing entity for archival films
260	Publication, distribution, etc. (Imprint)
260 ≠a	Place of publication, distribution, etc.
260 ≠b	Name of publisher, distributor, etc.
260 ≠c	Date of publication, distribution, etc.
300	Physical description
4XX	Series statements
5XX	Notes
6XX	Subject access fields
70X-75X	Added entries
76X-78X	Linking entries

Figure 6.27   Labels

Examples of labels found in existing systems:

1XX	Author		300	Collation
	AUTHR			Contains
	Main author			DESCR
100	Personal author			Descrip
245	Title statement			Descript
	Title			Description
	Title/author			Material
245 ≠a	Main title			Pagination
245 ≠b	Subtitle			Paging
245 ≠c	Authorship			Phys. desc.
245 ≠h	Format			Physical desc
	Medium		4XX	SERIE
250	Edition			Series
255	Math. data		5XX	Notes
260	Imprint		6XX, 7XX	Other entries
	Publ info		6XX	Subject
	Publication			Subjects
	Publication info			SUBJT
	Published		600	Personal subject
	Publisher		70X-71X	AAUTH
	PUBLR			Other au
260 ≠a	City			Other aut
	Place			Other authors
	Place of pub.		70X-75X	Added entries
260 ≠b	Publisher			Other entries
260 ≠c	Date		246, 74X, 73X	Add. title
	Pub. date			Alt title
	Published			Other ti

incomprehensible, and the fault lies squarely on the system's shoulders. See figure 6.28 for a summary of the display constants required by the USMARC format. International standards call for supplying International Standard Bibliographic Description (ISBD) punctuation in the display of a single record. ISBD punctuation is intended to aid in making bibliographic information comprehensible even to people who do not speak the language of the description. See figure 6.29.

The single record display of a record for a serial publication presents some special problems that are worth examining separately. Most serials users are looking for a particular volume of a serial that contains an article for which they have a citation. One field in the bibliographic record (the 362 field in the USMARC format) describes the volumes of the serial as published. Most libraries have another field or fields they use to describe which volumes are actually held in the library.[29] If the library does not have a complete run of the serial, this statement of holdings is going to be different from the description of the volumes of the serial as published, and the

Field	Indicator	Subfield code	Text
245	1_		I. Title. [Consider indicating whether or not a title is traced in this fashion, i.e., supplying both roman numeral and text constant.]
246			See figure 6.25
362		≠z	-- [dash should precede subfield ≠z]
440			Add parentheses around each transcribed series statement.
440		≠x	ISSN
440			I. Series. [Consider indicating the fact that a series is traced in this fashion, i.e., supplying both roman numeral and text constant.]
773	0_		In
505	0_		Contents:
505	1_		Incomplete contents:
505	2_		Partial contents:
505	__		[no display constant]
511	1_		Cast:
511	2_		Presenter: [Note: this display constant is now obsolete, but unless a conversion is done, the display constant should appear on older records with first indicator 2.]
511	3_		Narrator: [Note: this display constant is now obsolete, but unless a conversion is done, the display constant should appear on older records with first indicator 3.]
511	0_		[no display constant]
508			Credits:
510	0_		Indexed by:
510	1_		Indexed in its entirety by:
510	2_		Indexed selectively by:
510	3_		References:
510	4_		References:
516	♭_		Type of file:
516	8_		[no display constant]
520	__		Summary:
520	0_		Subject:
520	1_		Review:
520	8_		[no display constant]
522	♭_		Geographic coverage:
522	8_		[no display constant]
524	♭_		Cite as:
524	8_		[no display constant]
555	♭_		Indexes:
555	0_		Finding aids:
555	8_		[no display constant]

Figure 6.28   Display constants required by the USMARC bibliographic format

556	β_	Documentation:
556	8_	[no display constant]
565	β_	File size:
565	0_	Case file characteristics:
565	8_	[no display constant]
567	β_	Methodology:
567	8_	[no display constant]
581	β_	Publications:
581	8_	[no display constant]
586	β_	Awards:
586	8_	[no display constant]
6XX,	≠v, ≠x,	-- [substitute a double dash for each subfield code]
7XX	≠y, ≠z	
76X-78X		See figure 6.12

statement of holdings is going to be the more crucial for the user seeking a particular volume; it may well indicate that the library doesn't hold the volume sought, or that the volume sought is in an unexpected place, e.g., in remote storage. Currently, the 362 field usually appears before holdings information in bibliographic record displays and misleads users into thinking it is a statement of volumes actually held in the library. This might be one area in which a labeled display could be helpful. Perhaps the example in figure 6.30 may give system designers ideas for better single record displays for serials.

In the section earlier in this chapter on display of relationships among serials, we suggested that the initial display of titles matching a search indicate a serial's relationship with its earlier and later titles. If the system does not do this, however, it is important that the single record display indicate these relationships to the user. The display constants listed in figure 6.12 should be used to precede the serials linking notes in the single record display. Make sure the display is driven by the first indicator in the linking fields (USMARC 760-787 fields), which allows more complex relationships to be explained to the user by means of a 580 note that supersedes the display of the 760-787 fields.

250	Precede this area by a full stop, space, dash, space. [. --]
254-257	Precede this area by a full stop, space, dash, space. [. --]
260	Precede this area by a full stop, space, dash, space. [. --]
300	Precede this area by a full stop, space, dash, space [. --], or start a new paragraph.
4XX	Precede this area by a full stop, space, dash, space. [. --]
5XX	Precede each note by a full stop, space, dash, space [. --], or start a new paragraph for each.

Figure 6.29   ISBD punctuation

Internet world. -- Westport, CT : Meckler Corp., c1992-

v. ; 28 cm.

Volumes published:*   v. 3, no. 7 (Sept. 1992)-
Volumes held in this library:[†]
  In College Library: v. 7 no. 5-12 (1996)
  In storage: v. 5 no. 1-v. 7 no. 4

Continues: Research & education networking.

---

*Data from 362 field.
[†]Data from library's holdings fields.

Figure 6.30   An example of a single record display for a serial

It is common for the display of a single record in an OPAC to begin with a clutter of computer information such as record and screen numbers, call numbers, command lines, and function key definitions, rather than with the heading that determines the order in which this record is displaying relative to others that may have been retrieved in the same search. Displaying the relevant heading would be a more elegant display, as it would clearly situate the single record in the context of the overall search and therefore be more helpful for the user who can't remember where she or he is, how she or he got there, and where she or he could go next.[30]

AACR2R prescribes the order of the data elements in a cataloging record. Thus any online display that does not follow AACR2R order is not following nationally established standards. (See figure 6.31.) There is a good reason to follow the national standard order of fields: it has the effect of identifying and characterizing an item first as it embodies a particular work, identified by its author, if it has one, and uniform title, if it has one, and then as it embodies a particular edition of that work, with the most important information for identification and characterization first. This identification and characterization are important in their own right in that they help the user decide whether an item is useful or not; when the display is in main entry order, they also serve as an orienting device, reminding the user where he or she is in a display of multiple records.

We have not tried to deal with the complexities of the new USMARC holdings format, nor have we dealt with other types of information collected in integrated library systems, such as acquisition, circulation, and bindery information. However, we would like to make a general recommendation regarding the integration of such information into OPAC displays. The ideal should be to create a display that integrates availability and location data onto a single public screen, so that a user can immediately determine whether or not the item sought has been ordered, received, cataloged, checked in or out, sent to the bindery, declared missing, or withdrawn.

1XX
240
243
245
250
254-257
260
300
310
340
342
343
351
362
4XX
5XX, as follows [note that this order must be determined by the cataloger and preserved
    by the system]:
Nature, scope, or artistic form; includes system requirements
Frequency
Language of the item and/or translation or adaptation
Source of title proper
Variations in title
Parallel titles and other title information
Statements of responsibility
    Cast (511)
    Credits (508)
Edition and history
Material (or type of publication) specific details
Notation
File characteristics
Numbering and chronological designation
Publication, distribution, etc.
Donor, source, etc., and previous owner(s)
Place of writing
Published versions
Physical description
Accompanying material and supplements
Series
Dissertations
Audience
Access and literary rights
Reference to published description
Other formats
Summary (520)
Indexes
Contents (505)
Numbers borne by item
Copy being described, library's holdings, and restrictions on use
With notes (501)
Combined notes relating to the original
Ancient, medieval and Renaissance manuscripts notes (style of writing, illustrative
    matter, collation, other physical details, opening words)

Figure 6.31   Order of data elements prescribed by AACR2R

Conclusion

Display and arrangement of multiple headings matched and of multiple bibliographic records matched can be crucial in determining the success or failure of a user's search. Use of headings rather than bibliographical records in initial displays is highly recommended because a heading stands for an author, a work, or a subject, while a bibliographic record stands for a particular edition of a particular work. The former is much more likely to be the object of the user's search. Headings can also be more easily summarized and compressed, allowing the user readily to comprehend the scope and structure of even the largest and most complex retrievals.

Notes

1. Beverly Janosky, Philip J. Smith, and Charles Hildreth, "Online Library Catalog Systems: An Analysis of User Errors," *International Journal of Man-Machine Studies* 25 (1986): 580.

2. Michael Berger, *The User Meets the MELVYL System: An Analysis of User Transactions*, Technical Report no. 7 (Oakland, Calif.: Division of Library Automation, University of California, 1996), p. 56.

3. Allyson Carlyle, "Ordering Author and Work Records: An Evaluation of Collocation in Online Catalog Displays," *Journal of the American Society for Information Science* 47 (1996): 538–554.

4. *Library of Congress Filing Rules* (Washington, D.C.: Library of Congress, 1980), p. 9.

5. Nicholson Baker, "Discards," *New Yorker*, April 4, 1994, p. 69, 75.

6. Robert Alan, "Linking Successive Entries Based upon the OCLC Control Number, ISSN or LCCN." *Library Resources & Technical Services* 37 (1993): 403–413.

7. "Relator Terms for Archival Moving Image Cataloging," *Cataloging Service Bulletin* 31 (1986): 71–75.

8. Systems that do this include MULTILIS (from the Multilis Corporation) and one version of Dynix.

9. The Bibliographic Retrieval Services (BRS) system highlights matched keywords in this fashion. See Walt Crawford, *The Online Catalog Book: Essays and Examples* (Boston: G. K. Hall, 1992), p. 202.

10. Ideally, this date should be taken from the 260 field in monograph records but from the coded dates in the 008 field for serial records. The 260 dates in monograph records are designed to be more readable and expressive.

11. The display can be based on USMARC tags in the bibliographic record. The work itself could be represented by the following tags or combinations of tags: 100, 110, or 111, plus 240 or 245; 130; 700, 710, or 711, plus delimiter t; 730. Note that for such displays to work, catalogers must be using uniform titles to bring together all the editions of a work, regardless of title changes; unfortunately, these rules are optional in AACR2R.

12. In the USMARC format, 245 field, subfield c.

13. Gregory Wool, "The Many Faces of a Catalog Record," *Information Technology and Libraries* 15 (1996): 173–195.

14. Alan Seal, Philip Bryant, and Carolyn Hall, *Full and Short Entry Catalogues: Library Needs and Uses* (Bath, Eng.: Bath University Library, 1982).

15. *Using Online Catalogs: A Nationwide Survey: A Report of a Study Sponsored by the Council on Library Resources*, ed. Joseph R. Matthews, Gary S. Lawrence, and Douglas K. Ferguson (New York: Neal-Schuman, 1983).

16. Gary S. Lawrence, Vicki Graham, and Heather Presley, "University of California Users Look at MELVYL: Results of a Survey of Users of the University of California Prototype Online Union Catalog," *Advances in Library Administration and Organization* 3 (1984): 88.

17. Wool, "The Many Faces," p. 178–179.

18. 130 or 240 field in the USMARC format. In Wool's study, twenty-nine OPACs failed to display uniform titles. See Wool, "The Many Faces," p. 179.

19. In the USMARC format, 245 field, subfield c.

20. Wool, "The Many Faces," p. 179–180. Eleven OPACs failed to display the 490 field.

21. When the 490 field has a first indicator of 0.

22. 490 field with a first indicator of 1.

23. The cataloger determines, through the use of the first indicator, whether the 246 field should be used to generate a note and/or an added entry. Prior practice was to employ only two first indicators: 0 to indicate that there should be no note generated and 1 to indicate the need to generate a note. Systems with older records should be aware of this lack of consistency.

24. Walt Crawford, Lennie Stovel, and Kathy Bales, *Bibliographic Displays in the Online Catalog* (Boston: G. K. Hall, 1987).

25. Benjamin S. Fryser and Keith H. Stirling, "Effect of Spatial Arrangement, Upper-lower Case Letter Combinations and Reverse Video on Patron Response to CRT Displayed Catalog Records," *Journal of the American Society for Information Science* 35 (Nov. 1984): 344–350.

26. Charles R. Hildreth, "Online Public Access Catalogs: Evaluation, Selection and Effect," in *Conference on Integrated Online Library Systems* (St. Louis, Mo.: Genaway and Associates, 1987), p. 43–57.

27. Crawford, Stovel, and Bales, *Bibliographic Displays*, p. 3.

28. Ibid., p. 78.

29. The USMARC holdings format has recently become available to carry information about a library's serial holdings, but few libraries have used it yet. Most probably have devised local solutions for describing serial holdings. This situation should change over the next few years as implementation of the USMARC holdings format becomes more widespread. A good introduction to the USMARC holdings format may be found in Frieda B. Rosenberg, chapter 11, "Managing Serial Holdings," in Marcia Tuttle, *Managing Serials* (Greenwich, Conn.: JAI Press, 1996), p. 235–253.

30. Baker, "Discards," p. 81.

7

Demonstration of Relationships—Authors and Works—Summary— Desirable Defaults

Many online systems offer users a list of search types on the initial log-on screen. It is rare for these to correspond to the three most common searches, those addressed by the objectives of the catalog: a search for the works of an author, a search for a particular work, or a search for works on a particular subject. Subject searches will be dealt with in the following chapters, but here, we review desirable default searches and displays, for both a search for the works of an author and a search for a particular work. Of course, the system should offer the sophisticated user as much power and flexibility as it possibly can, and it should explain its powerful and flexible options as thoroughly as possible in readily accessible *HELP* screens, so the user who wishes to learn to become sophisticated can easily do so. However, the default searches offered to the novice user, or the user who just doesn't want to be bothered investing time in learning how to use a library catalog, are critical to convincing the user that the system is friendly.

Offer just one default search for the works of a particular author, and one default search for a particular work, and make it the best search you can possibly design. Consider the following suggestions:

Default Author Search

File Structure Decisions

For further discussion of the reasoning behind the following recommendations, please see chapter 4.

1. Avoid naming the file by using form fill-in to gather information from the user about the nature of the terms being used in her or his search. If the file must be named, it is probably better to call it the *Name* index than to call it the *Author* index, as the latter has too specific a meaning to cover all the kinds of names that will appear in this index.

2. Make a general search available for users who cannot be specific about the nature of the terms they are using in their search, e.g., users who seek the works resulting from a particular sequence of conferences.

Indexing

For further discussion of the reasoning behind the following recommendations, please see chapter 5.

1. Because personal authors' names are under authority control, it is strongly recommended that the default personal author search be a within-authority-record keyword search with a headings display (see below). When the search is for a single author, a keyword search for that heading within one authority record will prevent the false drops that occur on within-record matching of bibliographic records; for example, a search for James Stewart can retrieve a bibliographic record with both James Jones and Fred Stewart attached. Such a search will also allow you to display all the headings matched to allow the user to choose the correct name, if there is more than one person by that name.

Users may not expect to have to invert names in an online system, so a keyword search of personal names that does not require the words in the search to occur in a particular order is useful.[1] However, it does mean that a search on Frederick Lewis will also retrieve Lewis Frederick. The best solution would be to use form fill-in for novice users, and inversion and commas for more experienced users, to get the user to identify the surname and forename elements of the name. See below for further advantages to be gained from having the forename and the surname identified so that they can be flagged for special treatment.

Because catalogers do not make *see* references for "variants of variants," keyword matching within the authority record, rather than within a field, is recommended for an author search; this approach will ensure that a citation that uses one variant of the forename (in one 400 field, for example) and another variant of the surname (in another 400 field) would still retrieve the record. Keyword matching across the record will also allow you to display all the headings and cross-references from retrieved authority records in order to allow the user to choose the correct name, especially important if the search retrieves authority records for more than one person. If your authority file is linked to your bibliographic records, the user seeking a particular author can readily view that author's works.

For all these reasons, the best default search for an author is a keyword-within-record search of authority records, including all cross-reference fields.

2. It is known that forename specification can vary considerably in users' citations. Smart software would recognize that a name sought by the user, Newton, Martin Alfred, for example, could be represented in the catalog as Newton, M. A., Newton, Martin A., or Newton, M. Alfred. Such software could help users considerably (as well as aiding catalogers in applying authority control). If it is possible to ask users to identify surnames and forenames separately, for example on a form fill-in screen, it might be useful to stem the forename to the first initial and bring up for further selection by the user all headings that either begin with that initial or contain that forename anywhere in the forename element of the heading. Nickname dictionaries could be used to recognize that, for example, Bob Hayes and Robert Hayes might be the same person. Terms of address and other appendages to names, such as

Sir and Dr., could be put on a stop word list to be applied to forenames only, although an override may be needed for cases in which such terms are legitimate forenames.

3. Certain patterns that can be observed in surnames might allow for smart indexing of surnames specifically identified as such. For example, any surname that began with either "Mc" or "Mac" could be searched as either form. Any surname that began with an element such as "De," "De la," "Van," etc., De Grasse, for example, could be searched either with or without the space(s), i.e., either as De Grasse or as DeGrasse—perhaps even as Grasse.

4. It is recommended that the default indexing for corporate names be a within-hierarchically-related-group match of authority records. Catalogers make a separate authority record for each main heading and for each subdivision of the main heading. For example, there is one authority record for the Federal Bureau of Investigation (entered under UNITED STATES. FEDERAL BUREAU OF INVESTIGATION), which has a *see* reference from FBI. There is another authority record for the Uniform Crime Reports Section of the FBI (entered under UNITED STATES. FEDERAL BUREAU OF INVESTIGATION. UNIFORM CRIME REPORTS SECTION). In all current OPACs, the following search would fail: FBI UNIFORM CRIME REPORTS SECTION. If we could build smarter systems that recognize that the main heading has hierarchical force over all of its subdivisions, such a system would recognize the relationship between the UNIFORM CRIME REPORTS SECTION record and the FBI *see* reference and ensure that the user's search was successful.

5. Create a conference index that can search title and note fields (in addition to the corporate name fields).

6. Take a liberal approach toward normalization.

7. Use an implicit Boolean AND, but make it explicit on the display of search results, along with a suggestion of other Boolean operators available with an explanation of how the results would vary.

8. Consider the possibility of developing smart indexing programs that could search under all possible transliterations for a name in a transliterated language such as Chinese or Russian.

Display Decisions

For further discussion of the reasoning behind the following recommendations, please see chapter 6.

1. Any search that matches more than one person's or corporate body's name should result in a display of headings matched, not a display of bibliographic records.

2. The display of headings matched should arrange the headings following the principle of filing elements, such that all headings with the same initial element should display together and be subarranged using the secondary filing element, then the tertiary filing element, etc. Parenthetical qualifiers and separately subfielded elements of names should all be treated as secondary, tertiary, etc. filing elements. To this end, normalization should be applied very conservatively in display algorithms.

3. The display of a person's or corporate body's name should include the display of all subject subdivisions applied to that heading; the display of a corporate body's name should include the display of all of its corporate subdivisions.

4. The display of a person's or corporate body's name should include the display of all *see also* references that apply to that heading.

5. On searches that match on main headings only, compress all headings with the same initial filing element if the display of headings matched is longer than would fit on one screen, differentiating them only for users that choose a further display of headings with that initial filing element.

6. Make cross-references selectable, as opposed to requiring rekeying of the authorized heading.

7. Display the number of postings attached to each heading in a headings display.

8. The display of works under an author's name should be subarranged by the main entry for each work. As discussed above, the main entry for a work will occur as any one of the following combinations: (a) a 130 field; (b) a 245 field and no 1XX field; (c) a 1XX field and a 240 field; (d) a 1XX field and a 243 field; (e) a 1XX field and a 245 field and no 240 or 243 field; (f) a 730, 630, or 7XX or 6XX field with a delimiter t subfield.

9. The display of the records representing a work should be divided into (a) editions of the work, (b) works containing it, (c) works about it, and (d) other related works.

10. Editions of the work should be arranged by language and then by date of publication.

Default Work Search

File Structure Decisions

For further discussion of the reasoning behind the following recommendations, please see chapters 4 and 5.

Offer a name-title search of some kind. Possible approaches include the following:

1. A name-title search that permitted different kinds of searching algorithms to be applied to the name portion and the title portion of the search request would be best, because names are under authority control and titles usually are not. Also, it is not uncommon for titles in users' citations to appear in bibliographic records as subtitles, parallel titles,[2] or series titles.[3] If the system can search for the title separately from the author names, and do a different kind of search, it will be able to search more precisely for the work sought. A form fill-in approach that allowed users to supply subject terms as well might be useful for extremely garbled or incomplete citations to nonfiction works of which the subject is known. If the form fill-in could place the user's input terms in the context of the appropriate authority file (for names and subjects) or headings list (for titles) in a little window for each box on the form fill-in, the user could modify his or her search as necessary. A personal name search should be a within-record search of the authority file. A corporate name search should be a within-hierarchically-related-group match on authority records containing corporate names. The title search should be a within-heading match on all title fields in bibliographic records and a within-hierarchically-related-group match on authority records containing title fields.

2. A name-title search of the name-title index described in chapter 4 would not allow as many different title forms to be linked to as many different name forms as the previous solution, but it could, if designed properly, obviate the requirement that the user distinguish between the name and title elements of the search in cases in which citations are unclear.

Indexing

For further discussion of the reasoning behind the following recommendations, please see chapter 5.

1. If the work sought has a main entry that is different from the user's search, the option of a second search on the main entry would guarantee that the user had the opportunity to view all editions of the work, as well as works about the work sought and works related to it.[4]

2. The user may be searching for a particular work using the names of more than one author; if possible, ask the user to input each author's name separately, so that each name can be separately searched in the authority file.

3. Take a liberal approach toward normalization.

Display Decisions

For further discussion of the reasoning behind the following recommendations, please see chapter 6.

1. If the user's search retrieves just one work (i.e., there may be more than one record for its various editions, but all have the same main entry), the best display would be a summary screen of the bibliographic records retrieved, grouped into the following categories: (a) editions of the work; (b) works containing the work; (c) works about the work; and (d) works related to the work.

2. If the user's search retrieves more than one work, the best initial display would be a summary display of the main entries of the works retrieved, together with the titles, subtitles, and dates drawn from the bibliographic records representing each work. In large displays, compression of works with the same main entry would be useful.

3. In displays of serial works, display all linked titles (e.g., earlier and later titles).

4. Allow users the option of displaying the items in a series either in volume number order or by main entry.

5. The default display of a single bibliographic record should include all bibliographic fields in the record—including 130, 240, and 490 fields; note fields; and tracings—and should be an unlabeled (with one exception; see number 8 below) so-called card format display. Ideally, it should be possible for a user to select any heading in the tracings and navigate from it to other bibliographic records with that heading.

6. All display constants called for by the USMARC formats should be employed.

7. Fields should display in the order set by the cataloger, not in field number order.

8. The display of a single bibliographic record for a serial could be helpfully labeled to distinguish between volumes published and volumes held by the library, because users are known to confuse the two.

When the User's Search Fails,
What Should the System Do Next?

First of all, let us remind ourselves of what failure means in an OPAC. Research on search failure has tended to concentrate on searches that retrieve zero hits. However, a zero-hit search is a successful search if the author or work sought by the user is not in the library. Also, a search that retrieves something can be a failed search if that something is the wrong thing. The only definition of failure a computer program can recognize is the zero-hit search. A computer program should not be designed to assume that a zero-hit search is a failure, for the reasons just enumerated. However, perhaps no harm would be done if the software provided the user with the option of asking it to LOOK HARDER.

For author searches, a LOOK HARDER command could search some of the fields in bibliographic records that are not under authority control.[5] This might also be a good point at which to implement some of the more radical word-stemming and synonym-matching algorithms described above. For example, title words in a failed title search could be searched in their plural form, if they were initially in singular form, or vice versa. The name-title searches recommended above don't deal with titles that may appear in contents notes.[6] A keyword match within all title and contents fields in a single bibliographic record might be a good LOOK HARDER search for a known-work search that fails. Also, users who cannot differentiate between author words and title words in their citations (a particular problem with works of corporate authorship) could benefit if the latter search did *not* require that the differentiation between author and title words be made. Another possibility might be to display all headings that matched at least one keyword in a user's search, a kind of fuzzy matching approach. If the within-hierarchically-related-group matching recommended above is too resource-intensive for the default search, it could be used only in LOOK HARDER searching. Another possibility might be to try placing the first term in the user's search next to the nearest match in an A to Z list of headings, allowing the user to explore the list up or down from there.

Options to Offer Power Users

1. Allow power users to bypass form fill-in screens and GUI interfaces and simply type in a command string for any available search.

2. For sophisticated users seeking particular works, it would be wise to offer the option of left-to-right match searches with truncation against the name authority file, and against a title heading file that includes all title fields, for cases in which the keyword search does not work well, e.g., when there are too many common words in the name or title sought.

3. Always offer a phrase index (title or author) as an option for power users who are confident that they know the entry terms of the headings they seek.

4. Allow power users to search for a work or works with two or more authors using the names of the two or more authors.

5. In catalogs in which relator terms have been consistently applied to name headings, allow users the option of displaying the works of a person or corporate body subarranged by relator term.

Notes

1. Carlyle has found that current systems that rely primarily on phrase indexing tend to collocate authors or titles better in online displays than do current systems that rely on keyword indexing (within-record keyword indexing, that is; within-heading keyword indexing as recommended in this book is rare in current systems); she did not study author-title searches, however. See Allyson Carlyle, "The Second Objective of the Catalog: A Performance Evaluation of Online Catalog Displays" (Ph.D. diss., UCLA, 1994).

2. In the USMARC bibliographic format, found in the delimiter b subfield in the 245 field.

3. In the USMARC bibliographic format, found in 4XX and 8XX fields.

4. In USMARC format terms, the main entry may be defined as main entry of the record retrieved: (1) The combination of 1XX and 2XX fields; i.e., 100 and 240, if present, otherwise 245; 110 and 240, if present, otherwise 245; or 111 and 240, if present, otherwise 245; (2) 130 (uniform title); (3) 245 alone, if the item has no 1XX field. Main entry for works related in some way to the record retrieved; (4) 6XX plus delimiter t, i.e., 600, 610, or 611, plus delimiter t; this would occur on the record for a work about the work sought; (5) 630; this would occur on the record for a work about the work sought if the latter were entered under title; (6) 7XX plus delimiter t, i.e., 700, 710, or 711, plus delimiter t; this would occur on the record for a work related to the work sought or on the record for a work containing the work sought, e.g., an anthology; (7) 730; this would occur on the record for a work related to or containing the work sought if the latter were entered under title.

5. In the USMARC bibliographic format, these might include the delimiter c subfield of the 245 field (for subsidiary authors not traced, for example); the 505 contents note field (which was recently subfielded to distinguish author names from titles as an optional practice, a practice that is rarely followed in libraries); and the 508 and 511 fields, which contain production and performance credits, many of which will not be authority controlled.

6. In the USMARC bibliographic format, 505 fields (which were recently subfielded to distinguish author names from titles as an optional practice, a practice that is rarely followed in libraries).

Demonstration of Relationships—Subjects

Subject access is another mechanism for demonstrating relationships between records in a database. In the case of subject access, the objective is to help users find works that are related to each other because they are on the same subject or on related subjects. Contrary to some reports, the Council on Library Resources (CLR) catalog-use studies did not demonstrate conclusively that subject searching predominates over other kinds of searching; for one thing, "author-subject," "title-subject," and "author-title-subject" searches were counted as subject searches, although many such searches were probably known-work searches done by users who knew the subject of the work sought.[1] Nevertheless, it is clear from CLR findings that subject searching is desired and used by our patrons and indeed can be useful for known-work searches as well as for pure subject searches.

In an ideal catalog, a single search would retrieve all the works on a particular subject and display them to the user in a meaningful way. To achieve this ideal result, the catalog designer must make decisions on file structure, indexing, and display. Effective file structure ensures that only one file (or one virtual file) must be searched, rather than two or more files, to be sure one has seen all the works on a particular subject.[2] Effective indexing ensures that a single search retrieves all the works on a particular subject, rather than several searches being necessary. Effective displays ensure that all the works on a particular subject display together and that relationships to works on other related subjects are made clear. All three elements—effective file structure, effective indexing, and effective displays—are necessary for a catalog to be useful.

Notes

1. Joseph R. Matthews, Gary S. Lawrence, and Douglas K. Ferguson, eds., *Using Online Catalogs: A Nationwide Survey: A Report of a Study Sponsored by* the Council on Library Resources (New York: Neal-Shuman, 1983), p. 146.

2. See chapter 4.

8

Demonstration of Relationships—Subjects—File Structure Decisions

The Nature of Subject Access

Online catalogs offer users subject access by three different means—controlled vocabulary, free text, and classification.

Controlled Vocabulary

A controlled vocabulary, such as Library of Congress Subject Headings (LCSH), used in most libraries, has the advantage of increasing both recall and precision for users. It increases recall in that it allows users to find everything on the subject in which they are interested, including works on narrower topics, works on broader topics that might contain chapters on the topic desired, and works on related topics. It increases precision to the degree that it allows users to get everything on the desired topic, even if a number of synonyms exist describing the topic; and, at the same time, it allows exclusion of material on other topics described using the same words (homonyms). A perfect example of the power of the controlled vocabulary is provided by Thomas Mann, who works as a reference librarian at the Library of Congress: a library user was looking for books on the diplomacy leading up to the Gulf War. The LCSH heading PERSIAN GULF WAR, 1991—DIPLOMATIC HISTORY retrieved ten books on the topic—six in English and the rest in French, German, and Indonesian. Only one of the ten books retrieved had the word *diplomacy* in the title, so, as Mann points out, these ten books "would have been scattered to the winds without vocabulary control."[1]

LCSH has been attacked in recent years for failing to match user vocabulary. However, when the research that is cited in attacking LCSH is looked at closely, it can be seen that the frequent failures of subject searches in online public access catalogs, rather than being due to failure of LCSH, are usually due to the following reasons: (1) typographical errors and misspellings; (2) the failure of the catalog to include the cross-references that form part of LCSH; (3) the inability of the user to learn to use a complex system; for example, the user makes a wrong choice of index or incorrectly formulates a search; (4) poor system design, for example, large retrievals that result in the display of bibliographic records rather than of headings; (a display of headings would allow the user to scan through the retrieval quickly); and (5) simple collection failure; in other words, the library does not contain a book on that subject.

Michael Berger points out that such research has focused on the failure of a single search, while in his research, which studied users of the MELVYL system, he discovered that a user whose search fails to retrieve anything frequently retries it another way with better results—this occurred in 36 percent of zero-result searches.[2] Among other things, his findings mean that users do observe the structure of the vocabulary and modify their results accordingly. The biggest problem Berger identified was that of suboptimal searches, in which the user finds something, but not everything, on the desired topic.[3] The MELVYL system displays bibliographic records rather than matched subject headings to the subject searcher, and it does not search the LCSH cross-references; one wonders if so many suboptimal searches would occur if users were shown the headings matched by each search in the context of the LCSH syndetic structure, which could alert them to broader, narrower, and related headings of interest.

Figure 8.1 summarizes the previous research on LCSH effectiveness. It can be seen from figure 8.1 that the systems with the highest failure rates tended to be phrase-indexed systems, which require the user to know the order of the terms in a multiterm LCSH heading, as well as systems that display bibliographic records rather than headings in response to a subject search. One study found that, once searches with problems with typos, misspellings, collection failure, system errors, and lack of LCSH syndetic structure in the catalog are removed from the data, only 2 percent of all topical subject queries studied use language that is not in LCSH.[4]

Free Text

When the user *is* having trouble finding the correct controlled vocabulary term to use for searching, more effective online public access catalog design can help. For years, librarians have practiced a good trick to overcome this difficulty: they know that you can search on title words, or retrieve a record for a particular work you already know to be on a particular subject, in order to view the subject headings on the record to find controlled vocabulary for the desired topic. Online public access catalogs offer the opportunity to show this trick to our users and guide them from free text terms in titles to the controlled vocabulary used in subject headings. (By *free text*, we mean uncontrolled terms found in transcribed and composed fields in bibliographic records.)

In catalog design, it is important, however, to keep the controlled vocabulary and the free text vocabulary distinct, so that the power of the controlled vocabulary is not lost. Results of free text searches should always include, as one option, the continuation of the search using controlled vocabulary. Some existing systems have attempted to design mechanisms to provide users with this controlled vocabulary option (see figure 8.2).

Much discussed in the last few years has been the desirability of adding more subject-rich fields to bibliographic records, including contents notes, tables of contents summaries, and in-depth indexing with multiple subject headings, as opposed to the current practice of attempting to find a single coextensive subject heading for the work cataloged. Such proposals would inevitably increase the cost of cataloging and seem incompatible with the current emphasis on cataloging simplification, that is, reduction of the time spent on cataloging in order to save money.

Study and system	Keyword (KW) or phrase (P)	Cross-references available	Display of headings (H) or bib (B)	Date of study	Number of subject searches that failed expressed as percentage
Alzofon and Van Pulis —LCS	P	No	?	1984	32%*
Ballard and Smith —INNOPAC	P	No	H	1992	25% Of these, 75% (or 19% of all searches) were because of failure to match LCSH.
Berger —MELVYL system	KW and P	No	B	1994	48%* (KW) 57%* (P)
Carlyle —ORION	KW	Not present but studied	H and B	1984	5%
Cherry —FELIX	KW	Not present but studied	?	1992	Not calculated
Drabenstott —Dewey Online	KW and P	No	?	1988	34%* (KW) 72%* (P)
Drabenstott and Vizine-Goetz —SULIRS	KW	?	?	1994 (i.e., 1989?)	31%*
Drabenstott and Vizine-Goetz —ORION	KW	No	H	1994 (i.e., 1989?)	39%*
Hunter —BIS	P	?	?	1991	52% Of these, only 29% (or 15% of all searches) were because of "use of uncontrolled vocabulary"; the rest were because of typos, system errors, etc.
Kern-Simirenko —SULIRS	KW	No	?	1983	46%*
Kern-Simirenko —MELVYL system	KW	No	B	1983	35%*
Kern-Simirenko —LUIS/NOTIS	P	No	H	1983	39%*
Larson —MELVYL system	KW	No	B	1986	49%*
Lester —LUIS/NOTIS	P	No	H	1986-1987	60%*
Markey (corrected by Carlyle) —SULIRS	KW	Not present but studied	?	1984	50%
Moore —?	?	No	?	1981	30%*

(Continued)

Figure 8.1   Research studies of LCSH performance

Study and system	Keyword (KW) or phrase (P)	Cross-references available	Display of headings (H) or bib (B)	Date of study	Number of subject searches that failed expressed as percentage
Peters —WLN	P	Searched separately	?	1989	52% Of these, 5% (or 3% of all searches) were because of inability to choose correct controlled vocabulary; 40% (or 21% of all searches) were not in database; and 20% (or 10% of all searches) were because of typos and misspellings.
Tolle —Scorpio	KW	?	?	1982	Not reported
Tolle —SULIRS	KW	No	?	1982	53%* (p. 107)
Tolle —Dallas	?	No	?	1982	Not reported
Tolle —OSU-LCS	P	No	H	1982	Not reported
Tolle —OCLC	P	Yes	B	1982	Not reported
Van Pulis and Ludy —LCS	P	Yes	H	1988	16% reported 18% not found when searches replicated
Vizine-Goetz and Drabenstott —SULIRS	KW	Yes	?	1989	76%*
Wilkes and Nelson —IRIS (Geac)	P	No	H	1995	59% Breakdown: 7% (or 4% of all searches) duplicates 6% (or 3% of all searches) misspellings 46% (or 24% of all searches) no match
Wilkes and Nelson —MARION (DRA)	P	Yes	H	1995	Not reported

Note: Figures as published sometimes had to be recalculated to represent them as the overall number of failed searches.

*Figures include failure due to misspellings, typos, collection failure, and system errors.

Full citations for user studies are found in the bibliography of user studies in appendix A.

Figure 8.1—Continued

Even from the point of view of user service, these additions should be approached with great caution, as the wholesale inclusion of terms from these supplementary sources is not necessarily desirable. The addition of contents notes and summaries to

The approach is described, and then, when possible, citations are given to literature that includes sample screens:

BLIS (Biblio-Techniques Library and Information System, WLN)

After a search has been done, the *Index terms option* displays a list of controlled vocabulary used in one or more records retrieved in the last search.

CAS (Minnesota State University)

When a subject search retrieves zero hits, the system suggests a *term search*. The term search searches a keyword index of both title and subject fields. While this is a good idea, the weakness is that the computer can only spot a failed search when no records are retrieved. There are many other ways for a subject search to fail and yet retrieve some records.

CITE (Computerized Information Transfer in English)
(National Library of Medicine)

A search of keywords in titles, subject headings, scope notes, and cross-references, using a stemming algorithm that, for example, matches *nephr-* with *kidney*, gathers a pool of subject headings and terms from free text or uncontrolled fields that are then presented to the user for relevance judgment and weighting.

> Tamas E. Doszkocs, "Automatic Vocabulary Mapping in Online Searching," *International Classification* 10 (1983): 78–83.
>
> Tamas E. Doszkocs, "CITE NLM: Natural-Language Searching in an Online Catalog," *Information Technology and Libraries* 2 (1983): 364–380.
>
> Tamas E. Doszkocs, "From Research to Application: The CITE Natural Language Information Retrieval System," in *Research and Development in Information Retrieval*, ed. Gerard Salton and Hans-Jochen Schneider, Lecture Notes in Computer Science Series, 146 (Berlin: Springer-Verlag, 1983).
>
> Tamas E. Doszkocs, "Implementing an Associative Search Interface in a Large Online Bibliographic Data Base Environment," in *New Trends in Documentation and Information: Proceedings*, ed. Peter J. Taylor (published by Aslib for FID, 1980), p. 295–297.
>
> Tamas E. Doszkocs and B. A. Rapp, "Searching MEDLINE in English: A Prototype User Interface with Neutral Language Query, Ranked Output, and Relevance Feedback," in *Information Choices and Policies*, ed. Roy D. Tally and Ronald R. Deultgen (published for ASIS by Knowledge Industry Pubs., 1979), p. 131–139.
>
> Tamas E. Doszkocs and John E. Ulmschneider, "A Practical Stemming Algorithm for Online Search Assistance," in *Proceedings*, National Online Meeting (1983), ed. Martha E. Williams and Thomas H. Hogan (Medford, N.J.: Learned Information, 1983), p. 93–106.
>
> Charles R. Hildreth, *Intelligent Interfaces and Retrieval Methods* (Washington, D.C.: Cataloging Distribution Service, Library of Congress, 1989), p. 78–79.

(Continued)

Figure 8.2   **Some examples of the methods used by existing systems to link user searches to controlled vocabulary**

ILLINET Online

When a subject search retrieves zero hits, the user is given a message that explains that the search is being done in several steps, and that she or he should press the enter key to continue. If the user presses the enter key, a keyword search of titles is done; retrieved records are then displayed in a brief display with the following message: "These items have your subject words in their titles; their headings will be useful in your search. Enter the number(s) of the items for which you would like to see headings. Enter 99 to see headings from all items, or press <ENTER> to return to the list of items.
Number(s): 99 __ __ __ __ __ __ __ ."

> Leslie Troutman, "The Online Public Access Catalog and Music Materials: Issues for System and Interface Design," *Advances in Online Public Access Catalogs* 1 (1992): 3–35.

JOSIAH (Brown University)

When a subject search retrieves zero hits, a keyword search of titles is done automatically, and the user is asked if he or she wants to see the retrieved records to find subject headings.

> Walt Crawford, *The Online Catalog Book: Essays and Examples* (Boston: G. K. Hall, 1992), p. 332.

LCS/WLN (Library Control System/Washington Library Network)

If a user's subject search fails to find an exact match, LCS/WLN displays subject headings closest in the alphabet, with a message asking the user to press the enter key if the headings are not satisfactory. If the user presses the enter key, the search is redone as a title keyword search, and the user is asked to pick out relevant records. The first subject heading on a relevant record can be searched, if the user desires; any other subject headings on a record must be reinput.

> Crawford, *Online*, p. 309.
>
> Hildreth, *Intelligent*, p. 85.

LIAS (Libraries Information Access System, Pennsylvania State)

The initial search is done on a dictionary file that includes titles, names, and subjects. A phrase search is done, and if it matches on more than one kind of phrase, the type is summarized. Note, though, the dependence on left-most match. This means that the user finds only those titles and subject headings that begin with the same word his or her search begins with.

MELVYL System (University of California)

In Lookup mode, the subject search at one time automatically searched keywords in both title and subject fields. This design confounded free text and controlled vocabulary, so that the user knowledgeable about the power of the controlled vocabulary was unable to use it because of the noise introduced by a search that automatically searched free text as well. The design was later changed so as to suggest a title search when a subject search fails.

Figure 8.2—Continued

OASIS

Offers users a command, SUMMARIZE SUBJECTS, that lists all subject headings in a retrieved set, ranked by decreasing frequency of occurrence; the fifteen most frequently occurring subjects are shown to the user for possible rekeying and further searching.

> Michael K. Buckland, Mark H. Butler, Barbara Norgard, et al., "OASIS: A Front-End for Prototyping Catalog Enhancements," *Library Hi-Tech* 10, no. 4 (1992): 12.

PaperChase (Beth Israel Hospital, Boston)

(Description based on article by Cochrane, which lacks screen displays)

User types *SLE*
Computer asks if user wants:
    authors
    journals
    subjects

User chooses *subjects*
Computer lists words beginning with *SLE:*
    1. SLE
    2. SLED
    3. SLEEK
    4. SLEEP

User selects 1. *SLE*
Computer says *SLE* is in 109 titles and that the following MeSH terms might be of interest:
    1. Lupus Erythematosus, Systemic
    2. DNA
    3. Anti-Nuclear Factors
    4. Arthritis, Rheumatoid
    5. Antigen-Antibody Complex

User selects 1.
> (Apparently the system is suggesting MeSH terms that are attached to the 109 records with SLE in the title, perhaps listing first those that occur most frequently.)

> R. I. Beckley and H. L. Bleich, "Paperchase: A Computer-Based Reprint Storage and Retrieval System," *Computers and Biomedical Research* 10 (1977): 423–430; Pauline Cochrane, "Friendly Catalog Forgives User Errors (Paperchase)," *American Libraries* 13 (1982): 303–306, 448, 576; Gary L. Horowitz and Howard L. Bleich, "Paperchase: A Computer Program to Search the Medical Literature," *New England Journal of Medicine* 305 (1981): 924–930.

Systems That Allow Users to Navigate

Once a single record has been retrieved, the access points (i.e., tracings) are displayed in menu form; any one may be selected in order to pull up all records with that subject heading. Among these are:

(Continued)

1. BLIS (Biblio-Techniques, WLN), described in Curtis W. Stucki, "BLIS: Biblio-Techniques Library and Information System," *Library Hi-Tech* 11 (1985): 73–84.

2. CARL (Colorado Alliance of Research Libraries) "Express Search," described in Crawford, *Online*, p. 165.

3. Dynix "Related Works Menu," described in Crawford, *Online*, p. 240.

4. ILLINET online music subsystem (K command keeps the headings on a particular record; F with line number redoes the search), described in Troutman, "Online Public Access Catalog," p. 25–29.

5. Marquis "Related Works," described in Crawford, *Online*, p. 375.

6. NLS (Network Library System) at the University of Wisconsin-Madison, described in Donna Senzig, *Network Library System Public Access Catalog* (Madison: University of Wisconsin-Madison Board of Regents, 1985); *NLS User's Guide* (Madison: University of Wisconsin-Madison Libraries, 1985).

7. TINman, described in Helen L. Henderson, "TINman: Information Made Easy," in *Online Public Access to Library Files: Proceedings of a Conference Held at the University of Bath, 3-5 Sept., 1984,* ed. Janet Kinsella (Oxford, Eng.: Elsevier International Bulletins, 1985), p. 183–185; Kathleen T. Bivins Noerr and Peter L. Noerr, "A Microcomputer System for Online Catalogues," in *Future of Online Catalogues,* ed. A. H. Helala and J. W. Weiss (Essen, Germany: Gesamthochschulbibliothek, 1986), p. 360–392; Peter L. Noerr and Kathleen T. Bivins Noerr, "Browse and Navigate: An Advance in Database Access Methods," *Information Processing and Management* 21 (1985): 205–213.

8. Unicorn (LIKE command), described in Crawford, *Online*, p. 479.

Figure 8.2—Continued

the free text (transcribed or composed) fields available for searching (the title is currently available in most systems) would add to the amount of noise or false drops retrieved on any given search. Such searching, which tends to be within-record rather than within-field searching, would produce displays of massive numbers of records that could not be displayed by headings matched, or subarranged into subcategories to facilitate scanning, and it would be very difficult for users to determine quickly why each was retrieved, because the terms causing retrieval could be buried deep in each record and scattered across multiple fields. More and more OPACs are offering adjacency searching, which could reduce the multiple-field problem, but such searching is complex and requires sophistication and knowledge on the part of the user. Default in-depth indexing would exacerbate problems users are already having with retrievals that are too large; these problems get worse as our databases get larger over time[5] (see figure 8.3).

Some propose using mechanical algorithms to try to put the "most relevant" documents first, but computers are not nearly as good as humans at such recognition work, and such algorithms produce baffling and sometimes even ridiculous results.[6] They are also frustrating for users who can't figure out the retrieved documents' order.

Current practice ensures that once the user identifies a controlled vocabulary subject heading on the desired topic, works retrieved using that subject heading will

Anderson, Reich, Wagner,
et al., p. 12

Berger, "Information-
Seeking"

p. 59, 119: The greatest proportion of long searches
in his sample occurred as title keyword searches
(13 long searches) and subject keyword searches
(9 long searches). This constituted 72% of
all long searches in all objectives.

p. 60–61: Keyword searches generate 92% of
long search conditions (note that on the
MELVYL system, the system studied by Berger,
these are keyword-within-record searches,
making a display of headings matched
impossible).

p. 121: Subject searches retrieved an average of
137 records per search, 302 records per search
objective (a search objective is made up of
multiple searches on a single subject).

p. 119: Subject searchers viewed more screens,
displayed more records, and spent more time
per objective (than other types of searchers).

p. 131: Subject searchers tend to "issue imprecise
searches with large results."

Drabenstott and Vizine-Goetz

p. 158: Initial access points retrieved an average
of 200 bibliographic records on SULIRS,
350 headings on ORION

p. 169: Topical exact matches retrieved an average
of 1,150 bibliographic records on SULIRS,
700 headings on ORION
All topical queries retrieved an average of
231 bibliographic records on SULIRS,
362 headings on ORION

Graham, p. 27

37% of single keyword searches on GEAC resulted
in 100 or more hits.

Kaske and Sanders, p. 40

Kern-Simirenko, p. 32

Lynch, p. 112

The average search on the MELVYL system
retrieved 118 records.

Markey, "Favorable
Experiences," p. 150

(Continued)

Figure 8.3   **User studies that have reported user problems with reducing results
of subject searches**

Martin, Wyman, and Madhok, p. 3	The average retrieval on the MELVYL system was 97–125 records per search.
Matthews, Lawrence, and Ferguson, p. 124	In the CLR study, 27% of users checked this problem, making it the 8th ranked.
Pease and Gouke, "Patterns of Use," p. 288	17% of those who had changed from online catalog use to card catalog use switched because they had retrieved too many hits online.

Full citations for user studies are found in the bibliography of user studies in appendix A.

Figure 8.3—Continued

be substantially about that topic. If in-depth indexing is used as a default, many more works will be retrieved, and these additional works are likely to have scanty amounts of material on the topic.

With these caveats in mind, however, additional access to free text terms could help users under certain circumstances—if the terms are kept separate from controlled vocabulary and used either as a lead-in to controlled vocabulary or as a backup for problematic searches.[7] If the free text terms could be selected by human editors, it could help to reduce noise, although it would also increase the amount of time spent on a record by a cataloger. Use of free text terms may be particularly helpful in narrow specialist libraries for which LCSH is too broad, especially in subject areas where the terminology is particularly specific and well controlled; the ideal in such libraries, however, would be use of a specialized thesaurus. In any system that does offer searching of free text fields, it is imperative that default displays display all indexed fields, or at least all the fields causing the retrieval of that particular record, so that the user can always tell why the record was retrieved; highlighting of matched text can be very helpful here.

One unsolved problem in OPAC design is that of designing terminology to convey to users the difference between a search of subject headings (controlled vocabulary) and a search of free text or natural language (transcribed and composed) fields. Even our technical language is muddy and is frequently used inaccurately or ambiguously; see, for example, the quite different meanings for the term *keyword* discussed in chapter 3. Because so many users' searches do seem to match our controlled vocabulary, and because it is so difficult to convey explicitly to users the differences between the two types of searches, we would like to reiterate our suggestion that it is better to do a controlled vocabulary search as the default, and use free text searching when that fails.

Classification

The third kind of subject access that can be offered by online public access catalogs is classified or hierarchical access (subjects by category rather than by alphabet), provided by either the syndetic structure of LCSH (referring users to broader and narrower and related terms) or by classification numbers. Micheline Hancock-Beaulieu has shown that it is very common for users to move from broad concepts to narrow concepts or from narrow concepts to broad concepts in the process of expressing a topic, searching a catalog, modifying the catalog search, examining titles at the shelf, and selecting titles.[8] OPAC users interviewed by Debra Johnson and Lynn Connaway had noticed that their first searches tended to be too broad and specifically requested hierarchical displays of LCSH to aid them with this problem.[9] They also asked for a feature to help them browse the shelves (i.e., the shelf list) online.[10] Drabenstott and Vizine-Goetz observed a user, for example, whose initial search for the painter Magritte failed (due to a misspelling) and who next tried a search under SURREALIST ART-IST.[11] It would be wise for online catalog designers to *assume* that a user's initial search is likely to be broader or narrower than the category of material that the user is actually seeking (see figure 8.4).

Unfortunately, catalog users have always had significant problems in finding ways to broaden or narrow searches. Very few online public access catalogs have incorporated effectively either the syndetic structure of LCSH or the structure of classification schemes to allow users to browse up and down the hierarchical relationships, which, because they aren't being displayed to users, are thereby concealed in our subject heading and classification systems. Of course, revealing the structure of classification numbers requires developing human-readable translations of classification numbers, so that the numbers have meaning for library users.

Several subject heading systems, including Medical Subject Headings (MeSH) and Art and Architecture Thesaurus (AAT), have numerical notation that could be utilized to allow users to expand or contract searches. For example, one could imagine a user who has found a relevant MeSH heading being allowed to type in the command EXPAND or EXPLODE and thereby to retrieve all records with the heading found, as well as those that have narrower headings under that heading; this is currently possible in Medline. Hierarchical relationships in LCSH are being edited, so that broader and narrower heading relationships are more accurate than they have been in the past; once the editing has been completed, the same power could be offered to LCSH users.

Bates, "System Meets User," p. 370	35% of searches were too broad. 19% of searches were too narrow.
Knapp, p. 222	31% of subject search failures were due to the search being too broad.
Lilley, p. 42	93% of subject search failures involved incorrect specificity; of these, 65% were too broad. 35% were too narrow.
Markey, "Online," 1987, p. 42–43	A number of users expressed a need to see a list of terms related to the ones used initially. 37% of patron-entered terms were more general than their expressed topic. 13% were more specific.

Full citations for user studies are found in the bibliography of user studies in appendix A.

Figure 8.4   **Evidence that a user's initial search is likely to be broader or narrower than the category of material that the user is actually seeking**

In Mann's opinion, based on much experience at the reference desk at the Library of Congress, users often assume that the term they are searching includes all narrower topics under it, although currently that is an erroneous assumption.[12]

Classification numbers also offer opportunities for letting users narrow and expand searches within particular disciplines (see figure 8.5).

A fundamental principle of current subject cataloging practice is that classification divides the world first by discipline, while subject headings divide the world first by topic. Thus, a user who is interested in a topic, such as water, regardless of discipline, would be best served by an LCSH search. However, a user who wants to see only works on water that are written for hydraulic engineers, for example—a user for whom other works on water are only so much noise—might be better served by doing a classification search initially, because in the LC or Dewey decimal classifications commonly used by libraries, works that take a hydraulic engineering point of view are gathered together before being organized by topic.

Bibliofile: lets the user looking at a particular item use arrow keys to BROWSE ADJOINING WORKS.

> Charles R. Hildreth, *Intelligent Interfaces and Retrieval Methods* (Washington, D.C.: Cataloging Distribution Service, Library of Congress, 1989), p. 60.

CARL, Catalog Plus, CL-CAT, IMPACT (Autographics), INLEX, INNOPAC, IO+, LS/2000, MacLAP, MARCIVE, NOTIS, PALS, plus, Resource Librarian, Unicorn: users who are able to type in a call number can browse the shelf list in call number order from that point in the file; display includes author (sometimes), title (often abbreviated), and date (sometimes).

> Walt Crawford, *The Online Catalog Book: Essays and Examples* (Boston: G. K. Hall, 1992), p. 166, 177, 191, 255, 291, 301, 315, 344, 353, 364, 403, 417, 439, 452, 490.

DORS: A prototype system was designed by Songqiao Liu and Elaine Svenonius. It is designed as a separate classification search and offers users the option of browsing either a schedule display or a chain index display.

> Songqiao Liu and Elaine Svenonius, "DORS: DDC Online Retrieval System," *Library Resources & Technical Services* 35 (1991): 359–376.

GRC: lets the user looking at a particular item use arrow keys to move to the right or left of that item on the shelf.

> Hildreth, *Intelligent*, p. 93–94.

INNOPAC: a command is available at a display of a particular record that shows *items nearby on the shelf*.

> Crawford, *Online*, p. 299.

TINlib: Hildreth is working on an experimental version of TINlib that allows users to navigate from the display of a particular item into the Library of Congress classification, which is displayed using both terms from the schedule and subject headings associated with records classed under the numbers displayed.

> Hildreth, *Intelligent*, p. 73.

Figure 8.5   **Ways in which some OPACs are already beginning to allow users some degree of access to the classification structure**

Use of current classification systems to provide user access does present some problems. Currently, clear and concise translations of classification notation into human-readable text do not exist; what does exist was designed for catalogers, not users, and is often too technical. This means that it is hard to design displays that can be readily scanned and comprehended by users. Prototype systems that provide access to classification numbers using free text, LCSH, chain indexes, and classification schedules can be very confusing to users, who are presented with many cryptic options for various kinds of searches.

Another problem arises from the fact that current practice is to give each book or other item just one classification number, even if the book spans several disciplines. Also, many books are given classification numbers based on shelving practice, rather than on the discipline covered (e.g., analytics); some materials may not be given classification numbers at all if they are not shelved by classification number (e.g., items in remote storage stored by bar-code number). The situation would improve if cataloging practice changed to support true classed catalogs, in which interdisciplinary works may be given several classification numbers and in which classification is seen as a form of subject access, not a mere locating device.

Finally, the fact that classification practice may have changed over time may cause problems. Books in existing libraries may have both old and new forms of numbers, leading to a scatter of works on the same topic in the same discipline.

There are problems other than those due to current classification practice. Users do not always understand the concepts of broader or narrower terms, nor have they always realized that the cross-reference structure and the classification notation structure could be used to broaden or narrow searches. There is some evidence that users find classification schemes more difficult to understand and use than alphabetical lists.[13] Concepts such as *broader* versus *narrower* can be very difficult to impart to casual users of an online catalog; the vocabulary we use to discuss such concepts will be unfamiliar to most catalog users, although many of them may be able to observe such relationships without having a vocabulary to refer to them. Heretofore, we have been dependent on mechanisms such as *see also* references and numerical classification systems to record relationships such as that between a broader and a narrower term. It is probable that these mechanisms have not communicated these relationships very well in the past. Perhaps future systems should always offer the user the option of either the particular level of specificity selected *or* everything narrower as well. One way current catalogs could approach this function is to display the broader and narrower term relationships already identified in current lists, with selectable line numbers, and ensure that headings with their *see* and *see also* references are the default display for subject searchers.

On the bright side, classification has the advantage of being discipline-based for users who are oriented that way; only works on a topic that are written from the perspective of a particular discipline are grouped together; works on that topic done from the point of view of another discipline are elsewhere in the classification. Classification also has an advantage over topical subject heading access in that the arrangement of concepts is based purely on their subject relationships rather than on the alphabet. This causes related topics in a discipline to group together, rather than to scatter throughout the alphabet. And finally, the broader/narrower relationships in existing classification schemes are usually much better maintained than in subject heading lists such as LCSH, which tends to be more haphazard in demonstrating broader-narrower term relationships.[14]

Note that a system should never assume a one-to-one link between a subject heading and a classification number. Subject headings express topic first, while classification numbers express discipline first. Because a topic can be treated in more than one discipline, a single subject heading can legitimately be classed in several different classification numbers based on the primary disciplinary focus of the work cataloged. Drabenstott gives several examples of topical subject searches that retrieve bibliographic records with 30 to 100 different classification numbers.[15]

If the shelf list could be browsed in classification number order, with human-readable text to explain the meaning of the classification numbers, users could start at a relevant record, either a bibliographic record or a subject heading authority record (linked to classification numbers), and browse about in the classification looking for works on topics broader and narrower than the one found. Compression of classification numbers, so that broad classes can be seen together on the screen, could facilitate choice for the user.

Online systems offer us unparalleled opportunities to enable users to tap the power inherent in the structures we have built into our subject access systems. The hierarchical structures of our subject heading lists, such as LCSH and MeSH, and of our classification schemes may provide a way to guide users toward works on broader or narrower topics by means of online suggestion screens or menus,[16] by means of maps of subject relationships,[17] by means of travel on a map or a time line, or by means of EXPLODE commands such as those available on MEDLINE and other abstracting and indexing (A&I) services.[18] Stephen Walker has experimented with the use of the Dewey decimal classification to show users works related to those they have already judged relevant.[19] Geller and Lesk report on a user study of a system that features hierarchical menus of Dewey classification numbers and that allows a user to move from a subject heading to the classification menu at that spot with a single letter command.[20] HYPERCATalog is planned to incorporate links and relations between fields, records, and files and to provide access to classification systems and thesauri in the form of maps.[21] We need to develop software that allows the user to discover the relationships among subjects without having to predict them ahead of time and that as much as possible explains by example, rather than requiring the user to use or understand unfamiliar bibliographic vocabulary. We need to ensure that users always know where they are, how they got there, how to get back, and how to move up, down, and sideways in the hierarchy.

CARL's Everybody's Catalog uses the call numbers and other location devices in a catalog record to show a user where a desired book is located in the library on a graphic library map. Such a feature was specifically requested by OPAC users interviewed by Johnson and Connaway.[22] This could be a very useful feature to help make our collections less bewildering for users, especially in libraries that maintain more than one sequence of classification numbers—for example, in the reference department, in the serials section, in the children's section, and in the stacks.

Now that we have examined the nature of subject access, we are ready to ask what the implications are for the design of OPACs.

Relationship between the Authority File and the Bibliographic File

The power of the cross-reference structure itself to lead users from their terminology to the terminology used in the catalog should not be forgotten[23] (see figure 8.6). A shockingly small number of online public access catalogs offer their users access to the

Drabenstott and Vizine-Goetz (p. 59) found that 19% of exact match topical searches (constituting 9% of all queries studied) hit cross-references and 2% hit complex *see* references; for some reason, partial matches were not compared to *see* references (or, if they were, the results were not reported).

Frost (p. 179) examined the proportion of assigned subject headings on cataloged items that match words in the title and found

    11% exact match on complete heading
    12% exact match on heading minus subdivision
    30% keyword match
    14% partial match; of those,
        27% singular/plural differences
        28% language/translation differences
        27% no match, i.e., no words from the title matched any part of the
        assigned subject headings

Jamieson, Dolan, and Declerck (p. 279) compared words on title pages with *see* references to all subject headings assigned to the item and found that 84.5% of references from nonpreferred forms would not retrieve the record on a keyword search.

Lester (p. 216) found matching on cross-references from left to right with truncation boosted users' success rates from 42% to 65%. She found also (p. 211) that 9.8% of all failed subject searches matched *see* references.

Roose (p. 77) points out that one of the major findings of Lester's failure analysis study was that matching against the LCSH syndetic structure boosts users' success rates from 40% to 74%.

Wilkes and Nelson (p. 75–76) took failed searches done on an OPAC without authority control (i.e., cross-references or syndetic structure displayed to the public) and redid them on an OPAC with authority control; they found that of the 46% of subject searches that failed on the system without authority control, 74% (or 34% of all searches) would have found material had the system included cross-references, reducing the total number of failed searches from 46% to 12%.

Full citations for user studies are found in the bibliography of user studies in appendix A.

Figure 8.6   **Studies of the usefulness of subject cross-references**

full cross-reference structure of LCSH. At the time the CLR study was done, none of the catalogs studied allowed users to search LCSH cross-references. Most of the user studies showing high rates of failure of subject searches have been on systems that lacked LCSH cross-references. No controlled vocabulary list can be fairly judged without its cross-reference structure; LCSH, especially, performs badly without its cross-reference structure, because the problem of obsolete terms is frequently dealt with by means of a *see* reference from the current term. For example, as of April 1997, *Blimps* is a *see* reference to *Airships*.

Subject authority records contain a wealth of other information as well, including related term *see also* references, *see also* references to broader and narrower terms, scope notes, and complex reference notes (see figure 8.7). De rigueur for effective subject access is a subject authority file linked to the bibliographic file, with full cross-reference structure that is searched on every subject search and with *see also* references and scope notes displayed for users; such a system is surprisingly hard to come by, although there are a few, such as LC Access (developed at the Library of Congress). In addition, it would be particularly useful for subject searching if the problem with limiting authority file searches by date, etc., described in chapter 4, could be solved. This would allow users to do an authority file search, so as to be sure of good precision and recall, and still indicate interest only in historical materials or only in current materials.

Linking subject headings to bibliographic records provides other benefits as well. In a sense, the full bibliographic records can serve as scope notes, telling the user something about what a particular heading means through descriptions of the books to which it has been assigned.

In creating the links between the authority file and the bibliographic file, the problem (discussed in chapter 3) of information stored partially in the authority record and partially in the bibliographic record should not be forgotten. For example, there is nothing in the authority record to enable a display that distinguishes between the works by a person and the works about a person—it is the 600 tag in the bibliographic record that distinguishes the works about from the works by. Also, allowing users to limit authority file searches by date or language will require drawing information from bibliographic records.

Relationships among the Classification File, the Authority File, and the Bibliographic File

Work is currently being done on converting both the Dewey decimal classification and the Library of Congress classification to machine-readable form using the new USMARC classification format. When these records are ready for use by system designers, it will require considerable thought and ingenuity to make effective use of them in OPACs. Effective system design will enable one-to-many and many-to-one links between classification records and bibliographic records and between classification records and authority records (both name and subject). One-to-many and many-to-one links are necessary because of the following conditions: (1) one topical subject heading (found either in a bibliographic record or in a subject authority record) can link to more than one classification number when the topic has been

Elementary schools
    SEARCH ALSO UNDER headings beginning with the words Elementary school

Figure 8.7   An example of a complex reference note

treated by several different disciplines; (2) one classification number (found either in a bibliographic record or in a classification record) can link to more than one subject heading, especially when the subject heading has been subdivided in LCSH; this is also true when several subject headings exist that are of greater specificity than the most specific classification number available; all of them will then link to the single broader classification number; (3) one classification number can link to more than one bibliographic record when several works have been written on that topic from that disciplinary point of view; and (4) one bibliographic record can link to more than one classification number when libraries have begun to create true classed catalogs, which allow classing an interdisciplinary topic in all relevant disciplines by assigning more than one classification number to a single book. (Currently, most libraries assign just one classification number, even when more than one would apply, because they use the classification as a mere location device.) Thus, the relationships among these files must be made simultaneously as complex and as seamless as possible in order to allow the user to move back and forth from bibliographic records to subject headings to the classification as easily as possible.

Names and Works as Subjects

Do you assume a person looking for books about Beethoven or WordPerfect or the FBI or the Rocky Mountains would do a subject search, or do you assume that the person would do an author or name or known-work search? It seems probable that users think of a *subject* as *something that books (or other materials) are about.* Therefore, it also seems probable that users are likely to choose to perform a *subject search* when they are interested in knowing *about* something but do not know, or are unable to remember, a specific work that they wish to consult. It is not our intent to engage here in a philosophical discussion on the concept of *about* but simply to point out that users should not be expected to specify, and perform different kinds of searches for, the various sorts of subjects that appear in catalogs. Specifically, a user should not be expected to determine in advance whether what she or he wishes to know about is considered to be a personal name (e.g., Beethoven), a title (e.g., WordPerfect), a corporate name (e.g., the FBI), a geographic area (e.g., the Rocky Mountains), or what librarians call a *topical* subject (e.g., butterflies).[24] Lester found that nearly 29 percent of subject queries contained personal, geographic, or corporate names.[25] Drabenstott and Vizine-Goetz found that 18.2 percent of subject queries consisted entirely of elements of corporate, geographic, or personal names and that an additional 7.3 percent contained elements of these names in combination with topical elements.[26] Karen Drabenstott and Marjorie Weller found that personal names accounted for 11 percent of subject searches and that 8 percent contained geographic elements.[27] These percentages may be even higher in certain disciplines: in a study of humanities scholars searching DIALOG databases, Marcia Bates, Deborah Wilde, and Susan Siegfried found that 39.9 percent of search terms input by these scholars were either personal or geographic names.[28] Michael Berger found that users were confused about where to search for works by an author versus works about an author.[29]

Although it is probably not wise to assume that everyone looking for books about Beethoven or WordPerfect or the FBI or the Rocky Mountains will choose to perform a name or title search, it may not be wise to assume that everyone will perform a subject search for such books either. Some users will choose one search and some will choose the other. Also, we must not forget the user who is looking for works by Beethoven but will check out a book about him when it is serendipitously discovered. Ideally, the person who is looking for books about Beethoven would also be alerted to works by Beethoven in the library, just as the user looking for books about Word-Perfect would be told if the library owned actual copies of the computer program.

The best solution may be to double-post names and works as subjects—that is, make them searchable in subject indexes as well as in name-title indexes. Unfortunately, many systems are currently designed in such a way that this is not possible; for example, a system that allows users to search a name authority file linked to bibliographic records, or a subject authority file linked to bibliographic records, may be constrained by the need to have each heading controlled by a single authority record that must reside either in the name authority file or in the subject authority file but not in both; because of this constraint, such a system may not be able to allow double-posting. Clever solutions to this problem could certainly make current systems more user-friendly to users who benefit from seeing names as subjects. Effective displays that differentiate works by an author from works about the author will only be possible if a solution is found for the problem (discussed in chapters 3 and 6) of neither the authority record nor the bibliographic record containing all of the information needed to support such displays. (See also chapter 10 for an example of the ideal display.)

Such solutions could also help with the problem of geographic/jurisdictional names. Some names are only geographic;[30] an example would be "Rocky Mountains." Other names may be either geographic or jurisdictional; in other words, the entity may act as a government and, as such, be a corporate author[31] as well as a geographic entity;[32] an example would be "France," which is both a government and a geographic area. Because most online systems have separate name and subject authority files, these geographic/jurisdictional entities pose the problem that they need to be controlled in both files, because the same name, "France," may be used sometimes as a subject, as in a work about traveling in France, and sometimes as an "author," as in the case of French government documents. Different systems have solved the problem in different ways, which means that searching for geographic/jurisdictional entities may be unpredictable for users. Again, double-posting might be the best solution.

Genre and Form Access

What happens to the person interested in folktales? Will that person think of his or her query as a subject search? Would that person understand if it were necessary to specify in advance whether he or she wished for books about folktales or books that actually contain folktales? Would he or she understand that a subject search might only retrieve those books that are about folktales? It seems probable that retrieving both works about folktales and the folktales themselves with a single search would be desirable for users of the catalog.[33]

We are not suggesting that no distinctions should be made among these sorts of subjects in the catalog record, for such distinctions can be very useful in indexing records and in providing instructive displays, but merely that the user initiating a subject search should not be expected to understand these distinctions at the outset of a search.

Subject Search as a Default

If your catalog is predominantly used for subject searching, it might be desirable to assume a subject search, in that there is one less specification for your users to learn to include in their searches. Some medical systems make this assumption, as do abstracting and indexing databases. However, it should be clearly explained to users that this assumption is being made, as well as how to do other kinds of searching.

Naming the File

We have been referring to a subject search and to the subject file. At first glance, the term *subject* may have seemed to be fairly clear and straightforward and likely to be familiar to users. However, it should now be clear that *subject* can include, as it currently does in LCSH in the USMARC formats, performing animals, such as Lassie; fictitious characters, such as Bugs Bunny and Sherlock Holmes;[34] personal, corporate, and geographic names; and even some of the forms and genres that people may consider to be subjects. (According to Leslie Troutman, the ILLINET online music subsystem calls its subject file TYPE OF MUSIC, not SUBJECT, because subject headings for music are much rarer than form headings for type of music.[35]) There probably is no good term that could convey to the user the fact that all of these kinds of concepts are being lumped together in the subject file in a general library, although possibilities that might be considered include *category, works about or examples of,* and *subject or type of work.* A general search in which an index need not be specified would be a big help for a user confused about which type of search to do. If a general search is offered, however, heading displays should be carefully labeled to distinguish between subject headings and titles (see figure 8.8, for example); otherwise, a subject searcher might think she or he has retrieved everything on a subject when she or he has merely retrieved a book with a title consisting of the original search term.[36]

The classification file, too, will be hard to name. Perhaps the phrases *classified by discipline* and *alphabetical by topic, form, genre, etc.* could be used to signal to users the differences between these two types of subject access.

Conclusion

Library catalogs offer users several different types of subject access: topical subject access, access by form or genre category, and access by academic discipline (classification). Users cannot be expected to grasp the differences among these types of access and select them explicitly. Instead, effective file structure must enable users to pass seamlessly from one type of subject access to another, changing their view of the catalog until they reach the one that seems most helpful at the moment. If all of our subject access schemes are failing, effective file structure must provide a way to lead the user from free text terms to controlled headings. If we can design more effective file structures, we can ensure that users find all the works available on the subjects they seek, in the forms or genres they seek, or with the disciplinary approach they seek.

(1)	Chaos (Christian theology)	(subject)
(2)	Chaos (Christian theology) in literature	(subject)
(3)	Chaos, Deterministic	
	SEARCH: Deterministic chaos	(subject)
(4)	Chaos (German weekly)	(title)
(5)	Chaos in systems	
	SEARCH: Chaotic behavior in systems	(subject)
(6)	Chaos, Quantum	
	SEARCH: Quantum chaos	(subject)
(7)	Chaos (Theology)	
	SEARCH: Chaos (Christian theology)	(subject)
(8)	Chaos theory	(title)
(9)	Chaos theory in psychology	(title)
(10)	Chaos (Weimar, Thuringia, Germany)	(title)
(11)	Chaos (Woodbury, N.Y.)	(title)
(12)	Chaotic behavior in systems	(subject)

The person interested in chaos theory might be warned by the above display that no subject heading or cross-reference takes that form (although it appears in several titles) and that the works sought are under the subject heading CHAOTIC BEHAVIOR IN SYSTEMS.

Figure 8.8   An example of a labeled display, result of a general search

Notes

1. Thomas Mann, E-mail message to authors, March 12, 1996.

2. Michael George Berger, "Information-Seeking in the Online Bibliographic System: An Exploratory Study" (Ph.D. diss., UC Berkeley, 1994), p. 49, 152, 154–155.

3. Ibid., p. 155.

4. Karen Markey Drabenstott and Diane Vizine-Goetz, *Using Subject Headings for Online Retrieval: Theory, Practice and Potential* (San Diego, Calif.: Academic Press, 1994), p. 168.

5. Nicholson Baker, "Discards," *New Yorker*, April 4, 1994, p. 68, 81–83.

6. A good deal of research in the field of information retrieval is on the design of optimal relevance ranking algorithms. On the INSPEC database (online database produced by the Institution of Electrical Engineers), in October 1996, for example, there were 114 articles indexed since 1995 under the heading "relevance feedback."

7. The following USMARC bibliographic format fields might be candidates for free text indexing:

Title fields: 130, 240, 242, 245 delimiter a, delimiter b, and delimiter p, 246, 247, 400 delimiter t, 410 delimiter t, 411 delimiter t, 440, 490, 600 delimiter t, 610 delimiter t, 611 delimiter t, 630, 700 delimiter t, 710 delimiter t, 711 delimiter t, 730, 740, 800 delimiter t, 810 delimiter t, 811 delimiter t, 830

Note fields: 505, 520

Corporate name fields: 110, 111, 410, 411, 610, 611, 710, 711, 810, 811

Note that corporate names can be a rich source of free text vocabulary, because corporate bodies are often formed to do work in particular subject areas and will have those subject areas in their names. Eventually, indexes to the classification schedules should also be rich sources of free text terms that could be used to link users up to the controlled subject access provided by classification.

8. Micheline Hancock-Beaulieu, "Evaluating the Impact of an Online Library Catalogue on Subject Searching Behaviour at the Catalogue and at the Shelves," *Journal of Documentation* 46 (Dec. 1990): 318–338.

9. Debra Wilcox Johnson and Lynn Silipigni Connaway, "Use of Online Catalogs: A Report of

Results of Focus Group Interviews," typescript (Feb. 1992), 11, 13, 15, 20, 22, 28.

10. Ibid., p. 12, 15, 20, 22, 28.

11. Drabenstott and Vizine-Goetz, *Using Subject Headings*, p. 134.

12. Thomas Mann, personal communication to Martha Yee, 1995.

13. Valerie Geller and Michael Lesk, "An On-line Library Catalog Offering Menu and Keyword User Interfaces," in *Proceedings of the 1983 National Online Meeting Sponsored by Online Review, 1983, Apr. 12–14, N.Y., N.Y.*, comp. Martha E. Williams and Thomas H. Hogan (Medford, N.J.: Learned Information, 1983), p. 159–165; Christine L. Borgman, Sandra G. Hirsh, Virginia A. Walter, et al., "Children's Searching Behavior on Browsing and Keyword Online Catalogs: The Science Library Catalog Project," *Journal of the American Society for Information Science* 46 (1995): 663–684.

14. Note that the advantages of classification apply equally well to materials that don't require a classification number as a location device, such as electronic documents accessible over the Internet and items shelved remotely by bar-code numbers.

15. Karen M. Drabenstott, "Classification to the Rescue—Handling the Problems of Too Many and Too Few Retrievals," in *Knowledge Organization and Change: Proceedings of the 4th International ISKO Conference, 15–18 July, 1996, Washington, D.C.*, Advances in Knowledge Organization, vol. 5, ed. Rebecca Green (Frankfurt am Main: Indeks Verlag, 1996), p. 378–385.

16. Geller and Lesk, "An On-line Library Catalog," p. 159–165.

17. Charles R. Hildreth, *Intelligent Interfaces and Retrieval Methods* (Washington, D.C.: Cataloging Distribution Service, Library of Congress, 1989), p. 95–99.

18. Thomas H. Martin, *A Feature Analysis of Interactive Retrieval Systems* (NTIS PB-235 952) (Stanford, Calif.: Institute for Communication Research, 1974), p. 52.

19. Described by Janet Kinsella and Philip Bryant, "Online Public Access Catalog Research in the United Kingdom: An Overview," *Library Trends* 35 (spring 1987): 626.

20. Geller and Lesk, "An On-line Library Catalog."

21. Roland Hjerppe, "HYPERCATalog and Three Meta-schemata for Database Views," in *Online Public Access to Library Files: Second National Conference,* ed. Janet Kinsella (Oxford, Eng.: Elsevier International Bulletins, 1986), p. 102, 109.

22. Johnson and Connaway, "Use of Online Catalogs," p. 19, 20.

23. Baker, "Discards," p. 84.

24. These different sorts of subjects should appear in the following USMARC bibliographic format subject fields: 600 (personal name); 630 (uniform title); 610 (corporate name); 655 (form and genre) used for actual examples of the form or genre; 651 delimiter a or 650 delimiter z (geographic name); 650 (topical heading).

25. Marilyn Ann Lester, "Coincidence of User Vocabulary and Library of Congress Subject Headings: Experiments to Improve Subject Access in Academic Library Online Catalogs" (Ph.D. diss., University of Illinois at Urbana-Champaign, 1989), p. 263.

26. Drabenstott and Visine-Goetz, *Using Subject Headings*, p. 159. In this study, one of the systems used to collect the data (UCLA's ORION system) requires a "name" search, rather than a "subject" search when searching for personal and corporate names as subjects, which probably resulted in a lower percentage of subject searches containing these names.

27. Karen M. Drabenstott and Marjorie S. Weller, "Handling Spelling Errors in Online Catalog Searches," *Library Resources & Technical Services* 40 (1996): 117.

28. Marcia J. Bates, Deborah N. Wilde, and Susan Siegfried, "An Analysis of Search Terminology Used by Humanities Scholars: The Getty Online Searching Project Report Number 1," *Library Quarterly* 63 (1993): 29.

29. Berger, "Information-Seeking, p. 157.

30. Geographic names are placed in the 651 field delimiter a subfields or 650 field delimiter z subfields in the USMARC bibliographic format.

31. Such "jurisdictional" corporate names appear in 110, 610, or 710 fields in the USMARC bibliographic format.

32. That is, appear in 651 field delimiter a subfields or 650 field delimiter z subfields in the USMARC bibliographic format.

33. It should be pointed out that although the USMARC bibliographic format provides different fields for works about a form or genre (i.e., 650) and works that are examples of a form or genre (i.e., 655, 650 delimiter v), many Library of Congress subject headings for form and genre have historically been coded as 650 or 650 delimiter x, even when applied to examples of a form or genre. Form and genre

headings for music are a good example of this practice. Efforts are currently underway to identify form/genre headings and subdivisions in LCSH and to provide for their being coded appropriately in bibliographic records.

34. Martha M. Yee and Raymond Soto, "User Problems with Access to Fictional Characters and Personal Names in Online Public Access Catalogs," *Information Technology and Libraries* 10 (March 1991): 3–13.

35. Leslie Troutman, "The Online Public Access Catalog and Music Materials: Issues for System and Interface Design," *Advances in Online Public Access Catalogs* 1 (1992): 25.

36. This has always been a pitfall for catalog users. For an extended discussion, see Seymour Lubetzky, "Titles: Fifth Column of the Catalog," *Library Quarterly* 11 (Oct. 1941): 412–430.

9

Demonstration of Relationships—Subjects— Indexing Decisions

In this chapter, we examine ways that effective indexing can improve the chances of success for a user who is looking for works on a particular subject. We make recommendations for a default subject search, and we examine ways that systems could compensate for common user errors and variations in subject expression. System designers should remember the latter in particular when designing default searches; there is no guarantee that a user's description of a subject is going to match the way the subject sought has been identified in the catalog. Thus, it behooves a system to be as flexible as possible in matching a user's search to the records it contains.

We discussed in chapter 3 the four types of indexing—keyword indexing, phrase indexing, search key indexing, and permuted indexing—and it has been noted that the choice of indexing type has a profound effect on the overall design of the system. For example, systems offering keyword access usually allow cross-field searching. When a search looks for keywords across several different fields or headings, it may be impossible to arrange the results by the heading matched if matched words come from different headings or fields within the same record. Thus, it can be very difficult to design effective displays of multiple records in keyword-indexed systems. This is even more crippling for subject searchers than for known-work searchers, because the main entry display of bibliographic records that is the usual display offered is frequently more helpful for the latter than the former. The user doing a subject search may have to look at many records in their entirety to find out why they were retrieved. Keyword-searchable systems often have inconvenient stop-lists that can cause the failure of such searches as those for VITAMIN A or UNITED STATES—HISTORY. On the other hand, phrase-indexing systems tend to assume that a search will match just one subject heading. If steps are not taken to get around this rigidity, a user looking for a subject that does not have a single coextensive subject heading, that instead is covered by a combination of headings, may easily wind up with a failed search without understanding why the failure occurred. Phrase-indexing systems also demand that the user know the beginning words in headings sought and can be intolerant of users who do not know the word order of a particular subject heading. In a subject heading system like the LCSH, in which phrases are sometimes inverted and sometimes not (inconsistently and unpredictably), requiring users to know ahead of time whether their subject heading is inverted can impose a real hardship on the user and cause many search failures.

Entry Terms and Order of Terms

Phrase or search key indexes require that the user know entry terms. Requiring this kind of knowledge of library users is a particularly unfortunate choice for subject access, because the user is even less likely to think of the exact subject heading we have assigned than she or he is likely to think of the form of surname we have used for an author or the beginning word of a title.[1] It should be noted that most of the user studies showing high rates of failure of subject searches have been phrase-indexing systems. Phrase-indexing and search key–indexing systems have tended to introduce keyword indexing to solve this problem.

On the other hand, if the user does know the entry term, perhaps because he or she was smart enough to determine the subject heading ahead of time, he or she should be allowed the option of using the more precise phrase search. In pure keyword systems, the user is not allowed to specify that a particular word should occur at the beginning of a field. Some systems that began as keyword access systems, such as the MELVYL system, have added exact searches, using phrase indexing, to allow users to specify that they want a particular string of words to occur at the beginning of a field.

Should the user be required to input an LC subject heading exactly from beginning to end? Search key–indexing systems or phrase-indexing systems without implicit truncation require that the user know the correct order of terms after the first. Such a requirement is particularly unfortunate for subject searchers, because they usually have no idea what the actual subject heading is. The subject heading the user needs may have a parenthetical qualifier or subdivision supplied by catalogers to disambiguate homonyms or subdivide a large file into smaller subcategories for easier scanning. Examples of such headings are POWER (SOCIAL SCIENCES), LONDON (ONT.), and UNITED STATES—HISTORY—CIVIL WAR, 1865-1869. Such additions were never intended to be specified by the user; they were designed to appear with the heading to any user interested in that heading to aid in decision making.[2]

Implicit truncation in phrase-searching systems can help with some problems but not with a search that begins with the wrong entry term. The best solution is to allow a keyword search of the subject headings, with a within-heading match, and an initial display of matched headings. Allyson Carlyle's study of matches between user-input subject searches and LCSH headings on a keyword-within-heading-searchable system showed that only 5 percent of searches resulted in no match.[3] Lester found that keyword searching of LCSH (including the syndetic structure) boosted user success rates from 40 percent to 72 percent and was the single most effective procedure for improving match success.[4]

On the other hand, the rare user who *does* know the correct order of terms should be allowed to use this knowledge to make the search more precise. In systems offering pure keyword access, the user is not allowed to specify order. Some systems that are basically keyword-indexing systems, such as the MELVYL system, have added exact searches, using phrase indexing, to allow users to specify order when known.

Default Subject Search

In this section we discuss the following issues: (1) should the default subject search be a search of the controlled vocabulary? (2) should the default search be a search of headings in authority records as well as in bibliographic records? and (3) what co-occurrence rules should keyword searches follow?

Controlled Vocabulary

We argued rather forcefully in chapters 3 and 8 that the default subject search should be a search of the controlled vocabulary and that free text searching should be used only as a backup if controlled vocabulary searching fails, and even then it should be used as a gateway to the controlled vocabulary.

Authority Records and Bibliographic Records

Note that if the default subject search is to make use of cross-references, then authority records must be included in that search. However, some parts of LC subject headings exist only in bibliographic records and do not occur in the subject authority records that comprise LCSH. These parts are known as free-floating subdivisions.

Catalogers have a large number of free-floating subdivisions available for appending to subject headings when applicable; some common examples of free-floating subdivisions are —HISTORY, —DESIGN AND CONSTRUCTION, and —FICTION. This practice frees catalogers to construct certain kinds of subject headings as they are needed, rather than forcing catalogers to wait for the Library of Congress to receive a book on that particular topic and only then create the subject heading. However, there is a trade-off for this freedom. Free-floating subdivisions don't have authority records of their own, and subject headings that consist of a main heading and one or more subdivisions usually appear only in bibliographic records.[5] Because free-floating subdivisions can represent important pieces of the user's search, e.g., —HISTORY or —BIBLIOGRAPHY, it would not be a good idea to limit a subject searcher's search to headings in the subject authority file, as these free-floating subdivisions would not necessarily appear in subject authority file headings, although they might well appear in relevant subject headings in bibliographic records. There are potentially an infinite number of headings that could be legally constructed, many of which would be nonsensical in practice so in fact would never be used; thus, it is not practical to consider having the computer construct authority records for all available combinations. This means the default search must search both subject headings in authority records and headings derived from bibliographic records.

Co-occurrence Rules

We recommended earlier in this chapter, in the section on entry terms and order of terms, that the default subject search be a keyword-within-heading search. In making decisions about co-occurrence rules, it is important to be aware of some conditions that obtain with subject headings.

First, catalogers make a separate authority record for each main heading and each established subdivision of the main heading (however, see above for a discussion of free-floating subdivisions, which lack authority records). For example, there is one authority record for the subject heading ONLINE CATALOGS, which has a *see* reference from OPACs. There is another authority record for the subject heading ONLINE CATALOGS—SUBJECT ACCESS. In all current OPACs, the following search would fail: OPACs SUBJECT ACCESS. This is the problem of the hierarchically related group that we discussed in chapters 3 and 5. Ideally, the system would consider cross-references applying to a given subject heading as also applying to any other headings that consist of the original heading plus one or more subdivisions.

Second, it is not uncommon for a subject sought by users not to have a single coextensive subject heading but instead to be covered by a combination of two or more headings (see figure 9.1). In chapter 3, we saw an example of a biography (of Hunter S. Thompson). There we noted that because the subject of the biography is in one field, and the form subdivision for biography is in another, anyone who wanted to limit a subject search on a person to biographies only would have to have a cross-field search available.

Because it is not uncommon for a subject sought by users not to have a single co-extensive subject heading, but instead to be covered by two or more headings, a search that looks for co-occurrence within all subject fields in a single bibliographic record should always be available (see figure 9.2). Searches requiring across-heading matches should also look at cross-references, however. Also, it can be seen from the research cited in figure 9.2 that such searches are definitely in the minority. Because a within-heading search allows a display of headings that the user can scan for further decision making, and because a within-heading search would serve the majority of users, it should probably be the default, with an across-heading search available as a backup.

Another useful backup searching algorithm might be one that searched each keyword separately and in combination, and displayed subject heading combinations and authority records retrieved, for a relevance decision in which more than one heading or group of headings can be retained for further searching. This could be conceived

---

The topic *rock paintings at the Painted Rock Site in California* is covered by the two subject headings ROCK PAINTINGS—CALIFORNIA—SAN LUIS OBISPO COUNTY and PAINTED ROCK SITE (CALIF.). Also, Lois Mai Chan gives the following example: the title *Methods of Conducting a Wind Tunnel Investigation of Lift in Roll at Supersonic Speeds of Sweptback Wings* must be given the following subject headings to cover all aspects of the topic:

1. Airplanes—Wings, Swept-back—Testing.
2. Lift (Aerodynamics)
3. Rolling (Aerodynamics)
4. Aerodynamics, Supersonic.
5. Wind tunnels.*

---

*Lois Mai Chan, *Library of Congress Subject Headings: Principles and Application* (Littleton, Colo.: Libraries Unlimited, 1978), p. 166.

Figure 9.1   Examples of sought subjects covered by more than one subject heading

Carlyle, "Matching," p. 44	21%
Drabenstott and Vizine-Goetz, p. 168	4% of all subject searches
Markey, 1984, refigured in Carlyle, 1989, p. 39–40, 52	11%
Markey, 1987, "Online," p. 38	8% of all searches (38% of zero-hit searches)
Markey, 1991, "Online," p. 69	Subject queries producing zero retrievals were highest for queries that combined elements.
Van Pulis and Ludy, p. 528	9%

Full citations for user studies are found in the bibliography of user studies in appendix A.

Figure 9.2   User studies that counted the number of times a user's search matched on more than one subject heading

of as a Boolean OR search; possibly it would be helpful to consider retrievals that have the highest number of matched keywords the most relevant and display them first (see figure 9.3).

What about authority records? What co-occurrence rules should be used there? It might be useful to try co-occurrence within the 1XX and 4XX blocks combined of the authority record. That might help users with variants on multiple-term headings (see figure 9.4). However, inclusion of the 5XX block (the *see also* references), which can be extensive, might lead to quite a bit of irrelevant retrieval in some cases and should probably be avoided.

Typographical Errors, Misspellings, and Variant Spellings and Forms

We discussed in chapter 5 the problems that users are having searching OPACs due to users' inability to type and spell (see figure 9.5). Lester found that 17 percent of author searches failed because of spelling errors and that spelling correction programs could have boosted user success in subject searching from 40 percent to 42 percent.[6] Methods devised to compensate for the problems of typos, misspellings, and spelling variants include truncation, displaying alphabetically close subject headings, menu-choice rather than typing, stemming algorithms, and synonym dictionaries.

Truncation

As noted in chapter 3, in systems offering phrase indexing, implicit truncation is commonly used. Should implicit truncation occur at a point determined by the

Consider the user who is looking for works about Precambrian paleontology in California. Unbeknownst to this user, the Library of Congress subject headings do not allow PALEONTOLOGY—PRECAMBRIAN to be subdivided geographically. Thus, the cataloger has to add two headings to cover both aspects of this topic on relevant books, one PALEONTOLOGY—PRECAMBRIAN, and the other PALEONTOLOGY—CALIFORNIA. If the Boolean OR search described in the text was done, it would retrieve the following:

92 headings in LCSH that contain the word *Paleontology*

27 headings in LCSH that contain the word *Precambrian*

The third aspect of this user's search, the *California* part, is trickier. —CALIFORNIA is a geographic subdivision, which can be added to any subject heading that can be subdivided geographically; in other words, it is a type of free-floating subdivision. On ORION, the UCLA Libraries' online information system, a keyword search on subject headings with *California* added to them retrieves 34,071 headings (on October 26, 1996). It would probably not be that helpful to display 34,071 headings to this user just because they include the word *California*.

So perhaps the most helpful display to give this user in response to a Boolean OR search would be the following:

The OPAC found the following headings that included two of your three search terms:

1. Paleontology—Precambrian

2. *SEARCH ALSO* Paleontology—Proterozoic

3. Paleontology—California

One item in the catalog contains both of the matching headings:

4. Albert, Stephen Paul, 1947- Trace fossils of the Precambrian-Cambrian succession, White-Inyo Mountains, California. 1974.

If you would like to see headings that included one of your three search terms, choose one or more of the following:

5. Paleontology (92 headings)

6. Precambrian (27 headings)

7. California (34,071 headings)

Figure 9.3 **Boolean OR search for the user whose search matches more than one subject heading**

system—for example, seven characters in—or should it occur wherever the user ceases to input? The latter gives the user more power. The former might be useful as a backup if the initial search fails. Explicit truncation, available in most systems offering keyword access, requires the user to diagnose the problem and is little used even when available.[7]

Consider the user who does a keyword search on ON-LINE PUBLIC ACCESS CATALOGS. The LCSH heading for this topic is ONLINE CATALOGS. The authority record for ONLINE CATALOGS has cross-references from ON-LINE CATALOGS and from ONLINE PUBLIC ACCESS CATALOGS. If a keyword-within-heading search on ON-LINE PUBLIC ACCESS CATALOGS is done, it will fail; but if a keyword-within-authority-record search is done, it will retrieve this authority record and direct the user to the used heading. A keyword-within-authority-record search on ON-LINE PUBLIC ACCESS CATALOGS would match on the keywords underlined below:

    150_0 ≠a Online catalogs
    450_0 ≠a Catalogs, On-line
    450_0 ≠a On-line catalogs
    450_0 ≠a Online public access catalogs
    450_0 ≠a OPACs
    550_0 ≠a Library catalogs ≠wg
    550_0 ≠a Online information services ≠wg

Figure 9.4   An example of a user who would be helped by a within-record keyword search
            of authority records

Carlyle, "Matching," p. 44	6% of all subject searches failed to match due to singular/plural matching failure. 2% of all subject searches failed due to suffix variation.
Drabenstott and Vizine-Goetz, p. 168, 175	3% of all topical subject searches failed due to typos or spelling errors. 4% of all topical subject searches failed due to problems with singulars and plurals.
Ferl and Millsap, p. 87	26% of subject searchers made from one to ten typographical errors per searching session.
Hunter, p. 400	6% of all subject searches failed due to typos. 1% of all subject searches failed due to spelling errors.
Jones, p. 8	6% of all subject searches failed due to typos and spelling errors. 6% of all subject searches failed due to spelling variance (American versus British spelling, hyphenation match failures, etc.).
Lester, p. 195	253 out of 1,518 subject searches, or 17% of author subject searches, contained spelling errors.
Markey, 1987, "Online," p. 38	6% of all subject searches failed due to typos and spelling errors.

Full citations for user studies are found in the bibliography of user studies in appendix A.

Figure 9.5   Error analysis user studies that address the question of how often users make
            typographical and spelling errors in subject searches

Alphabetically Close Subject Headings

When a search results in no hits, it might be helpful to display a list of alphabetically close subject headings derived from an authority file or index. Note, however, that if the user has input more than one term, one of the terms must be chosen to begin the display of alphabetically close subject headings. For this reason, this approach is probably most appropriate in a phrase-indexed system in which users have indicated the entry term they desire by typing it in first and in which they expect to match only a single field or heading. However, a more complex approach might work in either system: each term in a multiterm search could be taken in turn and shown to the user near other headings that begin with that term.

Menu-Choice Rather than Typing

Touch-screen and point-and-click systems have been extensively developed to try to allow the user to recognize the subject sought, rather than having to specify it ahead of time by typing a description, which can introduce many kinds of errors. Touch-screen and point-and-click systems are essentially menu-based systems, which, as we discussed in chapter 2, can be very slow and cumbersome but do have the advantage of requiring minimal typing and spelling skills of catalog users. In menus arranged alphabetically, users must know entry terms to succeed, but including cross-references (authority file records) can increase users' chances for success. Some systems are now offering a kind of classified menu-based access, e.g., icons representing broad subject areas that lead to narrower subjects when clicked upon. As discussed, because there are a limited number of choices you can offer on a single screen, these menu-based systems can be frustrating for the user whose subject doesn't clearly fall into one of the initial categories (or whose subject falls into more than one of the initial categories).

Stemming Algorithms

Stemming algorithms are discussed in detail in chapter 5. The fact that typographical errors and spelling errors happen relatively infrequently bolsters the argument for using stemming algorithms only in backup searches to avoid unnecessary noise and overly large retrievals on routine searches. Also sobering is the finding on one study of the Okapi experimental online public access catalog that of the 3 percent of subject search failures that were due to misspellings and typographical errors, only eight out of thirty could have been corrected using a stemming algorithm developed for Okapi.[8]

Synonym Dictionaries

Synonym dictionaries are discussed in detail in chapter 5.

Fuzzy Match

There is some evidence that novice users tend to type in too many terms in their subject searches; when some of the terms match but others don't, the search will fail in most current systems (see figure 9.6).

Graham (p. 27), investigating the use of keyword searching on the GEAC system, found the following: searches with 3 or more keywords resulted in 48% zero-hit searches. Searches with 2 keywords resulted in 35% zero-hit searches. Searches with 1 keyword resulted in 10% zero-hit searches.

Lester, p. 176, found that exact matches averaged the same length as nonmatches.

Drabenstott and Vizine-Goetz (p. 157) found the initial searches averaged 1.8 words.

Full citations for user studies are found in the bibliography of user studies in appendix A.

Figure 9.6   Problems because of too many terms in a subject search

Berger and Moore, p. 19:

    Search: AIDS AND living
    LCSH heading: AIDS (DISEASE)

Drabenstott, *Enhancing*, p. 51

    Search: gifted and talented education
    LCSH heading: GIFTED CHILDREN—EDUCATION

Drabenstott, *Enhancing*, p. 58

    Search: communication international aspects
    LCSH heading: COMMUNICATION, INTERNATIONAL

Full citations for user studies are found in the bibliography of user studies in appendix A.

Figure 9.7   Some actual failed subject searches that might have benefited from fuzzy matching

Fuzzy matching refers to various algorithms that look for a less-than-exact match with a user's search (see figure 9.7). A common approach is to match on some of the terms input in the user's search, but not all. One might also conceptualize such an approach as an implicit Boolean OR search. Perhaps it would be helpful to consider the headings that have the highest number of matched keywords to be likely to be the most relevant, and display them first. Because such an approach may increase the possibility of bringing up materials that are not relevant, it should be left to the user's discretion whether it is applied to any given search. For example, USCInfo gives users a form fill-in screen and then offers users, as one of several options, "Find at least one of the words above."[9] Despite the fact that precision may be lost, permitting users to request a fuzzy match might be of help when initial searches fail. A display that then listed first all subject headings with multiple-term matches and then all subject headings with single-term matches might help the user get back into the controlled vocabulary. An option to use two or more identified headings to perform a search would be highly desirable.

Some keyword-searchable systems give the postings for all terms searched, even on nonfuzzy match searches, so that users can see how many items each term would retrieve and which terms would retrieve materials and which would not.

Stop Words

Keyword systems frequently find it necessary to maintain *stop-lists* consisting of words such as articles and prepositions that are so common that a search using one of them overloads the system. These stop-lists can contain words, such as *United States*, that can be critical for the success of some searches.

If the user inputs a search using a stop word, the system should not reject the whole search but should simply ignore the stop word, conduct the search, and inform the user of the stop word(s) ignored. Ideally, a system should permit a search that consists entirely of stop words. Such a search capability would not necessarily require the indexing of all stop words. Some alternatives might be to (1) allow catalogers to designate headings that consist only of stop words, so that these only could be indexed; (2) index any heading that consists entirely of stop words; or (3) exclude subject headings from application of the stop word algorithm; in other words, put *United States* and *a* on the stop word list for free text searches but not for subject headings. One of these approaches might be better for the user anyway than indexing all stop words for the occasional search that needs them to be indexed: the user's search under the approaches described above would retrieve only a few hits instead of the massive number that would be retrieved on a comprehensive stop word search. We would even go so far as to recommend approach number three for subject headings, as we are fairly sure that prepositions are so rare that subject headings could safely be excluded from application of any stop-list.

Implicit Boolean Operators

Should we assume that a user always needs to have two terms ANDed rather than ORed? Many keyword-searchable systems make this assumption. It has the advantage of saving the user keystrokes (and possible typographic errors) in the course of typing in the explicit operators. It also protects the user from having to know how to use Boolean operators. Some systems assume an adjacency operator between two keywords without an explicit Boolean operator; for example, a search for FOSTER CARE would be taken to mean *foster* must occur next to *care*. This may be doing too much on the user's behalf without letting the user in on how the search is being defined.

If a given operator is implicit when two or more keywords are entered in a search, it might be desirable, when the results of the search are displayed, to make the implicit operator explicit and offer alternatives, e.g., FOSTER AND CARE; FOSTER ADJ CARE; or FOSTER OR CARE.

Keyword Searches That Limit the User to One Term

When phrase-indexed systems add on so-called keyword access, the keyword access can be somewhat restricted compared to the keyword access offered on systems that were originally designed for keyword access. Some phrase-indexed systems limit the user to a single keyword in a keyword search.[10] If possible, the user should be allowed to formulate searches using two or more keywords.

Allowing Users to Limit a Search to the Topic Desired as a Primary Topic

It has been a long-standing practice among catalogers to place first in the subject part of the record the subject heading that most nearly summarizes the overall subject of the work cataloged. Subsequent subject headings may then be added for topics partially covered by the work. This practice provides the potential for system designers to devise methods to allow the user who is overwhelmed by a large retrieval to ask to see only the works that are completely about the topic desired, excluding works that are peripherally about the topic desired. Note, however, that many systems display USMARC fields in tag number order, rather than in the order determined by the cataloger (which is the correct way to display fields). If your system does this, you lose the ability to identify primary topics. For example, a book about France (651) with a secondary topic of wine (650) would have the order of these fields reversed in a system that displays fields in tag number order. For libraries that use MeSH, the first indicator in the 650 field is set to value 2, meaning "primary topic," by the National Library of Medicine in its cataloging.

Providing a Textual Index to the Classification

A number of candidates are available for providing textual indexes to the classification numbers, so that users can begin with a topical subject term and use that to enter the classified arrangement in order to browse it. First of all, the classifications themselves have indexes, for example, the Dewey relative index. Unfortunately, the indexes suffer somewhat from having been designed primarily for the use of catalogers, rather than catalog users. The second possibility might be a keyword index of the terms used in the classification schedules themselves; however, these terms have the same problem—they were designed for the use of catalogers, not catalog users. Library of Congress Subject Headings (LCSH), on the other hand, were specifically designed for user access; and by occurring on bibliographic records with classification numbers, LCSH could serve as a de facto index to the classification, if properly utilized. LCSH has the advantage of being designed as a public access subject-indexing tool, and it places concepts into a rich context of related terms to allow the user to specify her or his topical interest as accurately and precisely as possible before beginning an exploration of the classification.

Conclusion

Effective indexing decisions allow for discrepancies between a user's vocabulary for a subject and that used in the library's catalog, as well as accommodating the user whose vocabulary *does* match that used in the library's catalog. In the next chapter, we discuss the design of effective displays to help users make sense of the ways in which libraries provide subject access to their collections.

Notes

1. Drabenstott and Vizine-Goetz report that of all queries, including those that mix proper names and subjects, 25 percent match exactly, left to right, with no subdivisions, and 18 percent more match when order is not important. They also report that when only topical queries are studied, a mere .1 percent vary in word order; however, it may be that they have already weeded out those that match inverted cross-references; it may also be that the headings that would match if word order were not reported have already been counted as partial matches. See Karen Markey Drabenstott and Diane Vizine-Goetz, *Using Subject Headings for Online Retrieval: Theory, Practice and Potential* (San Diego, Calif.: Academic Press, 1994), p. 152.

2. Drabenstott and Vizine-Goetz (ibid., p. 166, 188, and 218) found that 9.9 percent of geographic queries and 3.8 percent of topical queries were partial matches due to the absence in the search of a qualifier present in the heading.

3. Allyson Carlyle, "Matching LCSH and User Vocabulary in the Library Catalog," *Cataloging & Classification Quarterly* 10, no. 1/2 (1989): 37–63.

4. Marilyn Ann Lester, "Coincidence of User Vocabulary and Library of Congress Subject Headings: Experiments to Improve Subject Access in Academic Library Online Catalogs" (Ph.D. diss., University of Illinois at Urbana-Champaign, 1989), p. 204, 267.

5. Free-floating subdivisions can occasionally be found attached to main headings in the authority file when it has been necessary to put them there to support cross-references; however, there are no authority records for the free-floating subdivisions by themselves except for those that happen also to function as main headings.

6. Lester, p. 194–195, 235.

7. This assertion is based on the findings of several researchers that many OPAC users resist learning very many different searching commands. See, for example, Thomas H. Martin, John C. Wyman, and Kumud Madhok, *Feedback and Exploratory Mechanisms for Assisting Library Staff [to] Improve Online Catalog Searching* (Washington, D.C.: Council on Library Resources, 1983), p. 3; Dorothy McPherson, "How the MELVYL Catalog Is Used: A Statistical Overview," *DLA Bulletin* 5, no. 2 (Aug. 1985): 17; John E. Tolle, *Current Utilization of Online Catalogs: Transaction Log Analysis* (Dublin, Ohio: OCLC, 1983), p. 108.

8. Drabenstott and Vizine-Goetz, *Using Subject Headings*, p. 176.

9. Walt Crawford, *The Online Catalog Book: Essays and Examples* (Boston: G. K. Hall, 1992), p. 497.

10. Stephen Walker and Richard M. Jones, *Improving Subject Retrieval in Online Catalogues. 1, Stemming, Automatic Spelling Correction and Cross-Reference Tables* (London: British Library, 1987), p. 12.

10

Demonstration of
Relationships—Subjects—
Display Decisions

In making display decisions, the catalog designer should assume multiple-record retrievals as the norm. Remember (from chapter 3) that one subject may be completely represented only by a group of authority records, including authority records that include various subject subdivisions.

Ineffective displays can render useless all of the expensive work done by catalogers and system designers to demonstrate relationships in the catalog. If two records representing works on the same subject are buried screens apart in an incoherent display, the relationship between them is not being demonstrated to the user. If the subject the user seeks is thirteen screens away from where the user expects to find it, it has been effectively lost; and the library might just as well not have purchased the material in the first place, because few will be able to find it to use it.

A number of user studies have noted that users of online public access catalogs frequently encounter long displays and have trouble scanning through them. (See figure 10.1.) One only has to consider the size of the files under UNITED STATES—HISTORY to realize why this might be so. One of Nicholson Baker's complaints is about the inability to scan through large retrievals quickly the way one could in the card catalog.[1] These findings and observations should *not* be used to justify showing users only *some* of a large retrieval, however, for there is evidence that *precision* (retrieval of all records on the desired subject and no records that are irrelevant) is more important to users than retrieval size.[2] Also, recent research by Brendan Wyly suggests that "the willingness to obtain location information for varying retrieval set sizes suggests that searchers were not immediately defeated by information overload problems as we might have expected."[3] Instead, better displays of large retrievals are needed. Effective display of the headings matched in a user's search can allow the user to pinpoint desired records with greater precision.

Display commands have added a layer of complexity to catalog searching that was completely absent in the card catalog, in which the user could flip cards or walk to another drawer in order to move about. It is frustrating for users now to have to learn how to tell a computer to move about on one's behalf. For example, Beverly Janosky, Philip Smith, and Charles Hildreth found that five out of twenty-eight subjects given

Anderson, Reich, Wagner, et al. p. 12.

Berger, "Information-Seeking," pp. 60–61:

> Keyword searches generate 92% of long search conditions (note that on the MELVYL system, the system studied by Berger, these are keyword-within-record searches, making a heading display impossible).
> p. 119:
> 72% of all the long searches on the MELVYL system were subject searches.

Drabenstott and Vizine-Goetz, p. 158:

> Initial access points retrieved an average of
> 200 bibliographic records on SULIRS
> 350 headings on ORION

Graham, p. 27:

> 37% of single keyword searches on GEAC resulted in 100 or more hits.

Johnson and Connaway, p. 8:

> OPAC (NLS, University of Wisconsin) users interviewed by Johnson and Connaway complained that subject searching often retrieved a large number of records and asked for better display algorithms to allow scanning through the retrieved records.

Kaske and Sanders, p. 40.

Kern-Simirenko, p. 32.

Lynch, p. 112:

> The average search on the MELVYL system retrieves 118 records.

Martin, Wyman, and Madhok, p. 3.

Matthews, Lawrence, and Ferguson, p. 124:

> In the CLR study, 27% of users checked this problem, making it the 8th ranked.

Pease and Gouke, "Patterns of Use," p. 288:

> 17% of those who had changed from online catalog use to card catalog use switched because they had retrieved too many hits online.

Van Pulis and Ludy, p. 529:

> For 90% of user-input subject headings matched in the LCS system, there were additional headings with further subdivisions on LCS.

Wiberley, Daugherty, and Danowski, p. 258:

> 26% of questionnaire respondents reported experiencing postings overload on LUIS (both subject and known-work searching, and including keyword-within-record searches).

Figure 10.1   **User studies that have reported user problems with reducing results of subject searches**

Wyly, p. 229:

> Subject searchers on MILO retrieved an average of 92 hits (probably bibliographic records, rather than headings, but this is not completely clear).
> Authority/subject searchers on MILO retrieved an average of 67 hits (probably authority records for subject headings, but this is not completely clear).

Note: Research that did not distinguish between author/work and subject searching is included here as well.

Full citations for user studies are found in the bibliography of user studies in appendix A.

an assigned author search failed to complete it successfully because of failure to master display commands.[4] Display commands should be carefully designed to be as simple and intuitive as possible; for example, use of the enter key for moving forward in a list seems fairly easy to remember. Make sure that the user can move backward or forward in a list and up and down in a hierarchy at any time. Make sure it is possible to jump many records or headings forward and backward, if so desired. There is nothing more frustrating than viewing a large retrieval in a system that allows you to view just one record at a time. Never require the user to return to the summary display in order to move on to the next record. Whenever possible, assign permanent unique line numbers and allow their use from anywhere.

Display and Arrangement of Multiple Headings

Need for Headings Displays

If a search retrieves records following co-occurrence rules that require a match within a single heading or authority record, and if more than one different heading matches the search or if a heading matched has subdivisions, the optimal default display would be by headings matched. Baker was probably referring to systems such as the MELVYL system, which displays bibliographic records not headings, when he wrote, "Card catalogues have the sense not to shuffle together alphabetically the myriad subheadings for 'labor' in the medical sense and 'labor' in the A.F.L.-C.I.O. sense; the on-line catalogues I've seen don't."[5] Compare the displays of results on a keyword search on PARIS in a collection of newsreels, shown in figure 10.2. Notice how display of the headings matched allows the user to make decisions about narrowing a search and to reject less-interesting topics or false drops. Now consider the display that could result from a keyword-within-heading search for WILLS (see figure 10.3). As can be observed from the example in figure 10.3, display of the headings matched also allows the user to see a kind of summary of the works retrieved and make decisions based on format, period of coverage, and other factors that may not have been specified in the initial search.

Another advantage to displaying headings is that the headings themselves provide the user with a context in which to interpret the various ways in which his or her input keywords have in fact been used in the catalog. The value as context of our

Subject headings matched with a keyword search:

Arc de Triomphe de l'Etoile (Paris, France)
Bands (Music)--France--Paris
Bicycle racing--France--Paris
Birds--France--Paris
Boxing--France--Paris--Matches
Carnival--France--Paris
Children's zoos--France--Paris
Concerts--France--Paris
Demonstrations--France--Paris

Bibliographic records matched with a keyword search on subject heading fields:

[Les Copains--students in Paris. Hearst vault material, HVMc5762r9A, D65497].
   [ca. 1963]
Die Deutsche Wochenschau. [Nr. 543]. [1941-02]
Hearst Metrotone news. [Vol. 1, no. 216]. [1929-11-23]
Hearst Metrotone news. [Vol. 1, no. 254]. [1930-04-09]
Hearst Metrotone news. [Vol. 1, no. 255]. [1930-04-09]
Hearst Metrotone news. [Vol. 3, no. 221]. [1931-12-09]
Hearst Metrotone news. [Vol. 3, no. 274]. [1932-06-11]
[Humez wins over Langlois! Hearst vault material, HVMc3941r7 D32092]. [1955-
   03-02]
[A new craze dance--the Monkiss. Hearst vault material, HVMc6178r4, D78560].
   [1965-12-20]
News of the day. [Vol. 23, no. 209--excerpt. International boxing! Paris, France].
   [1951-09-27]
UfA. Nr. 572. [ca. 1942-08]

Figure 10.2   Displays of results on a keyword search on PARIS in a collection of newsreels

precoordinated subject headings in systems such as LCSH and MeSH is often over-
looked by writers in our field. As Derek Austin points out, precoordination can express the relationship between two keywords;[6] for example, the concept *Television and
children* can be distinguished from the concept *Television programs for children*, because
our subject headings precoordinate the two concepts *television* and *children* in at least
two different ways.[7]

Michael Berger, in his study of MELVYL system users, found that topical subject
searches had the greatest number of long searches (72 percent of all long searches in
all search objectives), that topical subject searches had the highest error rate (56
percent errors per objective), and that topical subject searchers viewed more screens,
displayed more records, and spent more time per objective than known work searchers.[8] However, when one analyzes the types of searches that these users were doing,
one can see that the vast majority of the searches done were keyword-within-record
searches, which result in an immediate display of bibliographic records rather than a
heading display. Only 5 percent used the exact subject search, which results in a
heading display on the MELVYL system,[9] and even the heading display lacks the

Indians of North America--Wills.
Nahuas--Wills.
Wills.
Wills--California.
Wills--California--Handbooks, manuals, etc.
Wills--Cases.
Wills--Forms.
Wills--History.
Wills--North Carolina.
Wills--Scotland.
Wills--United States.
Wills--United States--Bibliography.
Wills--United States--Handbooks, manuals, etc.
Wills--United States--History.
Wills--United States--Popular works.

Figure 10.3 Display that could result from a keyword-within-heading search for WILLS

LCSH syndetic structure. One can't help but wonder if these users would have been able to search more successfully and more quickly if the default display had been a headings display, including the full LCSH syndetic structure. In a transaction log study of OPAC users, Wyly noted that "subject searching and authority-based subject searching do not seem to have been as prone to the information overload problem as were title keyword searching, author searching, and subject searches converted to title keyword searches."[10]

When extremely large numbers of headings are retrieved, such that hundreds of screens are necessary to display them, it might be useful to provide the user with a kind of table of contents for the retrieval. For example, NLS allows users to request a "guide display," which divides the retrieval into twenty alphabetical sections.[11]

Arrangement of Headings

A useful document to help in making decisions about the arrangement of multiple subject headings in an online public access catalog is *Headings for Tomorrow: Public Access Display of Subject Headings*.[12] It shows many display examples that contrast the results of following a strict alphabetical approach similar to that taken by most current OPACs and a structured approach that groups together items on the same subject more effectively.

If the headings matched have parenthetical qualifiers or subject subdivisions, the principle of filing elements discussed in chapter 6 can produce an elegant and useful display (see figure 10.4). The example in figure 10.4 using filing elements does not require users to know about additions to headings made by catalogers in order to subdivide large files, to disambiguate terms, and to make displays easier to scan. If the principle of filing elements is not followed, the user must know about these additions in order to find the headings in what can be multiple-screen displays. If filing elements are observed, the political scientist who is looking in the catalog for works about power will be reminded that engineers and theologians also use this term and

Display using filing elements:

Power (Mechanics)
Power (Mechanics)--Addresses, essays, lectures.
Power (Mechanics)--Statistics.
Power (Philosophy)
Power (Philosophy)--History.
Power (Social sciences)
Power lawn mowers.
Power of attorney.
Power presses.

Display not using filing elements:

Power lawn mowers.
Power (Mechanics)
Power (Mechanics)--Addresses, essays, lectures.
Power (Mechanics)--Statistics.
Power of attorney.
Power (Philosophy)
Power (Philosophy)--History.
Power presses.
Power (Social sciences)

Figure 10.4   Two examples of displays of subject headings, one using filing elements and one not

will be able to select POWER (SOCIAL SCIENCES). If filing elements are not observed, the sensible political scientist would not think of looking thirty screens ahead, past POWER LAWN MOWERS and POWER PRESSES. One online system that did ignore parenthetical qualifiers in the initial arrangement of multiple headings was OCLC's LS/2000. It is possible to program systems to do this as demonstrated by LS/2000, which probably looked for the presence of parentheses in controlled heading fields such as name headings, corporate headings, and subject headings.

Catalogers have developed other rather elaborate heading structures to ensure that multiple headings arrange themselves in a logical fashion. Unfortunately, some of these structures were designed to function in card catalogs filed by human beings and assume that a human brain will make the necessary connections. An example is the period subdivision that begins with the name of the period covered, rather than with a span of dates, e.g., UNITED STATES—HISTORY—CIVIL WAR, 1861-1865. In card catalogs, human beings would file this heading in chronological order (after 1850, before 1870), disregarding the alphabetic characters for the name of the period which begin the subdivision (Civil War). Most machines file these in strict alphabetical order, thus disrupting the logical chronological order that would be most helpful for users.[13] Whether or not this problem demands a record design solution or a system design solution, of course, is a matter for debate. If an "intelligent" machine filing program could be developed to arrange these in chronological order, it would save the expense of changing millions of existing records.

Because these period subdivisions are somewhat arbitrary, it is important to display them properly to users, who can't be expected to predict them ahead of time. A number of problematic subject searches reveal users struggling with ways to match their terms for historical periods with ours (see figure 10.5).

Catalogers never intended that users should have to be aware of the existence of subject heading subdivisions in order to formulate an effective search. The intent was that a search on the subject heading alone would retrieve a set of records that was then organized by subdivision to allow the user to scan through it easily. Unfortunately, many online systems interfile headings with subdivisions with other longer headings. See, for example, figure 10.6. Showing the heading with all of its subdivisions clumped together allows users to observe patterns that they might not otherwise observe. We have already given one set of examples in figure 10.5, when we listed actual searches in which users were trying to specify historical periods in ways that do not match the way they are expressed in catalogs. Users may also not be aware of the fact that geographic aspects of topics are most commonly expressed in the catalog by means of geographic subdivisions using noun forms, as in the WATER—CALIFORNIA example in figure 10.6. Another cause of subject search failure is the use of adjectival forms to express the geographical aspect. Actual searches that failed because of this problem are shown in figure 10.7. Obviously, there are other matching problems here besides the geographic one, but perhaps these users could come closer to the correct headings if they were shown displays of subject headings that revealed the pattern followed by headings containing geographic terms in LCSH.

---

tournaments medieval (p. 63)
1960s riots (p. 64)
jews in post war era (p. 69)
architecture in the 16th to 18th centuries (p. 84)
women in the work force in 1900-1950 (p. 85)
coins of the united states in 1943 (p. 86)
labor unions and depression and michigan (p. 86)*

---

*Drabenstott, Karen M., *Enhancing a New Design for Subject Access to Online Catalogs* (Ann Arbor: School of Information and Library Studies, University of Michigan, 1994).

Figure 10.5   **Actual searches that failed because of users' inability to match our terms for historical periods**

Water.
Water buffalo.
Water--California.
Water clocks.
Water--Congresses.

Figure 10.6   **An example of interfiling of headings with subdivisions with other longer headings**

american ceramists (p. 65)
swiss universities (p. 65)
iraqi political systems (p. 84)
french occupation in chad (p. 84)*

In fact, the correct subject headings for these searches are:

Potters--United States.
Universities and colleges--Switzerland.
Iraq--Politics and government.
Chad--History; and Chad--Politics and government.

*Drabenstott, Karen M., *Enhancing a New Design for Subject Access to Online Catalogs* (Ann Arbor: School of Information and Library Studies, University of Michigan, 1994).

Figure 10.7   **Actual searches that failed because of users' inability to match our geographic terms**

Compression

Some writers have begun to suggest that compression of headings could help with the problem of scanning through large retrievals.[14] Compression could mean, for example, that the initial display to the user would consist only of main subject headings; once the user chose one of the main headings, the subdivisions under that main heading would be displayed, as well as *see also* references.[15] There are dangers to this approach, because LCSH sometimes buries what some would consider to be the main topic in a topical subdivision; an example would be WATER—AERATION; a user looking for works on water aeration might not expect to have to choose the main heading WATER in order to find works on water aeration. Perhaps the solution to this problem is to reform subject heading practice. Pending such reform, sophisticated display programs could determine whether the user's initial search included term(s) found in subdivision(s); if not, main headings could be displayed first; if so, headings with subdivisions could be displayed on the initial display. Another possibility would be to offer a SUMMARIZE command to the sophisticated user who has done a search that has retrieved many screens of headings; such a SUMMARIZE command could display main headings only and could display subdivisions under those headings only when a particular heading in the summarize display was chosen by the user.

Consider how the example of wills as shown in figure 10.3 would look as a compressed display (see figure 10.8). One caveat, however. Library of Congress subject headings were not specifically designed to support elaborate compression, and some decisions will have to be made. See figure 10.9 for experimentation with potential display designs for three different situations: (1) user's keyword search matches more than one heading; (2) user's keyword search matches a single heading and that heading has subdivisions; and (3) user's keyword search matches on both headings and subdivisions.

1. Indians of North America--Wills.
2. Nahuas--Wills.
3. Wills.

Only if the user chose line 3 above would the following display result:
1. Wills--California.
2. Wills--Cases.
3. Wills--Forms.
4. Wills--History.
5. Wills--North Carolina.
6. Wills--Scotland.
7. Wills--United States.

The user who chose line 7 could see the following:
Wills--United States--Bibliography.
Wills--United States--Handbooks, manuals, etc.
Wills--United States--History.
Wills--United States--Popular works.

Figure 10.8   The example shown in figure 10.3 as a compressed display

1. Show just main headings, when more than one main heading is matched:
Results of a truncated keyword-within-heading search on STORM#:

Line no. for selection:	No. of titles:	Subject heading:
1		Brain storming
	50	SEARCH: Brainstorming
2	7	Building, Stormproof.
3		Cyclonic storms
	45	SEARCH: Cyclones
4		Desert Storm, Operation, 1991
	66	SEARCH: Persian Gulf War, 1991
5	310	Dust storms.
6	16	Magnetic storms.
7		Rain storms
	92	SEARCH: Rainstorms
8	10	Severe storms.
9	18	SEARCH ALSO: Microbursts
10	2	Stilling of the storm (Miracle)
11	5	Storm door industry.
12	120	Storm sewers.

(Continued)

Figure 10.9   Experimentation with compressed displays

13	97	Storm water retention basins.
14	13	Storm windows.
15	22	Storm winds.
16	675	Storms.
		SEARCH ALSO:
17	45	Cyclones
18	310	Dust storms
19	92	Rainstorms
20	10	Severe storms
21	323	Tornadoes
22	14	Storms in literature.

When line 16, *Storms,* is selected:

Storms

Line no. for selection:	No. of titles:	Subject heading:
1		By geographic area
2		By form, such as Dictionaries, or Handbooks
3		By historic period [Display only when chronological subdivisions are present?]
4	4	--Economic aspects

When line 2, By form, *such as Dictionaries, or Handbooks,* is selected:

Line no. for selection:	No. of titles:	Subject heading:
1	2	--Abstracts.
2	5	--Bibliography.
3	12	--Congresses.
4	3	--Dictionaries.
5	2	--Periodicals.
6	1	--Study guides.

OR:

Line no. for selection:	No. of titles:	Subject heading:
1	2	--Abstracts.
2	5	--Bibliography.
3	9	--Congresses.
4	2	--California--Congresses
5	1	--United States--Congresses
6	3	--Dictionaries.
7	2	--Periodicals.
8	1	--Study guides.

Figure 10.9—Continued

2. Show just subdivisions when a single main heading is matched:

A search on WATER DISTRICTS:

Line no. for selection:	No. of titles:	Subject heading:
1	1	--Economic aspects

By geographic area:

2	47	--California
3	3	--Colorado River
4	1	--Nevada
5	1	--New Zealand
6	1	--Poland--Prussia, West
7	1	--Prussia, East (Poland and Russia)
8	2	--United States
9	1	--Washington (State)
10	1	--West (U.S.)

3. Show headings and subdivisions when both main headings and subdivisions are matched:

A keyword-within-heading search on WATER QUALITY:

Line no. for selection:	No. of titles:	Subject heading:
1	5	Federal aid to water quality management--California.
2	1	Feed-water purification--Quality control--Congresses.
3	2	Fishes--Effect of water quality on.
4	2	Information storage and retrieval systems--Water quality.
5	2	Irrigation water--Quality.
6	47	Water quality.
7	1	Water quality--Africa, Central.
8	50	Water quality--California.
9	27	Water quality--California--Los Angeles.
10	1	Water quality--California--Mono Lake.
11	13	Water quality--United States.
12	75	Water quality management.
13	54	Water quality management--California.
14	1	Water quality monitoring stations.

(Continued)

OR, AS AN ALTERNATIVE TO THE ABOVE: compress main headings matched and display only subdivisions matched:

A keyword-within-heading search on WATER QUALITY:

Line no. for selection:	No. of titles:	Subject heading:
1	5	Federal aid to water quality management--California.
2	1	Feed-water purification--Quality control--Congresses.
3	2	Fishes--Effect of water quality on.
4	2	Information storage and retrieval systems--Water quality.
5	2	Irrigation water--Quality.
6	139	Water quality.*
7	129	Water quality management.*
8	1	Water quality monitoring stations.

*Subdivisions compressed

Figure 10.9—Continued

Placing the User in an A to Z List of Headings

It is possible to design displays that put a user's search in an alphabetic context of subject headings that is not limited to those matched by the initial search; this has been done by some systems. The user can then be allowed to scan up and down and select subject headings that did not match the initial search query (see figure 10.10). The displayed headings should include both authorized headings and cross-references (drawn from the authority file). A display of subject headings that are alphabetically close to the initial query is particularly useful for subject searching; users have always had trouble guessing what librarians called things. For example, users commonly have problems because they search the plural form, but LCSH uses the singular form, and vice versa.

It is easiest to produce a display of alphabetically close subject headings if the user's query was treated as a phrase search and matched against potential subject headings from left to right. In that case, the choice about where to begin the display is easy. In fact, such a display should probably be the default whether the user's initial search was a successful match or not.

However, when the user's initial query was a keyword-within-heading query, our recommended default subject search, the approach of putting the search into context of alphabetically close subject headings should be used *only* when the user's search matches nothing; otherwise, the default should be a display of all headings matched. It is a little more difficult to design a display of alphabetically close subject headings for a keyword-in-heading query. If the user's keyword search was on a single term, the initial display of headings, from which the user could scan up and down, should show the headings, if any, that *begin* with the first letters of the single term from the query.

Current search: LSH* CHAOS THEORY

1. Chaos (Christian theology)
2. Chaos (Christian theology) in literature
3. Chaos (Theology)
   SEARCH: Chaos (Christian theology)
4. Chaos, Deterministic
   SEARCH: Deterministic chaos
5. Chaos in systems
   SEARCH: Chaotic behavior in systems
6. Chaos, Quantum
   SEARCH: Quantum chaos

CHAOS THEORY IS NOT USED AS A SUBJECT HEADING IN OUR CATALOG;
COULD ONE OF THESE HEADINGS CLOSE BY IN THE ALPHABET SATISFY
YOUR QUERY?

7. Chaotic behavior in systems
8. Chaotic behavior in systems in literature
9. Chaotic motion in systems
   SEARCH: Chaotic behavior in systems
10. Chaouia (Berber people)

*That is, list subject headings (a left-to-right phrase-matching search)

**Figure 10.10   An example of a failed left-to-right subject search on CHAOS THEORY
placed in the context of alphabetically close subject headings**

For an initial query that includes more than one keyword, it might be possible in a windows-based system to display each keyword in the query in the context of subject headings that begin with that keyword, each in a separate window.

In all the approaches described so far, the user's success depends on the phrase or keyword(s) in her or his initial query being close to terms that begin subject headings. If the user needs to be shown terms that are in subdivisions or at the end of long phrase headings, these approaches still will not help. One of the authors suggests that the creation of an unposted, deduped uniterm index of words drawn from subject headings, in which each keyword in a subject heading or subdivision is extracted and put into an alphabetical list, could help users determine when the keywords in their searches do occur in subject headings and when they do not, regardless of location within the heading. The keywords that do occur could then be safely used in the keyword-within-heading search constructed using them, perhaps using the form fill-in technique. However, the other author hesitates to suggest the creation of a uniterm index of words drawn from subject headings, for at least two reasons: (1) because of the way such an approach strips each term of its context and therefore of much of the meaning provided by its context; and (2) because our current subject heading lists were not designed to be single-term thesauri, so there is much inconsistency in vocabulary across headings (e.g., *film* and *motion picture* are both used in headings).

If subject headings that are alphabetically close are displayed, it is important to communicate clearly to users that the display includes headings that did *not* match the initial search; otherwise users may assume that all displayed headings are relevant or at least matched their searches in some mysterious way.[16]

Display of Cross-References

As we have stated before (in chapter 6), it is best to display *see* references to users rather than matching on them automatically and taking users directly to bibliographic records, as the MELVYL system currently does; once *see* references are displayed, it is also best to allow the user to select a cross-reference rather than requiring the user to reinput the search (see figure 10.11).

It can also be very helpful to display related term *see also* references in such a way that users can select them without rekeying (see figure 10.12). The display in figure 10.12 is such a useful display for demonstrating broader and narrower terms for users that perhaps it should be used as the default display for any search that matches on a single subject heading. Such a default display should even be considered when a heading is selected subsequent to an initial search, such as in a navigation function, in which the user is shown all headings attached to a retrieved record, or retrieved group of records, and encouraged to choose from them for further searching. LC ACCESS, a system designed by the Library of Congress, uses this type of display; if a related term is selected, the system takes the user to that place in the headings list to see that heading in context, and so forth.

Line no. for selection:	Term:	No. of records:
12	Creativity (term used in this catalog: Creative ability)	43

Figure 10.11   An example of a selectable *see* reference

Line no. for selection:	Term:	No. of records:
1	Afro-Americans--Civil rights* *Related works are also found under the broader terms:*	469
2	Civil rights--United States	366
3	Race discrimination--United States *Related works are also found under the narrower terms:*	492
4	Afro-Americans--Suffrage	91
5	Black power--United States	33

Figure 10.12   Displays of related term *see also* references

6	Civil rights workers--United States	32
7	Poor People's Campaign	2
8	Selma-Montgomery Rights March, 1965	3[†]

Example of a display that would allow the user to ask for a term with all narrower terms under it:

Line no. for selection:	Term:	No. of records:
1	Crabs[‡]	13
	Synonyms: Brachyura	
	Related works are also found	
	under the narrower terms:	
2	Blue crabs	3
3	Dungeness crab	1
4	Fiddler-crabs	1
5	Freshwater crabs	2
6	Gecarcinidae	1
7	Ghost crabs	1
8	Hermit crabs	5
9	Leucosiidae	1
10	Portunidae	1
11	Sand-crabs	1
12	Tanner crabs	1
13	CRABS AND ALL NARROWER TERMS UNDER IT	
	Related works are also found	
	under the broader term:	
14	Decapoda (Crustacea)	14
	Other related works are found under:	
15	Cookery (Crabs)	1
16	Crab culture	1
17	Crab meat	1
18	Crabbing	3

---

*This line represents a compressed display of all works with the subject heading Afro-Americans--Civil rights, as well as all works with subdivisions under Afro-Americans--Civil rights; see the discussion of compression earlier in this chapter.

†Systems that do this include:

IMPACT: Walt Crawford, *The Online Catalog Book: Essays and Examples* (Boston: G. K. Hall, 1992), p. 255.

INNOPAC: Crawford, *Online*, p. 302.

LC ACCESS: Available by anonymous FTP (File Transfer Protocol) at ftp.loc.gov in the pub/lc.access directory.

NOTIS: Crawford, *Online*, p. 401.

‡This line represents a compressed display of all works with the subject heading Crabs, as well as all works with subdivisions under Crabs; see the discussion of compression earlier in this chapter.

Many systems will not display authority records to the public if there are no bibliographic records attached to them; such authority records are known as unposted authority records. If the collection has no bibliographic record with a particular subject heading attached to it, but it does have bibliographic records with that same subject heading with subject subdivisions attached, the *see* and *see also* related term references to the unsubdivided heading will not display to users. A smarter system would recognize that there is a relationship between a heading and its subdivisions, even though they are on separate authority records, and would display the cross-references pertaining to the main heading to anyone looking at that heading with one of its subdivisions.

A single authority record for a subject heading may have valuable information in it that is not formatted for display as a heading. For example, the authority record may contain a scope note that explains the usage of the heading, or it may have a complex *see* reference that is more like a note than a cross-reference, reminding users, for example, that headings beginning with a particular word might also be of interest to them. Many online systems lack public displays for authority records; in these systems, users are denied access to scope notes and complex *see* references altogether. Better public displays would integrate such information into the default display that resulted from the choice of a particular subject heading.

Display of Postings

Displaying the number of postings, or the number of records attached to each line of a summary display of headings or index entries, can help the user in decision making about the next step in searching; for example, a large posting might lead the user to try to think of ways to narrow the search. If the number of postings continues to appear on the screen after the user chooses to browse through the bibliographic records under a particular heading, it can give the user a sense of how far he or she has gone and how far he or she still has to go.

Multiple Subject Heading Lists (e.g., MeSH and LCSH)

It is common for a system to contain different headings for the same concept, because more than one subject heading list is being used to create records for the system; Carol Mandel has investigated this problem extensively.[17] For example, in an OPAC that combines the holdings of several libraries on a university campus, the medical library may be using MeSH, and the other libraries may be using LCSH. Thus, books on cancer may be found under either the heading CANCER (LCSH) or the heading NEO-PLASMS (MeSH); the situation is further complicated by the fact that each heading has a *see* reference from the other: CANCER, *see* NEOPLASMS (MeSH) and NEOPLASMS, *see* CANCER (LCSH).

The simplest display is a single alphabetical list in which the headings from all sources are intermingled. However, unless the source of the headings is shown in some way, such a list could be baffling to the user, at least in those cases where the form of heading for the same concept differs; when two lists use the same heading for the same concept, the headings could probably be safely merged. Users may not understand cryptic labels like *MeSH* and *LCSH*. Perhaps when MeSH is being used in conjunction with LCSH, labeling the MeSH headings (MEDICAL SUBJECT HEADING) would be sufficient for catalog users to understand that the heading comes from a different source than the other headings. The situation would be improved a great deal if we could develop sharable records constituting a syndetic structure to map between and among all of these lists, so that systems would be able to create something like the display shown in figure 10.13.

Some of our users are interested in works categorized as to form and genre, e.g., westerns or poetry. Charles Ammi Cutter even included this kind of access in his original objects of the catalog: "2. To show what the library has . . . (F) in a given kind of literature." (See discussion of the objects of the catalog in chapter 1.) The US-MARC bibliographic format contains a field for form and genre terms that allows these to be separately tagged from topical subject headings,[18] and there are a number of special lists of genre and form terms that can be put in this field. It is possible that those LC subject headings that are used to express genre or form will eventually be put in this field as well; the Library of Congress is currently studying the situation and trying to decide if this will be possible. The fact that form and genre terms are tagged separately from topical subject headings should allow us to let our users differentiate between works about and examples of a particular form or genre. Some systems might want to label terms in a single index as to whether they are used as genre/form headings (examples of) or topical subject headings (works about). Others might want to consider creating displays under a single heading (see figure 10.16 and the accompanying discussion later in this chapter).

It should not be forgotten that LCSH uses many form subdivisions. Designing effective displays of subject headings with form subdivisions helps users make choices regarding forms such as dictionaries, handbooks, dramatic or historical treatments of a topic, or indexes. If the recently approved subfield code for form subdivisions were widely implemented, compression screens could allow users to continue a search by looking only at form subdivisions of the chosen heading.[19]

Your search, BSU CANCER, retrieved:

Line no. for selection:	Term:	No. of records:
12	Cancer (Library of Congress subject heading)	33
	Neoplasms (Medical subject heading also used in this catalog)	553

Your search, BSU IRRIGATION, retrieved:

Line no. for selection:	Term:	No. of records:
2	Irrigation (Library of Congress subject heading)	78
	Irrigation (Medical subject heading also used in this catalog)	3

Figure 10.13   **An example of a display of a relationship between MeSH and LCSH if mapping were done**

Display and Arrangement of Multiple Bibliographic Records

This section will deal with the display of multiple bibliographic records. This is the obvious next display when a user's search has matched only one heading or when a user has selected a heading from a previous summary display of headings. However, it is also the easiest display to offer to searchers who have used co-occurrence rules that are across multiple fields or within a bibliographic record.

Records Retrieved by Matches on More than One Heading or Field

Once co-occurrence of keywords across multiple headings or fields is allowed, the option of displaying single headings is more problematic, because the keyword search could easily match one word in one heading and a second word in another heading. The easiest option is simply to display the bibliographic records retrieved. If the records are arranged by main entry, the works of authors who have written extensively on the subject and the editions of multiple-edition works will come together. Some systems may arrange records by title or by date; the latter options work against the second cataloging objective. If in the single record display of each selected record the keywords matched are highlighted, the user can quickly see why a particular record was retrieved; this highlighting can allow the user to scan through multiple records quickly.

Another option for the display of records retrieved on cross-field or cross-heading searches that might be explored is that of displaying only the fields or headings matched. When the fields matched are long note fields, this would make it difficult to compress long displays; perhaps sentences matched, rather than fields matched, could be tried when a field that is not a heading is matched. When two different headings are matched, the display could use the terms *paired with* to link the two headings (see figure 10.14).

Ranked Output

Some experimental systems have tried computer algorithms that weight retrieved records or subject terms based on factors such as (1) frequency of occurrence of terms in the database; (2) frequency of occurrence of terms in a previously retrieved group of records identified as relevant by the user; (3) closeness of match to the user's input search; (4) whether or not a matched heading is the first of several in a record; or (5)

Your search, FSU LIFT ON SWEPT-BACK WINGS, retrieved:

Line no. for selection:	Term:	No. of records:
12	Lift (Aerodynamics) paired with: Airplanes--Wings, Swept-back*	5

---

*This suggestion was made by Jo Crawford at the University of Wisconsin-Madison in a personal communication, September 1994.

Figure 10.14   An example of a possible cross-field match display

whether or not a matched heading is the narrowest term in a subject hierarchy. Display of multiple records or headings will be in weighted order, with the "weightiest" documents first. Such algorithms are dangerous in that (1) the results of applying them in any particular database are unpredictable; (2) the algorithms themselves are mechanical and unintelligent; and (3) the retrieval results are not necessarily truly relevant; for example, unusual or infrequently occurring words are weighted heavily as relevant, although they may not necessarily be closest to the user's information need. These algorithms are also invisible to the user and therefore can seem mysterious and out of control. There is some evidence that such algorithms actually drive users away from subject searching.[20] Finally, such algorithms can be quite costly in processing time.

Subarrangement of Bibliographic Records within One Subject Heading

It should not be forgotten that a very useful mechanism for the display of multiple records in online public access catalogs is the main entry based on authorship. Compare the examples in figure 10.15. In an online display of 100 records with the same subject heading, each record can be displayed only once. If the record is displayed alphabetically by main entry, the user can observe a number of useful things in the initial scan through the 100 records; the user can often observe which authors have written extensively on the subject, which corporate bodies are active in the field, which works are conference proceedings, and which are works of personal authorship. One could even argue that such a display can be a useful substitute for evaluation of the works available, what Patrick Wilson calls "exploitative control."[21] For example, it is at least possible that a general book by an author who has written extensively in the field would be valuable as an introduction to the field. If the records are arranged by main entry, the editions of multiple-edition works will generally come together. This will ensure that users are shown the latest edition of a work of nonfiction. Some systems may arrange these records by title or by date; the latter options work against the second cataloging objective of displaying the editions of a work together. Stephen Walker found that users preferred works to be in order by main entry so that editions of the same work appeared together.[22] Also, notice in the examples in figure 10.15 how the works on a subject tend to all have the same title words, usually very similar to the subject heading itself. Thus, title arrangement tends to be redundant and tends to cluster all works together under one letter of the alphabet. As mentioned earlier, some systems offer sort options to the user, such as author/title, title/author, date, or call number. This would be better than using title or date as the basis of a default arrangement of records.

Works about and Examples of a Genre or Form Heading

Current practice in LCSH is to design one heading string for a genre or form heading when it is used for works about that genre or form, and a different heading string when it is used for examples of that genre or form. Some examples are as follows:

Jazz [attached to sound recordings of jazz performances]

Jazz--History and criticism [attached to works about jazz]

Essay [attached to works about the essay form]

Essays [attached to the essays themselves]

Display of records under a subject heading with main entry based on authorship:

Online catalogs

1. Automating school library catalogs : a reader 1992.
2. Cheng, Chin-Chuan, 1936- Microcomputer-based user interface for library online catalogue [1985]
3. Clinic on Library Applications of Data Processing (23rd : 1986 : University of Illinois at Urbana-Champaign) What is user friendly? c1987.
4. Cochrane, Pauline Atherton, 1929- Improving LCSH for use in online catalogs : exercises for self-help with a selection of background readings 1986.
5. Crawford, Walt. Bibliographic displays in the online catalog c1986.
6. Crawford, Walt. The online catalog book : essays and examples c1992.
7. Crawford, Walt. Patron access : issues for online catalogs c1987.
8. End user searching in the health sciences c1986.
9. Fayen, Emily Gallup. The online catalog : improving public access to library materials c1983.
10. Hancock-Beaulieu, Micheline. Evaluation of online catalogues : an assessment of methods 1990.
11. Hennepin County Library Online Public Access Catalog Task Force report 1983.
12. The Impact of online catalogs c1986.
13. Markey, Karen. Online catalog use : results of surveys and focus group interviews in several libraries 1983.
14. Matthews, Joseph R. Public access to online catalogs c1985.
15. Mitev, Nathalie Nadia. Designing an online public access catalogue : Okapi, a catalogue on a local area network 1985.
16. Online catalog : the inside story : a planning & implementation guide c1983.
17. Tolle, John E. Current utilization of online catalogs : transaction log analysis 1983.

Display of records under a subject heading with main entry based on title:

Online catalogs

1. Automating school library catalogs : a reader 1992.
2. Bibliographic displays in the online catalog / Walt Crawford c1986.
3. Current utilization of online catalogs : transaction log analysis / John E. Tolle 1983.
4. Designing an online public access catalogue : Okapi, a catalogue on a local area network / Nathalie Mitev 1985.
5. End user searching in the health sciences c1986.
6. Evaluation of online catalogues : an assessment of methods / Micheline Hancock-Beaulieu 1990.

Figure 10.15   Records under one subject heading arranged by main entry compared with the same records arranged by title

7. Hennepin County Library Online Public Access Catalog Task Force report 1983.
8. The Impact of online catalogs c1986.
9. Improving LCSH for use in online catalogs : exercises for self-help with a selection of background readings / Pauline Cochrane 1986.
10. Microcomputer-based user interface for library online catalogue / Chin-Chuan Cheng [1985]
11. The online catalog : improving public access to library materials / Emily Fayen c1983.
12. Online catalog : the inside story : a planning & implementation guide c1983.
13. The online catalog book : essays and examples / Walt Crawford c1992.
14. Online catalog use : results of surveys and focus group interviews in several libraries / Karen Markey 1983.
15. Patron access : issues for online catalogs / Walt Crawford c1987.
16. Public access to online catalogs / Joseph R. Matthews c1985.
17. What is user friendly? / 23rd Clinic on Library Applications of Data Processing, University of Illinois at Urbana-Champaign c1987.

Display of musical works under a subject heading with main entry based on authorship:

1. Beethoven, Ludwig van, 1770-1827.
   Symphonies, no. 1, op. 21, C major
2. Symphonies, no. 2, op. 36, D major
3. Symphonies, no. 3, op. 55, E flat major
4. Symphonies, no. 4, op. 60, B flat major
5. Symphonies, no. 5, op. 67, C minor
6. Bizet, Georges, 1838-1875.
   Symphonies, C major
7. Borodin, Aleksandr Porfir'evich, 1833-1887.
   Symphonies, no. 2, B minor
8. Dvořák, Antonin, 1841-1904.
   Symphonies, no. 1, C minor
9. Symphonies, no. 2, op. 4, B flat major
10. Haydn, Joseph, 1732-1809.
    Symphonies, H. I, 6, D major
11. Ives, Charles, 1874-1954.
    Symphonies, no. 1
12. Mahler, Gustav, 1860-1911.
    Symphonies, no. 5, C sharp minor
13. Mozart, Wolfgang Amadeus, 1756-1791.
    Symphonies, K. 22, B flat major
14. Prokofiev, Sergey, 1891-1953.
    Symphonies, no. 1, op. 25, D major
15. Schubert, Franz, 1797-1828.
    Symphonies, D. 417, C minor
16. Tchaikovsky, Peter Ilich, 1840-1893.
    Symphonies no. 1, op. 13, G minor

(Continued)

Display of musical works under a subject heading with main entry based on title:

1. Symphonie no. 1 op. 21 ; Symphonie no. 7 op. 92 [sound recording] / Ludwig van Beethoven
2. Symphony no. 1 / Charles Ives ; Three essays for orchestra / Samuel Barber [sound recording]
3. Symphony no. 1, in C major [sound recording] / Georges Bizet
4. Symphony no. 1 in C minor : The bells of Zlonice ; The hero's song : op. 111 [sound recording] / Dvořák
5. Symphony no. 2, in B flat major, op. 4 [sound recording] / Dvořák
6. Symphony no. 1 in D, op. 25 : Classical ; Symphony no. 4, op. 47/112 : revised 1947 version [sound recording] / Sergey Prokofiev
7. Symphony no. 1, in G minor, op. 13 (Winter dreams) [sound recording] / Tchaikovsky
8. Symphony no. 2 in B minor [sound recording] / Borodin
9. Symphony no. 2 in D major, op. 36 ; Overture Coriolan, op. 62 ; Overture Prometheus, op. 43 [sound recording] / Ludwig van Beethoven
10. Symphony no. 3, in E flat major, op. 55 (Eroica) [sound recording] / Ludwig van Beethoven
11. Symphony no. 4, in B flat, op. 60 ; Symphony no. 8 in F major, op. 93 [sound recording] / Ludwig van Beethoven
12. Symphony no. 4, in C minor, D. 417 (Tragic) ; Symphony no. 5, in B flat major, D. 485 [sound recording] / Franz Schubert
13. Symphony no. 5 in B flat major, K. 22 / Mozart
14. Symphony, no. 5, in C minor, op. 67 [sound recording] / Ludwig van Beethoven
15. Symphony no. 5 in C sharp minor ; Symphony no. 10 in F sharp major [i.e., minor] [sound recording] / Gustav Mahler
16. Symphony no. 6 in D (1761) "Le matin" [sound recording] / Joseph Haydn

Figure 10.15—Continued

We suspect that users frequently find one heading string and not the other and therefore lose the serendipitous power of a display that puts both categories of material together. If current practice could be changed, a display such as that in figure 10.16 would be possible. Such a change might mean using the same heading string for both works about and examples of (as suggested in figure 10.16), or it might mean linking the authority records for pairs of headings (such as JAZZ; JAZZ—HISTORY AND CRITICISM) so that a search on either heading retrieved both headings and resulted in a display similar to that shown in figure 10.16.

Works by and Works about an Author

If the works about a person are double-posted in both the name/author and subject authority files, so that they can display both to a person doing a subject search and

Western films.

Works about:

1. Barbour, Alan G. The thrill of it all. 1971.
2. Cawelti, John G. The six-gun mystique. [1971?]
3. De Marco, Mario. Republic's wild & woolly western heroes, heroines, heavies & side-kicks. [1983?]
4. Eyles, Allen. The western : an illustrated guide. [1967]
5. Fenin, George N. The western : from silents to cinerama. c1962.
6. Kitses, Demetrius John. Horizons West : Anthony Mann, Budd Boetticher, Sam Peckinpah : studies of authorship within the western. 1969.
7. Lahue, Kalton C. Riders of the range : the sagebrush heroes of the sound screen. [1973]
8. Lahue, Kalton C. Winners of the West : the sagebrush heroes of the silent screen. [1971, c1970]
9. Parkinson, Michael, 1935- A pictorial history of westerns. 1972.
10. Short, John Rennie, 1951- Imagined country : environment, culture and society. 1991.
11. Smith, Harold. Saturdays forever : film adventure. c1985.

Examples of:

12. 3 godfathers. 1948.
13. The Alamo. 1960.
14. The border wolf. c1929.
15. Davy Crockett. 1955.
16. Frontier scout. c1938.
17. Geronimo! : the story of a great enemy. 1939.
18. I killed Geronimo. 1950.
19. Man from Oklahoma. 1945.
20. Pat Garrett and Billy the Kid. 1973.
21. Rio Grande. 1950.
22. Sons of the pioneers. 1942.
23. Toughest man in Arizona. 1952.
24. War party. 1965.

Figure 10.16   Desirable display for works about and examples of a genre or form

to a person doing a name/author search, work will have to be done to design effective displays of the works by and about an author, so that they are not intermingled in such a way as to confuse users. We recommend that the works by an author be displayed in a separate alphabet from the works about that author, clearly labeled as such; see the recommended display in figure 10.17.

Cummings, E. E. (Edward Estlin), 1894-1962.

Work(s) by:

1. 1/20
2. 1 x 1
3. 50 poems
4. 73 poems
5. 95 poems
6. Anthropos
7. Bal negre
8. By E.E. Cummings
9. Chaire
10. Christmas tree
11. CIOPW
12. Eimi
13. The enormous room
14. Him
15. Hist whist
16. The house that ate mosquito pie
17. I
18. Is 5
19. Kaminguzu shishu
20. Little tree
21. No thanks
22. Puella mea
23. Santa Claus
24. Tom
25. Tulips & chimneys
26. W

Work(s) about:

27. Adams, Robert Martin, 1915-
    Grasshopper's waltz, the poetry of E.E. Cummings. 1947.
28. Attaway, Kenneth R.
    E.E. Cummings' aloofness, an underlying theme in his poetry. 1969.
29. E.E. Cummings : a collection of critical essays. 1972.
30. Friedman, Norman.
    E.E. Cummings, the art of his poetry. 1960.
31. Kennedy, Richard S.
    Dreams in the mirror : a biography of E.E. Cummings. 1980.
32. Norman, Charles, 1904-
    E.E. Cummings : the magic-maker. 1964.
33. Whicher, Stephen E.
    The art of poetry : Cummings, Williams, Stevens. 1982.

Figure 10.17   Recommended display for works by and about an author

Display of a Single Record

It has been pointed out in chapter 6 that research that questions how much of the bibliographic record users really need has suffered from faulty research design. Because users doing subject searches are probably less familiar with the items found than users doing known-work searches, it is even more likely that full records would be useful to them; for example, a contents note could help a user in evaluation and choice. Display of the other access points on the record (i.e., the tracings) may suggest other relevant subject headings to the user or help the user find the works of an author who has written extensively in the field or a corporate body active in the field (see figure 10.18). Walker found that users preferred full records to brief displays because they listed other subject headings on a record (i.e., tracings).[23] Whether to label the subject tracings should be considered carefully. Many systems control personal name and work headings outside the subject authority file. If the display says SUBJECT(S): DBASE II (COMPUTER FILE) (a uniform title) or SUBJECT(S): SHAKESPEARE, WILLIAM, 1564-1616 (a personal name heading), the user is likely to think that these can be searched in the subject index; but in some systems they cannot be searched in the subject index, only in an author/name or title index.

We discussed in chapters 3 and 8 some of the dangers of adding free text data such as tables of contents to the searchable fields in bibliographic records. Whether you make them searchable or not, the addition of tables of contents as an optional display available from any bibliographic record could be a great help to the user in deciding whether a particular item is likely to be useful.

Display of the call number in a single bibliographic record raises some interesting issues because, in current cataloging practice, the call number is usually serving double duty as both a physical location device for a particular physical item and as a method of providing classified access based on discipline. Sometimes, however (e.g., items in remote storage shelved by bar code, electronic documents, or even records

---

A user interested in paper crafts has heard about a book called *Paper Circus* and looks it up by title. If the display includes a list of all the subject headings added to this record, the user may notice the subject heading PAPER WORK and find more books of interest by doing a subject search on that heading or by navigating from this display, if the system allows this:

West, Robin.
  Paper circus : how to create your own circus / by
Robin West ; photographs by Mark Wieland ; drawings by
Priscilla Kiedrowski. Minneapolis : Carolrhoda Books, c1983.
  72 p. : ill. (some col.) ; 25 x 22 cm.
  SUMMARY: Instructions for building a model circus complete with ringmaster, using construction paper and articles found around most homes.

1. Circus--Models. 2. Models and modelmaking. 3. Handicraft.
4. Paper work.

Figure 10.18   **An example of the usefulness of displaying the tracings**

in a true classed catalog, in which more than one classification number can be assigned to a work that takes an interdisciplinary approach to a topic), the classification number is *not* functioning as a location device. Whenever a catalog contains records for items for which this is the case, it ought to provide a way to differentiate in the display between the classification number as call number and the classification number as a type of subject access point.

Display of the Classification

Figure 10.19 contains a mock-up of a possible classification search of a catalog. It is intended to demonstrate one potential approach to trying to display the classification in a user-friendly and intuitive way. Notice from the displays in figure 10.19 how the ability to display a number in the context of its hierarchy is going to be crucial in the process of translating a classification number to a form that is comprehensible to catalog users. If, for example, a user were to start out with the class number GB 653.2, the translation *Collected works (Nonserial)* would be meaningless without its hierarchy to give it some context.

When looking at any hierarchy, the user should have the ability to select any point in the hierarchy in order either to see the classification context around the hierarchy at that point or to browse a virtual shelf list of materials represented in the catalog by looking at bibliographic records for items found in the shelf list at that point.

The user begins by doing a keyword-within-heading search for the subject WATER, and is given the following initial display:

Line no. for selection:	Term:	No. of records:
1	Water.	82,332
2	Water and architecture.	3
3	Water and civilization.	4
4	Water balance (Hydrology)	35
5	Water banking	4
6	Water bed industry	1
7	Water beds (Furniture)	2
8	Water beetles.	3
9	Water birds.	371
10	Water buffalo.	9

The user, seeing how many postings there are under the term *water*, bravely selects the heading and clicks on it. One of the options offered is, "Display subject broken down by academic discipline." The user chooses this option and gets the following initial display:

Figure 10.19   **A mock-up of a possible classification search of a catalog**

Geography and anthropology (G)
   Physical geography (GB)
Social sciences (H)
   Economic history (HC-HD)
Science (Q)
   Chemistry (QD)
   Natural history, biology (QH)
   Botany (QK)
   Microbiology (QR)
Agriculture (S)
   Animal culture (SF)
Technology (T)
   Hydraulic and ocean engineering (TC)
   Environmental technology, sanitary engineering (TD)
   Photography (TR)

This is a list of the general classification categories found on the bibliographic records that contain the LC subject heading WATER. The user can now select one or more desired disciplines above. At this point, the user should be offered at least two options: (1) look through the bibliographic records already retrieved that have the desired disciplinary focus; or (2) browse through the shelf list (i.e., the list of classification numbers assigned to books in the collection), starting at one of the selected classification points.

The following is a sample display if the user chooses the first option and asks to see <u>Physical geography (GB)</u>:

GB 653   Advances in hydroscience.
GB 661.2   Bowen, Robert. Surface water. 1982.
           Caro, Paul. De l'eau. English. Water. 1993.
GB 665   Lanz, Klaus. The Greenpeace book of water. 1995.
GB 671   Wendt, Herbert, 1914- Quellen, Strome, Meere. English.
           The romance of water. 1969.

At any point, the user should have the ability to click on any classification number and see its hierarchy. For example, if the user clicked on GB 653 in the above display, the following display should result:

G Geography and anthropology
     GB Physical geography
          GB 651-2998 Hydrology. Water
               GB 653-653.2 Collected works (Nonserial)
               GB 653 Individual authors

The single-record display of an item of interest should also provide the user with a pathway into the classification. If the user finds one particular record that is exactly the type of thing sought, the option to browse the virtual shelf list around that particular book should be offered at that point as well. In fact, on the single-record display, it might be wise to try to clarify for users that the classification number serves a dual function as both a physical location device and a means of organizing books and other documents by discipline rather than topic (as subject heading lists such as LCSH and MeSH do). For example, the single-record display could offer the user two choices: (1) "How to find this [book, videocassette, journal, etc.]," and when this option is chosen, the OPAC could provide a map of the library pinpointing where (on what floor, on what shelf, etc.) the desired item is located; or (2) "To find other items that take the same disciplinary approach to the subject as this item," and when this option is chosen, the user could browse the classification around the classification number assigned to the item displayed, as demonstrated above. If OPACs could make this distinction between the classification as physical location device and the classification as subject access tool, it would make it much easier to build classified catalogs in which it is possible to assign multiple classification numbers to the same item and in which items that are *not* physically located by means of classification numbers (e.g., items in remote storage stored by bar code, analytics) can still be shown to users with other works that take the same disciplinary approach.

Although we have emphasized that the classification number should not be regarded as a simple location device, it might be helpful to allow the user to have the option to print search results in call number order to aid in locating items in the library.[24]

There is one unresolved snag in attempting to make better use of the classification to provide hierarchical discipline-based subject access in OPACs. The problem occurs because the classification schemes in use by libraries allow catalogers to synthesize numbers as needed using tables, such as geographic tables. It would take some built-in intelligence in the OPAC software for these synthesized numbers to be decoded into sensible displays for users.

Conclusion

Better and more logical displays of subject headings, classification numbers, and the bibliographic records that bear them can help users navigate through our OPACs much more effectively than they can now. Use of headings rather than bibliographic records in initial displays is highly recommended, as headings can be more easily summarized and compressed, allowing the user readily to comprehend the scope and structure of even the largest and most complex retrievals.

Notes

1. Nicholson Baker, "Discards," *New Yorker,* April 4, 1994, p. 68, 81–83.

2. Mark T. Kinnucan, "The Size of Retrieval Sets," *Journal of the American Society for Information Science* 43 (Jan. 1992): 72–79.

3. Brendan J. Wyly, "From Access Points to Materials: A Transaction Log Analysis of Access

Point Value for Online Catalog Users," *Library Resources & Technical Services* 40 (July 1996): 234.

4. Beverly Janosky, Philip J. Smith, and Charles Hildreth, "Online Library Catalog Systems: An Analysis of User Errors," *International Journal of Man-Machine Studies* 25 (1986): 580.

5. Baker, "Discards," p. 81.

6. Derek Austin, "Vocabulary Control and Information Technology," *Aslib Proceedings* 38 (Jan. 1986): 1–15.

7. Note that this ability of our subject heading systems to put a user's search terms in complex precoordinated relationships with each other is one of the strengths of our controlled vocabularies. Moreover, it is a way in which our subject heading systems perform much better than do uncontrolled systems such as many abstracting and indexing services and the World Wide Web, which tend to lift single terms out of their context and not control their relationships. When indexing is limited to single terms, the relationship between two terms can no longer be expressed; for example, works about the two concepts being discussed would be put together both at (1) television and at (2) children, and the user could no longer be presented with the choice of works about the effect of television on children or works that list television programs designed for children, two quite different topics.

8. Michael George Berger, "Information-Seeking in the Online Bibliographic System: An Exploratory Study" (Ph.D. diss., UC Berkeley, 1994), p. 119.

9. Ibid., p. 120.

10. Wyly, "From Access Points," p. 230.

11. Dennis Auburn Hill, *User's Guide to the Library Computer Catalog: Network Library System (NLS) Catalog User's Guide*, 4th ed. (Madison: University of Wisconsin-Madison, 1993), p. 16.

12. *Headings for Tomorrow: Public Access Display of Subject Headings*, ed. Martha Yee (Chicago: American Library Association, 1992).

13. Robert P. Holley, "Report to the RTSD CCS Subject Analysis Committee on Filing Conventions for Period Subdivisions," typescript (1981).

14. Bryce Allen, "Improved Browsable Displays: An Experimental Test," *Information Technology and Libraries* 12 (June 1993): 203–208; Mark Kinnucan, "Fisheye Views as an Aid to Subject Access in Online Catalogues," *Canadian Journal of Information Science* 17, no. 2 (1992): 25–40; Gary S.

Lawrence, "Online Catalogs and System Designers," in *The Impact of Online Catalogs*, ed. Joseph R. Matthews (New York: Neal Schuman, 1986), p. 8; Dorothy McGarry and Elaine Svenonius, "More on Improved Browsable Displays for Online Subject Access," *Information Technology and Libraries* 10 (Sept. 1991): 185–191.

15. LS/2000 did this (Walt Crawford, *The Online Catalog Book: Essays and Examples* [Boston: G. K. Hall, 1992], p. 339).

16. Karen M. Drabenstott, "Online Catalog User Needs and Behavior," in *Think Tank on the Present and Future of the Online Catalog: Proceedings*, ed. Noelle Van Pulis (Chicago: American Library Association, 1991), p. 70.

17. Carol A. Mandel, *Multiple Thesauri in Online Library Bibliographic Systems* (Washington, D.C.: Cataloging Distribution Service, Library of Congress, 1987).

18. 655 field in the USMARC bibliographic format.

19. MARBI discussion papers 74 and 79 [cited 17 November 1997]; available from gopher://marvel. loc.gov:70/11/services/usmarc/marbipro/marbidp

20. John Akeroyd, "Information Seeking in Online Catalogues," *Journal of Documentation* 46 (March 1990): 36, 44, 45, 51.

21. Patrick Wilson, *Two Kinds of Power* (Berkeley: University of California Press, 1968), p. 25.

22. Stephen Walker, "The OKAPI Online Catalogue Research Projects," in *The Online Catalogue: Developments and Directions*, ed. Charles Hildreth (London: Library Association, 1989), p. 100.

23. Ibid.

24. Some systems already allow displays of subject retrievals by classification numbers; among them are TECHLIB plus (Crawford, *Online*, p. 461; TECHLIB plus is one option that a site can choose to offer); and Winnebago (ibid., p. 526).

11

Demonstration of Relationships—Subjects—Summary—Desirable Defaults

As discussed in chapter 2, many online systems offer users a list of search types on the initial log-on screen, and it is rare for these to correspond to the three most common searches, those addressed by the objectives of the catalog: a search for a particular work, a search for the works of an author, and a search for works on a particular subject. Now let's discuss how to offer the user the best possible default search for a particular subject. Of course, the system should offer the sophisticated user as much power and flexibility as it can, and it should explain its powerful and flexible options thoroughly in readily accessible *HELP* screens, so that the user who wishes to learn to become sophisticated can easily do so. However, the default searches offered to the novice user, or the user who just doesn't want to be bothered investing time in learning how to use a library catalog, are critical to convincing the user that the system is friendly.

Offer just one default search for a particular subject, and make it the best search you can design. Consider the following facts about subject headings:

1. Free-floating subdivisions don't have authority records and appear only in bibliographic records; also, free-floating subdivisions can cover important pieces of the user's search, e.g., —HISTORY, or —BIBLIOGRAPHY.

2. As noted in chapter 9, sometimes there is no single coextensive subject heading to cover a given topic. When this happens, it is routine cataloging practice to use two or more headings to cover the topic. However, research reveals that a minority of users do searches that match on more than one subject heading.

3. As noted in chapter 8, LCSH still has many examples of headings that use obsolete terminology, relying on a *see* reference from currently used terminology to get users to the term, which is not likely to be sought initially.

4. Sometimes free text is needed as a lead-in to the controlled vocabulary, but *not always*, and if free text and controlled vocabulary are always indexed together, or even if the default initial search is on both, it can destroy the precision of a search being done by someone who is being served by the controlled vocabulary. The vast majority of users are well served by the controlled vocabulary, judging by the research findings described in chapter 8.

5. Catalogers make a separate authority record for each main heading and each subdivision of the main heading. For example, there is one authority record for the subject heading ONLINE CATALOGS, which has a *see* reference from OPACs. There is another authority record for the subject heading ONLINE CATALOGS—SUBJECT ACCESS. In all current OPACs, the following search would fail: OPACs SUBJECT ACCESS. Perhaps some day we can build smarter systems that recognize that the main heading has hierarchical force over all of its subdivisions; such a system would recognize the relationship between the subject subdivision SUBJECT ACCESS and the OPACs *see* reference and ensure that the user's search was successful.

Based on the above facts, consider the following suggestion: the ideal subject heading default search would be conducted in stages, first looking for a match within a single-heading hierarchical group in an authority file that includes both cross-references and all assigned headings with free-floating subdivisions. If the initial search fails, a backup search (with the permission of the user) might be offered.

The following more detailed recommendations are offered:

File Structure Decisions

For further discussion of the reasoning behind the following recommendations, please see chapter 8.

1. Keep controlled vocabulary and free text vocabulary in separate indexes.

2. The default search should be on controlled vocabulary only, including the complete syndetic structure, and including all headings derived from bibliographic records (to ensure that free-floating subdivisions are included in the search).

3. Names and works as subjects should be indexed in both the name and name-title indexes and in the subject index.

4. Geographic-jurisdictional names as subjects should be indexed in both the name and name-title indexes and in the subject index.

5. Genre-form headings, either as topics or as exemplars, should be included in the general subject index.

6. A general search should be available for users who don't know whether their topic of interest is a *name* or a *subject*.

Indexing

For further discussion of the reasoning behind the following recommendations, please see chapter 9.

1. The default search should be a keyword-within-hierarchically-related-group match on subject headings and cross-references.

2. Subject headings should be excluded from control by any stop-listing algorithm that may be employed by the system.

3. A search using two or more terms should employ an implicit Boolean AND, but this should be made explicit on the display of the results, together with suggestions about other options and how those results might differ.

4. The user should never be limited to the use of one term in his or her keyword search.

Display Decisions

For further discussion of the reasoning behind the following recommendations, please see chapter 10.

1. The initial display should be a display of headings matched.

2. Headings matched should be arranged following the principle of filing elements, such that all headings with the same initial element should display together and be subarranged using the secondary filing elements, then the tertiary filing elements, etc. Parenthetical qualifiers and separately subfielded elements of headings should all be treated as secondary, tertiary, etc., filing elements.

3. The display of a subject heading should include all subdivisions applied to that heading (although these may be compressed, as in number 4 below).

4. When the headings display goes onto more than one screen, compress all headings with the same initial filing element, differentiating them only for users that choose a further display of headings with that initial filing element.

5. If the compressed display still is longer than five screens, provide a guide screen.

6. Make cross-references selectable.

7. Allow the user to select a heading and all narrower terms under it, if so desired.

8. Display unposted subject authority records and all cross-references from these records whenever the heading has been used with subdivisions.

9. Display scope notes from subject authority records.

10. Display the number of postings attached to each heading in a heading display.

11. Display together but label headings from different controlled vocabularies, such as LCSH and MeSH.

12. Display multiple bibliographic records attached to one subject heading in main entry order.

13. Display together but differentiate exemplars of and works about a form or genre.

14. Display together but differentiate works by and works about an author.

15. The default display of a single bibliographic record should include all bibliographic fields in the record, including 130, 240, and 490 fields; note fields; and tracings; and it should be an unlabeled (with the exception of classification numbers, as discussed in chapter 10) so-called card format display. Ideally, it should be possible for a user to select any heading in the tracings or the rest of the record and navigate from it to other bibliographic records with that heading.

16. Design effective displays to lead the user into the classification from either a single-record display or a display of subject headings.

When the User's Search Fails, What Should the System Do Next?

First of all, the system really has no way of knowing automatically when a user's search has failed. The assumption that a zero-hit search is a failure is a dangerous one, as is the assumption that a search that retrieves something is successful. If the library does not contain any books on the subject the user is interested in, a zero-hit search is a successful search. The computer should never be allowed to assume that a zero-hit search is a failure. On the other hand, a search that retrieves records may have retrieved no relevant materials and, therefore, be a failed search if the collection does in fact contain relevant materials. Only the user is really qualified to determine whether a search has failed. Perhaps a solution would be to offer a LOOK HARDER command or key that can be activated at any point in a user's search and lead to problem-solving software that could help correct for some of the more common searching problems. It is important to explain to the user what the software is going to do. The following are some of the kinds of solutions that might be tried, alone or in combination, to help the user who is having trouble with a subject search:

If the user is retrieving too little:

1. Ask the user if she or he can identify a bibliographic record that is like the works she or he is looking for, e.g., a bibliographic record for a work already known to the user or a bibliographic record for a work retrieved using free text terms in titles or notes; then offer a navigation feature to find other similar works using either classification or controlled vocabulary or both. Some suggest that this approach should be possible from an initial display of multiple records; for example, if the user can point to five relevant records, the system could search on all subject headings and classification numbers attached to those five records. If this is tried, resultant displays should be heading displays, including cross-reference structure (and perhaps classification numbers with textual explanations and displays of the hierarchy around them), rather than long lists of bibliographic records that might have many different headings and classification numbers on them. Simply presenting lists of records, which can easily represent "sets of excessive size and divergent attributes,"[1] without summarizing does not give the user the tools with which to give the system feedback on which subject headings and classification numbers are in fact retrieving useful materials.

2. If the user has input more than one keyword, search each keyword separately in the authority file (including cross-references and all heading subdivision combinations on bibliographic records), and give the user a list of all subject headings that matched at least one keyword; the user can then choose relevant subject headings from the list. Make sure your search includes cross-references on unposted authority records for headings that are present in the file with subdivisions. Beware of floating subdivisions here; perhaps if one of the keywords matches a subdivision, the subdivision alone should be displayed with an explanation, and the user should be allowed to keep the subdivision or not, as desired. A display of every heading with that subdivision could overwhelm the user with unwanted subject headings. Alternatively, do a keyword search within multiple-subject-heading fields in a bibliographic record. The former search, if possible, would be preferable, however, because of the inclusion of cross-references.

3. Match each term in the search against an online dictionary; if a term is not found in the dictionary, ask the user to verify that it is spelled correctly.

4. More extravagantly, establish a synonym dictionary, and match the user's search against that to see if alternative spellings, singular/plural variance, suffix stemming, etc., might facilitate a match with the controlled vocabulary.

5. It may be that there is no document about the specific topic sought by the user, but there might be documents on the next broader topic that would contain chapters on the desired subject. For example, the library may not have a book on cockroaches, but an encyclopedia or handbook on insects might contain much useful information. Offer the user the opportunity to broaden the search, using the hierarchy

built into the classification and subject heading systems used, e.g., related term *see also* references, especially those coded as broader terms, or classification numbers broader than relevant numbers in the classification.

6. Try placing the first term in the user's search next to the nearest match in an A to Z list of headings, allowing the user to explore the list up or down from there.

7. If the within-hierarchically-related-group matching recommended above is too resource-intensive for the default search, it could be used only in LOOK HARDER searching.

If the user is retrieving too much:

1. If the user has not yet looked at a display of subject headings, offer the user a display of all the subject headings retrieved; the more compression that can be practiced the better (see chapter 10), so that the headings take up as few screens as possible in order to allow the user to scan the headings quickly and make a choice as to the most relevant.[2]

2. Ask the user if he or she is interested only in works treated from the perspective of a particular discipline, e.g., engineering or sociology or fine arts; if so, display only works classified in that particular discipline. Alternatively, display a list of the disciplines retrieved from which the user may select.

3. Ask the user if she or he is interested only in particular languages, or only in works published after a particular date, or only in particular forms (e.g., dictionaries, bibliographies, encyclopedias, directories, or handbooks)[3] or physical formats (e.g., motion pictures, sound recordings), or only in the holdings of particular libraries, and limit searches as the user desires. See also chapter 12.

4. Limit the search to the topic as primary topic (i.e., the search must match on the first subject heading in a bibliographic record).

Options to Offer Power Users

1. For sophisticated users who know the exact subject heading they seek, the option of left-to-right matching with truncation should be offered.

2. Allow power users who know that the topic in which they are interested is represented by two or more subject headings to specify a search that looks for keyword co-occurrence across subject fields in a single bibliographic record.

3. Allow power users specifically to request that a subject search be limited to the topic as the primary topic (i.e., the first subject heading on a bibliographic record).

Notes

1. Michael K. Buckland, Mark H. Butler, Barbara A. Norgard, et al., "OASIS: A Front End for Prototyping Catalog Enhancements," *Library Hi-Tech* 10, no. 4 (1992): 11.

2. The NLS CITE command does this. See Dennis Auburn Hill, *User's Guide to the Library Computer Catalog: Network Library System (NLS)*

Catalog User's Guide, 4th ed. (Madison: University of Wisconsin-Madison, 1993), p. 34. Buckland et al. call this a SUMMARIZE command (see note 1).

3. Note that both form subdivisions added to subject headings and certain classification numbers can be used to limit searches to particular form types.

Other Relationships and Future Developments

PART

IV

12

Other Relationships

So far we have discussed the very important relationships among the editions of a work, the works of an author, and the works on a subject. However, there are other relationships in which our users may be interested. For example, a user may wish to retrieve all the works that can be run on a particular kind of equipment (e.g., a 16 millimeter projector or a compact disc [CD] player); in other words, users may want to view a list of all the works with particular physical characteristics (e.g., 16 millimeter films or CDs). They may also wish to limit a search to works of a filmmaker in a particular physical format, for example, films by Fellini that are available on videodisc.

Works in a particular physical format can be identified by means of coded data in the USMARC bibliographic or holdings record.[1] These codes are quite detailed and could be used to let users limit searches to quite specific physical formats, such as half-inch VHS videocassettes or wire recordings. Many systems use these codes very broadly in limiting commands, but few let users employ the power inherent in the specific codes by letting users both limit by and search directly on physical format, even though physical format information is encoded in existing records.[2] Physical format access could be quite useful, and more work needs to be done in this area. Also useful to many people would be software to allow them to specify various combinations of USMARC codes to be searched in order to generate printouts of large groups of records.

See figure 12.1 for a set of suggested physical format categories that might be useful for limiting, direct searching, or batch printing, along with the location of codes in the USMARC bibliographic or holdings format that can identify these formats. This table just scratches the surface in terms of what is actually available in the USMARC formats. Specialized collections that have active preservation programs or have lots of users with technical expertise could well use more detailed access. For example, in a motion picture archive, USMARC codes identifying various color processes and wide-screen processes might support preservation projects, such as preservation of films shot in three-strip Technicolor, or film programming projects, such as a night of Cinema-Scope films. A couple of warnings, however: (1) 007 fields can be found in both bibliographic records and holdings format records; ideally, the limiting algorithm could use codes found in either place; and (2) as shown in figure 12.1, codes in 008 fields can also be found in 006 fields ever since format integration; ideally, the limiting algorithm could use codes found in either place.

Format	USMARC field	Byte(s)	Code(s)
Archivally controlled materials	leader	06	p (and leader 08/a)
Art original	008 006	33 16	a
Art reproduction	008 006	33 16	a
Audiocassette	007	01	s (*only when* 007/00 is s)
Cartographic material	leader	06	e or f
Chart	008 006	33 16	n
Compact disc	007	03	f (*only when* 007/00 is s)
Computer file	leader	06	m (or 007/00/c)
Diorama	008 006	33 16	d
Filmstrip	008 006	33 16	f
Flash card	008 006	33 16	o
Game	008 006	33 16	g
Globe	007	00	d
Graphic	008 006	33 16	k
Kit	leader	06	o
Manuscript	leader	06	d, f, or t
Map	007	00	a
Microscope slide	008 006	33 16	p
Model	008 006	33 16	q

Figure 12.1   Suggested physical format categories that might be useful for limiting, direct searching, or batch printing

Format	USMARC field	Byte(s)	Code(s)
Motion picture	008 006	33 16	m
Motion picture— 16 mm.	007	07	d (*only when* 007/00 is m)
Music	leader	06	c or d
Picture	008 006	33 16	i
Realia	008 006	33 16	r
Reel-to-reel tape	007	01	t (*only when* 007/00 is s)
Slide	008 006	33 16	s
Sound disc	007	03	b, c, or d (*only when* 007/00 is s)
Sound disc, 33⅓	007	03	b (*only when* 007/00 is s)
Sound disc, 45	007	03	c (*only when* 007/00 is s)
Sound disc, 78	007	03	d (*only when* 007/00 is s)
Sound recording	leader	06	i or j
Technical drawing	008 006	33 16	l
Toy	008 006	33 16	w
Transparency	008 006	33 16	t
Videodisc	007	01	d (*only when* 007/00 is v)
Videorecording	008 006	33 16	v
Videorecording— VHS	007	04	b (*only when* 007/00 is v)

Users of rare book collections may want to find all the publications of a particular publisher or printer, and users of other kinds of collections may want works on a subject from a particular publisher.[3] Systems serving rare book collections or children's collections should consider indexing the publication/distribution area of the record. This type of search can also be very useful in any library for users with incomplete citations, e.g., "a book published recently by Wiley on semiconductors" or "an edition, published by Scribners, of one of Macaulay's works."

Indexing place of publication can also be valuable.[4] Users of rare book collections may be interested in publishing or printing in a particular place. Place of publication can also be useful in combination with other searches or limits, for example, when a user is looking for newspapers from a particular city.[5]

A useful limit is one that limits a search to serial publications. Serials can be identified by means of a code b or s in the 7th byte in the leader *or* (for nonprint serials) a code s in the 0 byte of the 006 field.

A number of systems allow users to limit a search to materials in a particular language (using the USMARC language codes located in bytes 35 to 37 in the 008 field in the bibliographic format), materials published before or after a particular date (using the dates found in bytes 7 to 10 *and* 11 to 14 in the 008 field—be sure to use *both*), materials to be found in particular libraries, or, as discussed above, materials in a particular format. This can be quite useful for the knowledgeable user, but system designers should be aware of the dangers. Limits can inadvertently prevent all the editions of a particular work from appearing, and it might be in the user's best interests for them to do so; for example, a user who limits his or her search for a scientific text to its publication date, 1994, might fail to discover a newer edition just published in 1998. A user looking for current material on a subject might limit a search somewhat arbitrarily to items published in the last two years and miss a highly significant work published just three years ago. To be used effectively, limits require some knowledge on the user's part about what is in the database. Limiting is done blindly when the user does not know what is there. Effective displays of subject headings with subdivisions can allow the user to make decisions less blindly than search limiting does. With effective displays, the user can see everything in the database laid out before her or him and make choices based, for example, on geographic area, period of coverage, or form.

Michael Buckland et al. suggest giving users the option of displaying a large retrieval as a matrix based on language, library location, and date.[6] This does at least protect users from having to limit blindly, without any sense of what is contained in the database; they can see a picture of the retrieval and get an idea of how many items fall into the various categories, before making choices. Unfortunately, OASIS, the application described by Buckland et al., requires the user to select a particular box in a grid, which is a somewhat cumbersome procedure.

If limits are offered, they should be available for all searches. Unfortunately, probably no current systems allow limiting of searches done through the authority file, rather than directly in the bibliographic file.

Notes

1. Specifically in the 007 field in the US-MARC bibliographic and holdings formats.

2. According to a posting on USMARC-L from Giles Martin, dated Aug. 9, 1994, the Australian Bibliographic Network has an enhanced search system called Supersearch, which allows users to search on much of the coded data in the MARC record, translated into English language terms.

3. In the USMARC bibliographic format, publishers are found in subfield delimiter b in the 260 field. Systems that do index this subfield include NLS (see Dennis Auburn Hill, *User's Guide to the Library Computer Catalog: Network Library System*

(NLS) Catalog User's Guide, 4th ed. [Madison: University of Wisconsin-Madison, 1993], p. 28) and ORION, which offers an FPB (Find Publisher) search.

4. In the USMARC bibliographic format, place of publication is found in the 260 delimiter a subfield.

5. In the USMARC bibliographic format, newspapers are coded n in 008 byte 21.

6. Michael K. Buckland, Mark H. Butler, Barbara A. Norgard, et al., "OASIS: A Front End for Prototyping Catalog Enhancements," *Library Hi-Tech* 10, no. 4 (1992): 10.

13

Future Developments

The records currently available for use in OPACs are rich with content and structure that have not yet been tapped by means of effective system design. The library and information science profession has as its knowledge base two valuable and unique elements: research about catalog user behavior and extensive experience with the complexity of the bibliographic universe. It is our professional duty to bring this knowledge base to bear on designing systems that are both powerful and easy to use. A number of improvements in system design would tap structure and information that already exist in our records to make better catalogs than the world has ever seen. As Nicholson Baker points out, not to design effective systems is a kind of "incidental book-burning."[1]

One of the major problems in known-work searching arises from the fact that the thing sought by the user, the work, can easily exist in the catalog in more than one record, very loosely linked together, if at all. Heretofore, we have been unable to invest in the authority work necessary to create distinctive alphabetical headings for each work that could be used to link all editions together. Perhaps future databases can record such relationships without requiring the construction of alphabetical headings, either through work-based records or relational links between records. This would enable us to ensure that no matter what kind of search a user employed to arrive at a record for a particular edition of a work, the catalog could display all editions of that work on demand, without making the user learn about main entries or type new searches. Other kinds of linkages, too, could be very useful: editions that themselves have editions could be linked into subsets. Records for works that contain other works and records for the works contained (i.e., analytics) could be linked in ways that allow one display option to be the order in which the parts appear within the whole, e.g., the stories on a newsreel in order. Works that have a chronological relationship, e.g., serials that change title over time, could be linked in ways that allow a chronological display. Mechanical linkage of a subject heading and all of its subdivisions or of a classification number with all numbers beneath it in the hierarchy might have the potential to improve indexing and displays for subject searching.

It is possible that experimentation might reveal that different record structures than those currently employed might better correspond with users' objectives. Current record structure is based on current publication practice; separate bibliographic records are made for each separately published edition. If publication practice changes with the advent of the information superhighway, as it has begun to do, the change presents us with the opportunity to structure our records in ways that better correspond with users' expectations. If new systems are properly designed, linkage of all the editions of a work, for example, might occur almost automatically, as new versions are electronically tacked onto the old.

Much of the subject information in our records remains untapped. Perhaps future systems will allow true classification browsing, in which classification searching is an integral part of any search, with the classification accessible from any individual record or subject heading and with user-friendly readable text to guide the user through the classification from any point.

In the introduction to this book, we listed a number of improvements to OPACs that would hinge on improvements in cataloging practice and that were therefore not discussed in this book, which focuses on improvements in system design. If these improvements in cataloging practice could be made in the future, they too could lead to improvement in OPAC function. True classed catalogs, in which a work might be assigned more than one classification number, might be possible. Complete integration of the subject authority file should also be aimed for, integrating authority records for floating subdivisions and integrating into the authority file all headings with subdivisions; the complete syndetic structure, including related term cross-references; and full authority records with scope notes and complex references. Mapping between subject heading lists, such as MeSH and LCSH, could enable terms from these lists to live together more harmoniously.[2] All of these developments could ensure that the complete syndetic structure, including cross-references to free-floating subdivisions, is available to and easily navigable by the user of the catalog. If catalogers can develop better distinctions among works about, examples of and pictures of, and between proper names and concepts, all of these can be better sorted out for users.

In general, future systems should work to make life as easy as possible for the user, requiring the user to type as little as possible and at the same time providing smarter programs that prompt the user to indicate the types of information he or she is including in his or her search, so that the search can be designed with greater precision and can be tailor-made for the particular problems presented by personal names, corporate names, titles, or subject headings. Displays should summarize and compress multiple headings and allow the user to browse up and down multiple levels, to facilitate scanning large retrievals. In general, authority files and bibliographic files should be better integrated, so that the distinction between the files is invisible to the user.

Future systems may provide users direct access to the power of USMARC format coding, as Anne Lipow urges.[3] This could allow them to manipulate records in more complex ways and even design their own indexes and searches. Geographic and time codes of various kinds in existing USMARC records could be used to design online maps or time lines through which users could travel at will.

The future undoubtedly holds multilingual systems that allow users to search successfully in any language. OPAC automation is becoming more complex as new technologies that permit the integration of images into the OPAC are employed. The increased complexity of the technologies results in more variety within the OPAC—

variety as to what the OPAC can contain and retrieve, such as images and even sound, as well as textual data. Variety has also increased in the interfaces that are possible to an OPAC: client-server systems permit a variety of interfaces to the same database. The ability to link users to catalogs (and other bibliographic databases for that matter) at remote sites has blurred the distinction between separate library catalogs and in effect decentralized the catalog. It is no longer necessary for an OPAC user to be limited to searching one central catalog: she or he may search several different catalogs from a single workstation or through a single interface.

All new technologies begin with a proliferation of nonstandard and incompatible practices, but eventually market forces result in standardization. The classic example is the lack of standardized tracks at the beginning of the history of railroads. Perhaps in time we can hope for a move to standardize searching, indexing, and display software across all information organization systems, so that users need not master the complexity they must today to cruise the information superhighway.[4] We may see the development of a universal "author" directory to which all contributors of documents to the information superhighway must link their documents as they contribute them. The services of scholars may be enlisted to create a universal dictionary, with all possible synonyms, variants, and broader and narrower terms linked together, so that subject searches could be constructed for users without their having to imagine all synonyms, variants, and broader or narrower terms.

The frustrations users are currently experiencing with Web searches that routinely produce forty thousand hits in no discernible order may ultimately produce a resurgence in interest in the creation of catalogs that employ human intelligence to reduce the inherent complexity of the bibliographic universe to an apparent simplicity.

The future holds out exciting possibilities for better ways to present information to the users of our OPACs, but it should not be forgotten that our basic objectives remain, as they were in Cutter's day, to help users find the subjects, authors, and works they seek.

Notes

1. Nicholson Baker, "Discards," *New Yorker,* April 4, 1994, p. 84.

2. There is a project at Northwestern University to attempt to do this for NOTIS, but it probably will not produce sharable records.

3. Anne Grodzins Lipow, "Teach Online Catalog Users the MARC Format? Are You Kidding?" *Journal of Academic Librarianship* 17 (May 1991): 80–85.

4. Gary Klein's study is revelatory of the anarchy that currently prevails and includes a discussion of the implications for attempting to create the appearance of standardization in superimposed interfaces. See Gary M. Klein, "A Bibliometric Analysis of Processing Options Chosen by Libraries to Execute Keyword Searches in Online Public Access Catalogs: Is There a Standard Default Keyword Operator?" typescript (1993).

User Studies Consulted

Akeroyd, John. "Information Seeking in Online Catalogues." *Journal of Documentation* 46 (March 1990): 33–52.

Alzofon, S. R., and N. Van Pulis. "Patterns of Searching and Success Rates in an Online Public Access Catalog." *College & Research Libraries* 45 (March 1984): 110–115.

Anderson, Rosemary, Victoria A. Reich, Pamela Roper Wagner, et al. "Library of Congress Online Public Catalog Users Survey: A Report to the Council for Library Resources." Washington, D.C.: Library of Congress, Office of Planning and Development, 1982. (ERIC ED 231384)

Ayres, F. H., Janice German, N. Loukes, et al. "Author versus Title: A Comparative Survey of the Accuracy of the Information Which the User Brings to the Library Catalogue." *Journal of Documentation* 24 (Dec. 1968): 266–272.

Ballard, Terry, and Jim Smith. "The Human Interface: An Ongoing Study of OPAC Usage at Adelphi University." *Advances in Online Public Access Catalogs* 1 (1992): 58–73.

Bates, Marcia J. "Factors Affecting Subject Catalog Search Success." *Journal of the American Society for Information Science* 28 (May 1977): 161–169.

———. "System Meets User: Problems in Matching Subject Search Terms." *Information Processing and Management* 13 (1977): 367–375.

Berger, Michael George. "Information-Seeking in the Online Bibliographic System: An Exploratory Study." Ph.D. diss., UC Berkeley, 1994.

Berger, Michael. *The User Meets the MELVYL System: An Analysis of User Transactions.* Technical Report no. 7. Oakland: Division of Library Automation, University of California, 1996.

Berger, Michael George, and Mary Jean Moore. "The User Meets the MELVYL System." *DLA Bulletin* 16, no. 1 (fall 1996): 13–21.

Borgman, Christine L., Sandra G. Hirsh, Virginia A. Walter, et al. "Children's Searching Behavior on Browsing and Keyword Online Catalogs: The Science Library Catalog Project." *Journal of the American Society for Information Science* 46 (1995): 663–684.

Brown, Margaret C. "The Graduate Student's Use of the Subject Catalog." *College & Research Libraries* 8 (July 1947): 203–208.

Carlyle, Allyson. "Matching LCSH and User Vocabulary in the Library Catalog." *Cataloging & Classification Quarterly* 10, no. 1/2 (1989): 37–63.

———. "The Second Objective of the Catalog: A Performance Evaluation of Online Catalog Displays." Ph.D. diss., UCLA, 1994.

Cherry, Joan M. "Improving Subject Access in OPACs: An Exploratory Study of Conversion of Users' Queries." *Journal of Academic Librarianship* 18 (May 1992): 95–99.

Crawford, Walt. "Long Searches, Slow Response: Recent Experience on RLIN." *Information Technology and Libraries* 2 (June 1983): 176–182.

Dickson, J. "Analysis of User Errors in Searching an Online Catalog." *Cataloging & Classification Quarterly* 4 (spring 1984): 19–38.

Drabenstott, Karen M. *Enhancing a New Design for Subject Access to Online Catalogs.* Ann Arbor: School of Information and Library Studies, University of Michigan, 1994.

Drabenstott, Karen Markey, and Diane Vizine-Goetz. *Using Subject Headings for Online Retrieval: Theory, Practice and Potential.* San Diego, Calif.: Academic Press, 1994.

Drabenstott, Karen M., and Marjorie S. Weller. "Failure Analysis of Subject Searches in a Test of a New Design for Subject Access to Online

Catalogs." *Journal of the American Society for Information Science* 47 (1996): 519–537.

———. "Handling Spelling Errors in Online Catalog Searches." *Library Resources & Technical Services* 40 (1996): 113–132.

———. "Improving Personal-Name Searching in Online Catalogs." *Information Technology and Libraries* 15 (1996): 135–155.

See also Markey, Karen

Dwyer, Catherine M., Eleanor A. Gossen, and Lynne M. Martin. "Known-Item Search Failure in an OPAC." *RQ* 31 (winter 1991): 228–236.

Ferl, Terry Ellen, and Larry Millsap. "The Knuckle-Cracker's Dilemma: A Transaction Log Study of OPAC Subject Searching." *Information Technology and Libraries* 15 (1996): 81–98.

Frost, Carolyn O. "Title Words as Entry Vocabulary to LCSH: Correlation between Assigned LCSH Terms and Derived Terms from Titles in Bibliographic Records with Implications for Subject Access in Online Catalogs." *Cataloging & Classification Quarterly* 10, no. 1/2 (1989): 165–180.

Fryser, Benjamin S., and Keith H. Stirling. "Effect of Spatial Arrangement, Upper-Lower Case Letter Combinations and Reverse Video on Patron Response to CRT Displayed Catalog Records." *Journal of the American Society for Information Science* 35 (Nov. 1984): 344–350.

Fuller, Elizabeth E. "Variation in Personal Names in the Catalog." Typescript (1986), 28p.

Golden, Gary A., Susan U. Golden, and Rebecca T. Lenzini. "Patron Approaches to Serials: A User Study." *College & Research Libraries* 43 (Jan. 1982): 23–30.

Golden, Susan U., and Gary A. Golden. "Access to Periodicals: Search Key versus Keyword." *Information Technology and Libraries* 2 (March 1983): 26–32.

Gouke, Mary Noel, and Sue Pease. "Title Searches in an Online Catalog and a Card Catalog: A Comparative Study of Patron Success in Two Libraries." *Journal of Academic Librarianship* 8 (July 1982): 137–143.

Graham, Tom. "The Free Language Approach to Online Catalogues: The User." In *Keyword Catalogues and the Free Language Approach: Papers Based on a Seminar Held at Imperial College, London, 19th October, 1983*, ed. Philip Bryant, p. 21–30. Bath, Eng.: Bath University Library, 1985.

Hancock-Beaulieu, Micheline. "Evaluating the Impact of an Online Library Catalogue on Subject Searching Behaviour at the Catalogue and at the Shelves." *Journal of Documentation* 46 (Dec. 1990): 318–338.

Hunter, Rhonda N. "Successes and Failures of Patrons Searching the Online Catalog at a Large Academic Library: A Transaction Log Analysis." *RQ* 30 (spring 1991): 395–402.

Jamieson, Alexis J., Elizabeth Dolan, and Luc Declerck. "Keyword Searching vs. Authority Control in an Online Catalog." *Journal of Academic Librarianship* 12 (Nov. 1986): 277–283.

Janosky, Beverly, and Philip J. Smith. "Online Library Catalog Systems: An Analysis of User Errors." Typescript (1983), 106p.

Janosky, Beverly, Philip J. Smith, and Charles Hildreth. "Online Library Catalog Systems: An Analysis of User Errors." *International Journal of Man-Machine Studies* 25 (1986): 573–592.

Johnson, Debra Wilcox, and Lynn Silipigni Connaway. "Use of Online Catalogs: A Report of Results of Focus Group Interviews." Typescript (Feb. 1992), 32p.

Jones, Richard. "Improving OKAPI: Transaction Log Analysis of Failed Searches in an Online Catalogue." *Vine* 62 (May 1986): 3–13.

Kaske, Neal K., and Nancy P. Sanders. *A Comprehensive Study of Online Public Access Catalogs: An Overview and Application of Findings*. Dublin, Ohio: OCLC, 1983.

Kern-Simirenko, Cheryl. "OPAC User Logs: Implications for Bibliographic Instruction." *Library Hi-Tech* 1, no. 3 (1983): 27–35.

Kinnucan, Mark T. "The Size of Retrieval Sets." *Journal of the American Society for Information Science* 43 (Jan. 1992): 72–79.

Klein, Gary M. "A Bibliometric Analysis of Processing Options Chosen by Libraries to Execute Keyword Searches in Online Public Access Catalogs: Is There a Standard Default Keyword Operator?" Typescript (1993).

Knapp, Patricia B. "The Subject Catalog in the College Library." *Library Quarterly* 14 (April and July 1944): 108–118, 214–228.

Kranich, Nancy C., Christina M. Spellman, Deborah Hecht, et al. "Evaluating the Online Catalog from a Public Services Perspective: A Case Study at the New York University Libraries." In *The Impact of Online Catalogs*, ed. Joseph R. Matthews, p. 89–140. New York: Neal-Schuman, 1986.

Larson, Ray Reed. "Workload Characteristics and Computer System Utilization in Online Library Catalogs." Ph.D. diss., UC Berkeley, 1986.

Lawrence, Gary S., Vicki Graham, and Heather Presley. "University of California Users Look at MELVYL: Results of a Survey of Users of the University of California Prototype Online Union Catalog." In *Advances in Library Administration and Organization*, p. 85–208. Greenwich, Conn.: JAI Press, 1984.

Lester, Marilyn Ann. "Coincidence of User Vocabulary and Library of Congress Subject Headings: Experiments to Improve Subject Access in Academic Library Online Catalogs." Ph.D. diss., University of Illinois at Urbana-Champaign, 1989.

Lilley, Oliver L. "Evaluation of the Subject Catalog: Criticism and a Proposal." *American Documentation* 5 (April 1954): 41–60.

Lipetz, Ben-Ami. *User Requirements in Identifying Desired Works in a Large Library*. New Haven, Conn.: Yale University Library, 1970.

Lynch, Clifford A. "Cataloging Practices and the Online Catalog." In *ASIS '85*, ed. Carol A. Parkhurst, p. 111–115. Proceedings of the ASIS Annual Meeting, vol. 22. White Plains, N.Y.: Published for the American Society of Information Science by Knowledge Industry Publications, 1985.

McPherson, Dorothy. "How the MELVYL Catalog Is Used: A Statistical Overview." *DLA Bulletin* 5, no. 2 (Aug. 1985): 16–18.

Malinconico, S. Michael. "The Library Catalog in a Computerized Environment." In *The Nature and Future of the Catalog: Proceedings of the ALA's Information Science and Automation Division's 1975 and 1977 Institutes on the Catalog*, ed. Maurice J. Freedman and S. Michael Malinconico, p. 46–71. Phoenix, Ariz.: Oryx Press, 1979.

Markey, Karen. "Alphabetical Searching in an Online Catalog." *Journal of Academic Librarianship* 14 (Jan. 1989): 353–360.

———. "Favorable Experiences with Online Catalog Features from the Perspective of Library Patrons and Staff." In *Productivity in the Information Age: Proceedings of the 46th ASIS Annual Meeting, 1983*, ed. Raymond F. Vondran, Anne Caputo, Carol Wasserman, et al., p. 161–166. Proceedings of the ASIS Annual Meeting, vol. 20. White Plains, N.Y.: Knowledge Industry Publications, 1983.

———. "Integrating the Machine-Readable LCSH into Online Catalogs." *Information Technology and Libraries* 7 (Sept. 1988): 299–312.

———. "Online Catalog User Needs and Behavior." In *Think Tank on the Present and Future of the Online Catalog: Proceedings*, ed. Noelle Van Pulis, p. 59–83. Chicago: American Library Association, 1991.

———. "Online Catalog Users and Subject Authority Information." In *Authority Control Symposium: Papers Presented during the 14th Annual ARLIS/NA Conference, New York, N.Y., Feb. 10, 1986*, ed. Karen Muller, p. 31–53. Tucson: Art Libraries Society of North America, 1987.

———. *Subject Searching in Library Catalogs before and after the Introduction of Online Catalogs*. Dublin, Ohio: OCLC, 1984.

See also Drabenstott, Karen

Martin, Thomas H., John C. Wyman, and Kumud Madhok. *Feedback and Exploratory Mechanisms for Assisting Library Staff [to] Improve On-line Catalog Searching*. Washington, D.C.: Council on Library Resources, 1983.

Matthews, Joseph R., Gary S. Lawrence, and Douglas K. Ferguson, eds. *Using Online Catalogs: A Nationwide Survey: A Report of a Study Sponsored by the Council on Library Resources*. New York: Neal-Schuman, 1983.

Moore, Carole Weiss. "User Reactions to Online Catalogs: An Exploratory Study." *College & Research Libraries* 42 (July 1981): 295–302.

Pease, Sue, and Mary Noel Gouke. "A Comparison of Patron Success in an On-line Catalog and a Large Union Card Catalog." In *Options for the 80s: Proceedings of the Second National Conference of the Association of College and Research Libraries*, ed. Michael D. Kathman and Virgil F. Massman, p. 97–205. Greenwich, Conn.: JAI Press, 1982.

———. "LCS Users: A Study of Current Use." In *Crossroads*, p. 96–101. (Library and Information Technology Association (U.S.) National Conference, 1st, 1983, Baltimore, Md.) Chicago: American Library Association, 1984.

———. "Patterns of Use in an Online Catalog and a Card Catalog." *College & Research Libraries* 43 (July 1982): 279–291.

Peters, Thomas A. "When Smart People Fail: An Analysis of the Transaction Log of an Online Public Access Catalog." *Journal of Academic Librarianship* 15 (Nov. 1989): 267–273.

Roose, Tina. "Online Catalogs: Making Them Better Reference Tools." *Library Journal* 113 (Dec. 1988): 76–77.

Seal, Alan. "Experiments with Full and Short Entry Catalogues: A Study of Library Needs." *Library Resources & Technical Services* 27 (April/June 1983): 144–155.

———. "Research into Online Catalogues." In *Online Public Access to Library Files: Conference Proceedings*, ed. Janet Kinsella, p. 133–144. Oxford: Elsevier International Bulletins, 1985.

———. "What's in It for You: Research on the Content of Catalogue Entries." *Catalogue & Index* 51 (winter 1978): 6–8.

Seal, Alan, Philip Bryant, and Carolyn Hall. *Full and Short Entry Catalogues: Library Needs and Uses.* Bath, Eng.: Bath University Library, 1982.

Seymour, Carol A., and J. L. Schofield. "Measuring Reader Failure at the Catalogue." *Library Resources & Technical Services* 17 (winter 1973): 6–24.

Shore, Melinda L. "Variation between Personal Name Headings and Title Page Usage." *Cataloging & Classification Quarterly* 4 (summer 1984): 1–11.

Sinnott, Elisabeth. "Fewer Errors Resulting from the Users' Misconception of the OPAC in 1992 than a Decade Ago: A Comparative Study of No Direct Hits and Zero Hits in Author Searches." *Cataloging & Classification Quarterly* 18, no. 1 (1993): 75–102.

Specht, Jerry. "Patron Use of an On-line Circulation System in Known-Item Searching." *Journal of the American Society for Information Science* 31 (Sept. 1980): 335–346.

A Study of an Online Catalog from a Public Services Perspective (New York University Libraries, Nancy C. Kranich, principal investigator). Washington, D.C.: Office of Management Studies, Association of Research Libraries, 1984.

Tagliacozzo, Renata, Lawrence Rosenberg, and Manfred Kochen. "Access and Recognition: From Users' Data to Catalogue Entries." *Journal of Documentation* 26 (Sept. 1970): 230–249.

Tate, Elizabeth L. "Main Entries and Citations: One Test of the Revised Cataloging Code." *Library Quarterly* 33 (April 1963): 172–191.

Taylor, Arlene G. "Authority Files in Online Catalogs: An Investigation of Their Value." *Cataloging & Classification Quarterly* 4 (spring 1984): 1–17.

Thomas, Catherine M. "Authority Control in Manual versus Online Catalogs: An Examination of 'See' References." *Information Technology and Libraries* 3 (Dec. 1984): 393–397.

Tolle, John E. *Current Utilization of Online Catalogs: Transaction Log Analysis.* Dublin, Ohio: OCLC, 1983.

Van Pulis, Noelle, and Lorene E. Ludy. "Subject Searching in an Online Catalog with Authority Control." *College & Research Libraries* 49 (Nov. 1988): 523–533.

Walton, Carol, Susan Williamson, and Howard D. White. "Resistance to Online Catalogs: A Comparative Study at Bryn Mawr and Swarthmore Colleges." *Library Resources & Technical Services* 30 (Oct./Dec. 1986): 388–401.

Watson, Mark R., and Arlene G. Taylor. "Implications of Current Reference Structures for Authority Work in Online Environments." *Information Technology and Libraries* 6 (March 1987): 10–19.

Wiberley, Stephen E., and Robert Allen Daugherty. "Users' Persistence in Scanning Lists of References." *College & Research Libraries* 49 (1988): 149–156.

Wiberley, Stephen E., Robert Allen Daugherty, and James A. Danowski. "User Persistence in Displaying Online Catalog Postings: LUIS." *Library Resources & Technical Services* 39 (1995): 247–264.

———. "User Persistence in Scanning Postings of a Computer-Driven Information System: LCS." *Library & Information Science Research* 12 (1990): 341–353.

Wilkes, Adeline, and Antoinette Nelson. "Subject Searching in Two Online Catalogs: Authority Control vs. Non-Authority Control." *Cataloging & Classification Quarterly* 20, no. 4 (1995): 57–79.

Wyly, Brendan J. "From Access Points to Materials: A Transaction Log Analysis of Access Point Value for Online Catalog Users." *Library Resources & Technical Services* 40 (July 1996): 211–236.

Yee, Martha M., and Raymond Soto. "User Problems with Access to Fictional Characters and Personal Names in Online Public Access Catalogs." *Information Technology and Libraries* 10 (March 1991): 3–13.

Cataloging Classics for the Inquiring System Designer

Appendix B

Brault, Nancy. *The Great Debate on Panizzi's Rules in 1847–1849: The Issues Discussed.* Los Angeles: School of Library Service and the University Library, 1972.

Chan, Lois Mai. *Library of Congress Subject Headings: Principles of Structure and Policies for Application.* Washington, D.C.: Cataloging Distribution Services, 1990.

Cutter, Charles Ammi. *Rules for a Dictionary Catalog,* 4th ed., rewritten. Washington, D.C.: U.S. Govt. Printing Office, 1904.

International Conference on Cataloguing Principles (1961 : Paris). *Statement of Principles,* annotated ed. with commentary and examples by Eva Verona. London: IFLA Committee on Cataloguing, 1971.

Lubetzky, Seymour. *Principles of Cataloging.* Los Angeles: Institute of Library Research, 1969.

Appendix

C

Searching Catalogs on the Internet

A continuously updated list of catalogs searchable on the Internet, along with Telnet addresses, entitled *Accessing On-Line Bibliographic Databases*, by Billy Barron and Marie-Christine Mahe, can be obtained by anonymous FTP from

ftp.utdallas.edu:/pub/staff/billy/libguide

It can also be found on the Web at

http://www.cni.org/pub/net-guides/barron/

Index

Martha M. Yee is cataloging supervisor at the UCLA Film and Television Archive at UCLA. She has written extensively on cataloging and OPACs.

Sara Shatford Layne is head of the cataloging division at the Physical Sciences and Technology Libraries at UCLA. She has taught workshops on OCLC and AACR2R.